PATTERNS OF INTERNATIONAL COOPERATION IN THE CARIBBEAN 1942–1969

A JNO. E. OWENS MEMORIAL FOUNDATION PUBLICATION

PATTERNS OF INTERNATIONAL COOPERATION IN THE CARIBBEAN 1942–1969

HERBERT CORKRAN, JR.

SOUTHERN METHODIST UNIVERSITY PRESS • DALLAS

© 1970 : SOUTHERN METHODIST UNIVERSITY PRESS : DALLAS

Library of Congress Catalog Card Number 74-128122

□ CONTENTS

□ PREFACE

Early in 1956 when I arrived to become vice consul at the American Consulate on the island of Aruba, in the Netherlands Antilles, I was told by the principal officer that among my miscellaneous duties as the junior officer would be that of "librarian." In this capacity I would have to receive and dispose in some fashion of the myriad press releases and other assorted printed material that flowed in great volume to the Consulate with every mail sack. I soon found on my desk certain homey, down-to-earth publicity releases—material which actually taught me a great deal about life in the West Indies—emanating from a strange organization of which I had never before heard: the Caribbean Commission. From that chance encounter began the research of which this book is the culmination.

When I left the Foreign Service to return to academic work my professors at Indiana University were as fascinated as I was by the existence of this little international organization in a region of the world where there were really no nations as such and where there consequently should have been no international organization. They encouraged my academic interest in this phenomenon, and thus since 1960 I have followed with sympathetic concern the changing patterns of international cooperation in the Caribbean. I have tried over the years, with several publications, to give some well-deserved publicity to these truly remarkable and creative innovations in international organization coming from a region of the world where they might least be expected. This book, then, will attempt to summarize and document more than a quarter of a century of the efforts of the West Indies to evolve a useful set of structures for regional cooperation.

The compilation of this material would not have been possible without the very generous cooperation of many busy people who were kind enough to discuss the affairs of their agencies with me and to make pertinent suggestions with regard to documentation and additional sources of information. My only hesitancy in mentioning any names at all in this connection is the fear that I might inadvertently omit someone to whom thanks are due.

Nevertheless I must certainly record here my sincere gratitude first of all to Professor Edward H. Buehrig, of Indiana University, who initially encouraged me to attempt this research, and through whose intercession I received a travel grant for my first extensive visit to Puerto Rico in 1961. To many people in the Department of State in Washington I owe a word of thanks, but especially to Mrs. Frances McReynolds Smith and her associates formerly in the Office of Dependent Area Affairs. More recently Mr. Edward T. Long of the State Department's Bureau of Inter-American Affairs has been generous with help and documentation.

To acknowledge properly the assistance given to me by the Caribbean Commission would require reciting the names of virtually the entire staff. Nevertheless special thanks are certainly due to Mr. Clovis F. Beauregard, who was secretary general of the Caribbean Commission and of the Caribbean Organization; to Mr. C. P. Erskine-Lindop, who was the administrative secretary of the Commission; and to Miss Enid Baa, who was the librarian of the Commission.

Likewise with CODECA, the agency which succeeded the Caribbean Commission and Caribbean Organization, it would require naming almost the entire staff. Needless to say, however, this book would not have been possible without the cooperation and help of Dr. Luis A. Passalacqua Christian, Executive Director of CODECA until 1969. Valuable assistance was also given to me by Mr. Adrian Diaz Ruiz, director of operations and economics officer of CODECA. During my final visit to CODECA in the summer of 1969 the acting director, Mr. Manuel Velázquez Borges, was extremely courteous and helpful in discussing the affairs of the Agency and making documentation available. And, as always, special thanks are due to the librarian; in the case of CODECA this was Mrs. Paulita Maldonado de la Torre.

Both the Caribbean Commission and CODECA supplied me with office space, access to files, and other generous assistance on the occasions when I visited them in Puerto Rico.

In the Puerto Rican government thanks must be recorded to a host of busy people, but especially to Mr. E. Zapater, former director of the Caribbean Training Program of the Department of State of Puerto Rico; the late Mr. Ernesto Ramos Antonini, speaker of the House of Representatives of Puerto Rico; Mr. Angel Calderon Cruz, assistant secretary of state of Puerto Rico; and Mr. Zoltan Meszaros, director of the Foreign Trade Program of the Commerce Department of Puerto Rico. And in the new administration in Puerto Rico I owe a special debt of gratitude to Dr. Roland I. Perusse, special assistant to Governor Ferré, who generously made the facilities of his office available to me in 1969.

Dr. Richard C. Morse, director of the Institute of Caribbean Studies of the University of Puerto Rico in 1961, gave me valuable assistance, and he arranged for me to have full access to the facilities of the University of Puerto Rico. His successor, Professor Thomas Mathews, has also been very helpful in recent years.

A word of appreciation should also certainly be expressed to Professor John M. Claunch, former chairman of the Government Department at Southern Methodist University, who encouraged me to continue my research and writing on this international phenomenon, and who arranged for me to have time off from a busy teaching schedule to make several trips to the West Indies. His successor as chairman, Professor Cecil Johnson, has been equally sympathetic and accommodating during this past academic year.

A final word of acknowledgment is certainly due to my wife and children who had to face with courage and good humor the ruin of summer vacation plans as a family while I pursued this research interest in the Caribbean.

For more than four hundred years the Caribbean has survived wars, hurricanes, volcanic eruptions, earthquakes, piracy, slavery, colonialism, fear, suspicion, ignorance, and neglect. This book is about the individual and institutional efforts of those who during the last twenty-seven years have been working to overcome these obstacles to a better life for the West Indies.

HERBERT CORKRAN, JR.

Dallas, Texas
September 1, 1969

☐ INTRODUCTION

"The Chair recognizes the delegate from Barbados." Those historic words were uttered in 1946 by an American, Mr. Charles W. Taussig, who in his capacity as United States co-chairman of the Caribbean Commission was presiding over the second session of the West Indian Conference.[1] To the world of the late 1960s, thoroughly accustomed to the pageantry of international gatherings where delegates of many races and cultures from formerly colonial and dependent areas rise to speak as sovereign equals for the new nations they represent, this recognition by the chair of a delegate from a small island in the Caribbean may not seem of unusual significance. But Barbados was a colony of Great Britain in 1946, not an independent country, and its delegate was an elected member of the island's colonial legislature. This occasion in 1946 marked the first time in history, according to Mr. Taussig, that the leaders of as many as fifteen dependent areas had gathered in an international conference to speak for themselves. Although this conference of 1946 and subsequent sessions of the West Indian Conference did not take up "political" questions, the very act of convening such conferences, whose delegates were representatives of dependent peoples, was of deep political significance. Furthermore, the West Indian Conference marked the beginning of a truly remarkable series of experiments in regional integration through intergovernmental structures in the Caribbean, in the course of which several more "firsts" were recorded in the realm of international organization.

SURVEY OF THE SUCCESSIVE ORGANIZATIONS IN THE CARIBBEAN

In order to chart the terrain which this study will attempt to survey, I offer the following brief introduction to the principal agencies and structures which it will be the purpose of this book to describe in detail.

Anglo-American Caribbean Commission

The Caribbean Commission, sponsor of the West Indian Conference, was originally constituted in 1942 as the bipartite Anglo-American Caribbean Commission, its creation inspired in large part by the need to cope with wartime emergencies. For the shortage of shipping and the disruption of world markets had accelerated the long-term economic decline of the islands and territories to the point where the responsible governments were forced to take drastic relief measures. Moreover, France and Holland were occupied by Germany, and Great Britain was still gravely threatened by Nazi might. Thus the defense of the European colonial and dependent territories in the Caribbean—to say nothing of the question of the future sovereignty over these areas in the event of a final German victory in Europe—was of great concern to the free world. The Nazi submarine campaign was making deep inroads on what was left of Caribbean shipping and had brought the people of many isolated islands close to actual starvation. Finally the United States, in exchange for a number of destroyers, had acquired from Britain the right to establish bases in the Caribbean; this gave the United States a direct interest in the welfare of the British islands which was added to its concern for its own dependencies in the area, Puerto Rico and the American Virgin Islands.

The Anglo-American Caribbean Commission did yeoman service in coordinating British and American efforts to solve the common wartime problems of the Caribbean area. It also made surveys and studies of ways to cope with the permanent and long-range economic and social problems. While the war was still on it actually got many long-term projects started. However, there were many observers who felt that despite the stated purposes of the Commission, which looked toward a permanent agency for cooperative endeavors, the organization would fall apart once the war-inspired incentive for cooperation was ended. The affairs of the area, they said, would return to the normal prewar pattern, when the various colonies, despite their many common economic and social problems, had far more intercourse with their home-country governments than with each other, and when any sort of negotiation affecting a group of colonies had to proceed via lengthy diplomatic procedures involving Washington, London, Paris, and The Hague.

Caribbean Commission

The Commission did not collapse with the end of the war. Instead it was broadened and transformed in 1946 to include France and the Netherlands, acting on behalf of their respective areas in the Caribbean. The West Indian Conference sessions were scheduled on a regular basis, and the Commission undertook many significant projects which over a period of fifteen years produced substantial achievements in agriculture, trade, fisheries, education, health, and related areas of special concern to the peoples of the West Indies. The Commission and the West Indian Conference provided forums for the discussion of long-standing problems. The Commission developed a regional awareness of common needs and aspirations. It secured technical help and guidance from the outside. And, not the least of its achievements, it promoted the political awakening of the area.

By the mid-1950s, considerable constitutional evolution in the direction of greater autonomy and self-government had occurred in Puerto

Rico and elsewhere in the West Indies. To the native leaders of this movement the Caribbean Commission, with its four national sections representing the metropolitan powers, seemed more and more anachronistic—a
nagging reminder of the colonialism which they were in the process of
shaking off. Pressures began to mount for a restructuring of their regional
organization to place its affairs more squarely in the hands of the regional
islands and territories themselves.

Caribbean Organization

Prodded by the Puerto Rican delegates to the West Indian Conference
of 1957, the Caribbean Commission called a special session of the West
Indian Conference in 1959 which proceeded to draw up the charter for a
new international organization to succeed the Caribbean Commission.
The new agency was to be called the Caribbean Organization. This in itself was an unprecedented development in international relations, for in
effect here were four metropolitan powers saying that a formal agreement
among them should be revised and supplanted, not by themselves, but by
delegates of their dependent or associated territories.

The principal institutional change in the evolution from Caribbean
Commission to Caribbean Organization was that of replacing the four-
power Commission with a Caribbean Council. Delegates to the new Council were to be from the Caribbean territories rather than from the
metropolitan powers. The actual members of the new organization were
likewise to be the Caribbean countries themselves. The only exception to
this new pattern was that the French Republic, because of the constitutional status of the French Caribbean territories as parts of France itself,
had to be retained as a member of the new Council and of the Caribbean
Organization "on behalf of" Guadeloupe, Martinique, and French
Guiana. West Indian Conferences were to be discontinued since in effect
the West Indian Conference had been elevated in the new arrangements
to actual control of the organization.

From its inauguration in 1961 the new Caribbean Organization had
broadly the same terms of reference as the old Commission, and it began
by continuing and developing the work started by the Commission.

The Caribbean Organization survived for a little more than three
years. The Organization was unfortunately beset almost from the beginning with constitutional, procedural, budgetary, and even political problems with which it was powerless to cope. Factors contributing to the
demise of the Organization included the political breakup of one of its
major members, the West Indies Federation, in 1962; the awkward position of France as a continuing member of an otherwise all-Caribbean
organization; and the impatience of Puerto Rico at the slow progress
which the Organization was said to be making in the face of the overwhelming needs of the West Indies.

Once again prodded by Puerto Rico, the fifth meeting of the Caribbean Council late in 1964 voted to disband the Organization. The Secretariat wound up its activities and closed on June 30, 1965.

CODECA

On the very next day, however, that is on July 1, 1965, began still another phase of institutional efforts at cooperation in the Caribbean. In urging the termination of the Caribbean Organization, Puerto Rico was already well along in its planning for an institutional structure to succeed the Organization. This involved the establishment of a new public corporation, to be an agency of the Puerto Rican government, which with the joint efforts of all the Caribbean territories would hopefully be able at last to turn effective cooperation and exchange into a reality. This project involving transition from formal to informal international cooperation in the Caribbean was debated and approved by delegates from the West Indies islands at a Conference on Economic Coordination in the Caribbean, held in Puerto Rico in May of 1965. From its title in Spanish, Corporación de Desarrollo Económico del Caribe, was derived the tag CODECA by which the new agency became known from its inception.

As a public corporation of Puerto Rico rather than an international organization CODECA would supposedly be able to bridge the differing political systems and degrees of autonomy in the region by entering into contracts with counterpart agencies in other territories for the effective carrying out of worthwhile regional projects.

The election of November 1968 brought to power in Puerto Rico an administration less enthusiastic about international cooperation centering on Puerto Rico, and this spelled the end for the time being of the CODECA experiment.

Meanwhile in other parts of the Caribbean alternative strategies for cooperation and integration were being attempted in piecemeal fashion. International cooperation in the Caribbean has thus exhibited a wide range of structures, reflecting the growing autonomy of the region in the face of an awkward variety of governmental patterns remaining in the area. Evolution has proceeded from first, a joint Anglo-American agency to next, a four-power agency but with regular participation by the local territories, then to an international organization run almost entirely by the Caribbean territories themselves but with the sanction of the metropolitan powers and with the participation still of France, to, in latter years, a pattern of informal cooperation centered on a public corporation of the Puerto Rican government and with the metropolitan powers banished at last from the scene.

It is the aim of this book to document and interpret these experiments and innovations in intergovernmental cooperation dating back to the formation in 1942 of the Anglo-American Caribbean Commission. Since that year, of course, the world has witnessed the flourishing of an enormous network of global and regional international organizations. In addition to the United Nations itself, with its affiliated specialized and functional agencies, such as the World Health Organization and the Food and Agriculture Organization, we have the regional bodies which include the Organization of American States, the Organization of African Unity, and the League of Arab States. We have also the military alliance organizations such as the North Atlantic Treaty Organization (NATO), the Southeast Asia Treaty Organization (SEATO), the Central Treaty Organization (CENTO), and the Warsaw Pact. In Western Europe there have grown up the remarkable supranational Community structures centering on the European Economic Community, or Common Market. The success of these agencies has served as model and inspiration for the rival European Free Trade Association (EFTA) and also for attempts at, and proposals for, various types of common markets in other historically associated regions of the world, including the Caribbean. The U.N., too, has found it advisable to decentralize much of its economic activities through its regional commissions: Economic Commission for Europe, Economic Commission for Latin America, Economic Commission for Asia and the Far East, and Economic Commission for Africa. In addition there are many other international organizations, large and small, in all parts of the world, for almost every conceivable joint international endeavor.

International Cooperative Technical Assistance

One phenomenon which is apparent in all of these organizations and commissions is that they engage in what might be called *international cooperative technical assistance.* This is true of even the military alliances. By some variation on the theme of Parkinson's Law it appears that these alliance organizations, having set up a headquarters staff for military cooperation primarily, nevertheless always seem to find the necessary resources to engage in functional programs of international economic and technical cooperation. NATO has its fellowship programs, its technical centers, and it also sponsors conferences, meetings, and seminars devoted to the discussion of matters of interest to member countries.[2] SEATO has community development centers, technical training centers, and a cholera research laboratory.[3] Its publications and press releases devote considerably more space to these activities than to military maneuvers. Even CENTO has its Technical Assistance Program and Economic Committee.[4]

It would be nonsense, of course, to allege that simply because the Caribbean Commission was engaging in international cooperative technical assistance prior to the start of such activities by most other international organizations, therefore the Commission was the inventor and originator of these practices. We know that the U.N.'s functional agencies, for example, owe much of their background precedents in international cooperation to the work of the International Labor Organization and to other bodies associated with the League of Nations in the 1920s and 1930s.

Nevertheless the world of international organizations is in a very real sense a community of shared experiences, if for no other reason than that the same diplomats often serve successively as delegates to the assemblies and councils of different international organizations. The practices developed in the Caribbean very early in the postwar era were known to and approved by officials from government agencies of Great Britain, the United States, France, and the Netherlands. Some of these people participated later in the foundation of other international bodies. Thus their experiences with the Caribbean Commission could very well have entered into the planning for the inauguration of similar projects in other regions of the world.

It can be said with certainty that at least one international agency, the South Pacific Commission, was designed in direct imitation of the Caribbean Commission. The same U.S. Department of State official who helped write the agreement establishing the Caribbean Commission and who attended most of its early sessions also shared in the drafting of the agreement for the South Pacific Commission.* Of even greater significance than that, the secretary general of the Caribbean Commission and then of the Caribbean Organization, Mr. Clovis F. Beauregard, told me he had every reason to believe that certain practices of the Caribbean Commission were copied by the men who set up similar services in the Bureau of the Colombo Plan (for Cooperative Economic Development in South and Southeast Asia). He based this belief not only on the obvious similarity of the operations but more especially on the fact that certain British diplomats known to him by name helped set up the Colombo Plan operation after having served on the Caribbean Commission.

If indeed the Colombo Plan owes certain of its activities to the pioneering done by the Caribbean Commission, then the favor was returned by the Caribbean Organization, successor to the Caribbean Commission, which attempted to formulate a Caribbean Plan modeled frankly after the document which gave the Colombo Plan system its name.

It is thus apparent that for a fuller understanding of the techniques and practices of international organizations generally it is of value to study one set of such institutions in particular. As a case study, then, this book will center its attention on the Caribbean international agencies, not only because those agencies may well have contributed significantly to some of

*Mrs. Frances McReynolds Smith

the modern practices of international technical cooperation, but also because of the interesting succession of different international patterns which evolved in an effort to keep pace with the changing political status of the countries concerned. Still another reason for detailing this experience is the relative lack of attention that has been given to international cooperation in this hybrid region, which is neither North Atlantic nor Latin America, and which is still dotted with remnants of the imperial past.

Definition of Geographic Area

Actually to define the area covered by this study is made difficult not only because of the political changes in the territories involved but also because the successive international agencies chronicled here have each had somewhat different membership rosters or areas of concern.

At its widest extension the area which figures in this description of international cooperation will take in all of the territories in the general Caribbean region which as of 1946 were colonial or dependent areas. This would include the British Bahama Islands; British Virgin Islands; Jamaica; and all of what were then called the British West Indies islands, including Trinidad. French islands in the West Indies consist of Guadeloupe, Martinique, and their dependencies. Included in the Dutch realm are the Netherlands Antilles, consisting of three groups of three islands each: Saba, St. Martin, and St. Eustatius in the Windward chain; and Curacao, Aruba, and Bonaire, just off the north coast of Venezuela. American dependencies, of course, consist of Puerto Rico and the American Virgin Islands. Countries served by the Caribbean Commission and by its successor also included four *mainland* territories which because of their dependent status were not eligible in their own right for any other international association. In Central America, neighboring Guatemala, is British Honduras, which is still a colony. Then on the north coast of South America, east of Venezuela, there are the traditional three Guianas: British, French, and Dutch. Dutch Guiana is now officially called Surinam, and, along with the Netherlands Antilles, it is an Equal Partner of the Realm. French Guiana is a *département* of France, as are the islands. Technically these are not dependencies any more than Hawaii is a dependency of the United States. British Guiana emerged into independence as the state of Guyana on May 26, 1966.

Among the islands, Jamaica, Trinidad, and Barbados became fully independent during the years covered by this study, and certain of the other British islands have evolved into a new semi-independent status in which each is to be called an "Associated State of the United Kingdom." Future political progress toward greater autonomy or independence for the American, French, and Dutch territories is still problematical. The recent political evolution and the future prospects of all of these territories are discussed at some length in chapters 8 and 12.

The political geography of the Caribbean includes also the three independent island states of Cuba, Haiti, and the Dominican Republic. Although each of these republics participated to a limited extent in certain of the activities of the Caribbean Commission and Caribbean Organization, they were never really a part of the international structures dealt with in this book. As independent countries of long standing they were entitled to full membership in the United Nations and the Organization of American States.

It would be difficult to imagine any part of the world *less* likely to be the scene of regional cooperation and even regional international organization than the Caribbean area. This region has been, and still is, crisscrossed with boundaries which not only isolated these territories from each other but also bound most of them with political, economic, linguistic, and cultural ties to separate metropolitan powers thousands of miles away. Thus the fact that not only did international structures arise in this politically conglomerate region, but that they actually pioneered new techniques in international cooperation, makes it all the more worthwhile to recount this history of international cooperation in the Caribbean.

PATTERNS OF INTERNATIONAL COOPERATION
IN THE CARIBBEAN 1942–1969

1 □ THE HISTORICAL BACKGROUND

SOCIAL AND ECONOMIC CONDITIONS

The decade before World War II found the colonial islands and territories of the Caribbean sunk deep in poverty and backwardness. The per capita wealth was extremely low. The people were beset by disease, malnutrition, high mortality rates, and ignorance. There was little or no industrial development, and most of the regions were carrying a population density far out of proportion to the resources available for the support of their people even at miserably low standards of living. The economies of the colonies consisted for the most part of small-scale, native subsistence farming, supplemented by the production of sugar, bananas, cocoa, coffee, and other export crops which were highly vulnerable to world market fluctuations. The worldwide economic depression of the early 1930s brought unprecedented hardship and suffering to the colonies.

There was also the growing problem of racial tension. Except for Puerto Rico and the smaller Dutch islands, more than 90 percent of the people in the Caribbean colonial areas were Negroes. The economic hardships of the period naturally fell most heavily on this part of the population. Underlying racial antagonisms were therefore deepened as the contrast grew starker between the situation of the Negro majority and that of the small, but economically and politically dominant, white minority group in each colony.

Beginning in 1935 in the British island of St. Kitts, there occurred a series of labor and hunger riots and strikes, accompanied by a degree of violence and bloodshed which at times reached almost insurrectionary proportions. The disturbances spread to Barbados, Trinidad, and British Guiana among the British possessions; while at the same time depressed conditions in Puerto Rico were giving rise to similar disturbances there. Reaching a climax in 1937 and 1938, these riots resulted in some 40 to 50 deaths and 479 personal injuries in the British territories, and 26 deaths and scores of injuries in Puerto Rico.[1] The seriousness of these troubles was thus described by one writer in 1944:

The most important developments affecting the Caribbean in a century and a half have been the emancipation of slaves early in the nineteenth century and the spontaneous wave of riots and strikes that engulfed the islands at various times

3

during 1935–1938. The second initiated profound political change no less than the first . . . . For the first time in history the black masses, as distinct from the middle class colored intellectuals, were demonstrating a heretofore unsuspected labor solidarity throughout the Caribbean and demanding concessions.[2]

Moyne Commission

Both Great Britain and the United States reacted by sending commissions, committees, and individuals to the Caribbean to investigate the troubles. The most noteworthy analysis was that made by the British West Indian Royal Commission, under the chairmanship of Lord Moyne (Walter Edward, Baron). This Commission, consisting of eight commissioners in addition to Lord Moyne and the vice chairman, reached Jamaica and began its work in November 1938. The Moyne Commission report was completed in 1939, but it was not released for publication until 1945.[3]

The Royal Warrant of August 5, 1938, to the Moyne Commission stated the following purposes of the mission: "To investigate social and economic conditions in Barbados, British Guiana, British Honduras, Jamaica, the Leeward Islands, Trinidad and Tobago, and the Windward Islands, and matters connected therewith, and to make recommendations."[4] That the Commission had its work cut out for it is evidenced by the following statement which appears in the preface to the report:

In Jamaica, as elsewhere, the number of persons desiring to give evidence was so great that we could not find time to hear all of them without seriously limiting our opportunities of traveling about the Islands and making ourselves familiar with conditions at first hand. We therefore made it a rule to give preference to evidence submitted on behalf of groups of persons and organizations, and to avoid the repetition of evidence already given.[5]

The commissioners traveled 9,900 miles and in twenty-six different communities they interviewed 370 witnesses or groups of witnesses; the evidence which they collected was condensed and recorded in 798 memoranda.[6]

The published Moyne Commission report covers 480 pages, setting forth in great detail, complete with statistics and photographs, the miseries of the area. The Commission's general economic survey concludes with the following observation:

The trend of world conditions, which was generally favourable in the nineteenth century, has become generally adverse today to the development of tropical communities basing their economic life on the export of agricultural commodities. This fact both adds to the gravity of the economic difficulties of our West Indian colonies, and complicates, in ways that will become apparent later, the problem of relieving them.[7]

The Commission found appalling social and economic conditions everywhere. Unemployment was extremely high due largely to the seasonal nature of sugar production, the principal export crop. "The plight of the unemployed, aggravated by the seasonal character of employment, is serious to the point of desperation. There is no unemployment insurance in the West Indies and public assistance in the form of poor law relief is usually confined to the old and infirm."[8] Wage rates were found to be distressingly low. It was reported that women workers in Barbados, for example, normally received what was at that time the equivalent of about twenty cents a day (one shilling) when they worked, while the men received about thirty cents (one shilling, six pence) a day. On Jamaica wages for cane-cutting ranged between about twenty-five cents and eighty cents per day, and these were the highest rates paid for agricultural laborers anywhere in the survey area.[9]

The conditions in housing, health, nutrition, and education were desperate. The situation with respect to agricultural technology, industrial productivity, craftsmanship, and incentives for work was deteriorating badly. In short, the findings with regard to every common social problem presented a picture of almost unrelieved gloom. The proportion of illegitimacy was found to be "seldom less than 60 per cent and often in the neighborhood of 70 per cent of the population."[10] Housing conditions were described as "deplorable" in most areas:

It is no exaggeration to say that in the poorest parts of most towns and in many of the country districts a majority of the houses is largely made of rusty corrugated iron and unsound boarding . . . . Sanitation in any form and water supply are unknown in such premises, and in many cases no light can enter when the door is closed. These decrepit homes, more often than not, are seriously overcrowded, and it is not surprising that some of them are dirty and verminous . . . . In short, every condition that tends to produce disease is here to be found in serious form.[11]

In its conclusion, the Moyne Commission summarized the problem of the British West Indies.

The problem of the West Indies is essentially agrarian. Their populations came or were brought, to establish and carry on the cultivation of tropical produce . . . . At the time of our appointment, West Indian industries with few and local exceptions were suffering from a severe depression, which made itself chiefly felt in the amount of employment available in rural as in urban areas . . . .

At the same time, the cumulative effect of education, the press, wireless, the spectacle of the standards of living of the white people, and the reports of West Indians who have lived and worked abroad, particularly in the United States of America, has been to create a demand for better conditions of work and life. This demand has found expression from time to time in disorders and bloodshed . . . .

Furthermore, the population of the West Indies shows a steady and rapid rise; in particular, the high birth rate and decrease in infantile mortality are being and will increasingly be reflected in a proportionately still greater increase in the population of working age.

The crux of the West Indian problem is then, that a demand for better living conditions is becoming increasingly insistent among an expanding population at a time when world economic trends seriously endanger even the maintenance of present standards.[12]

Here, then, was a comprehensive survey of the situation in the British Caribbean colonies as of 1939. Many of the conclusions reached by the Moyne Commission would have applied with equal force to the French and Dutch colonies. So disturbed was the British government by the conditions in the West Indies, as revealed by the Moyne Commission, that the report was kept secret during the war, for fear that if released to the public it would be used by the Nazis for propaganda purposes.[13] Yet, despite the many demands of war, in fact right at the time of the Battle of Britain, the Parliament, in 1940, voted for a program of welfare and development in all of the British colonies, and allocated one million pounds of the total annually for use in the West Indies. Thus was reversed the traditional policy that colonies must be self-supporting. The precedent was established that colonies might look to the mother country for economic and social welfare assistance. A permanent comptroller for welfare and development in the West Indies, in the person of Sir Frank Stockdale, was appointed to administer the funds allocated for the area. Sir Frank established headquarters on the island of Barbados, and later became, along with Charles Taussig, one of the founders of the Anglo-American Caribbean Commission.[14] Clearly the riots and the Moyne Commission report had been a profound shock to the British government. The ground was prepared for further and more far-reaching changes to come in the years ahead.

American Official Investigations

Meanwhile the American government was greatly concerned over conditions in Puerto Rico and the Virgin Islands of the United States. Committees of both the Senate and the House of Representatives investigated economic conditions in those islands and looked critically into the administration of their affairs. The findings of these investigative groups presented to the American people a picture of great suffering and despair, in both Puerto Rico and the Virgin Islands. Senator Dennis Chavez of New Mexico, a member of the Committee on Territories and Insular Affairs, took the lead over a period of several years in investigating Puerto Rican conditions, through the use of extensive hearings in Washington, as well as through personal visits to the island by the subcommittee which he headed. Puerto Rico had been hard hit by the depression, and like the British colonies it suffered from chronic unemployment engendered by the disastrous single-crop economy. The Chavez committee in its preliminary report of 1943[15] found that the average income for a Puerto Rican family with 5.6 dependents was $350 per year, and that 35 percent of the families earned less than $200 annually. Unemployment was found to be on the increase. Local industries were practically at a standstill due to the lack of supplies normally imported from the United States.[16]

Included in this report was a statement by General Phillip B. Fleming, of the Federal Works Agency. General Fleming spelled out in greater detail the extent of the crisis in Puerto Rico.

Over 12 per cent of the island's population was totally unemployed in August, 1942, and unemployment conditions have not improved since then.

At the depth of the depression in the United States in March, 1933, unemployment was estimated at 11 per cent of the total population. The unemployment crisis in Puerto Rico is now more severe than it was in continental United States at its worst.

Wartime conditions which have reduced unemployment in the continental United States to less than one per cent of our population have at the same time skyrocketed unemployment in Puerto Rico.

Dependency in the island is of vast proportions. About half of the population is in great need. Complete economic collapse has been prevented only by assistance from the Federal Government.

In the past, Puerto Rico has imported most of its food from the continent. There is now a serious food shortage and malnutrition is prevalent.[17]

Rexford G. Tugwell, governor of Puerto Rico from 1941 to 1946, has amply publicized the miseries of Puerto Rico in his book, *The Stricken Land*.[18] His summary of the common plight of both the British and American dependencies in the prewar years is worth quoting at length.

Until Lord Moyne's investigation and the establishment of the [Anglo-American Caribbean] Commission, the Caribbean islands had been slipping almost imperceptibly into a Sargasso Sea of neglect. Their apogee had been more than a century in the past when sugar had been an asset rather than just another embarrassing surplus. Their transformation into liabilities had been unacknowledged by the governments which had profited from them in earlier days and which now refused to recognize, much less pay, the debt. Their people had fallen further and further away from a civilized scale of living, their downward curve crossing the rising one of the people whose wards they were. Wages at a shilling a day in the British islands, and the almost complete lack of social services, were facts which represented well enough to anyone with imagination what the situation had become by the beginning of the war. And then the cutting of intercourse by the submarines had severed what hold they still had on civilization. The great nations, in their preoccupation with more pressing matters, had simply let them go.[19]

WORLD WAR II CRISIS FOR THE ISLANDS

By 1940, however, the pressing matter which concerned both Great Britain and the United States—namely, the war then underway in Europe—was serving to focus renewed attention on the Caribbean dependencies. Even more significantly, the war crisis was working toward an international cooperative approach to the problems of the Caribbean colonies.

Act of Habana, 1940

There was, first of all, the frightening prospect that a victorious Nazi Germany might attempt to enforce a transfer to itself of sovereignty over the British, French, and Dutch colonies in the Caribbean. For its part, to meet this threat, the United States government dispatched a note to the German government, on June 17, 1940, stating that "in accordance with its traditional policy relating to the Western Hemisphere, the United States would not recognize any transfer, and would not acquiesce in any attempt to transfer, any geographic region of the Western Hemisphere from one non-American power to another non-American power."[20] Clearly, however, some concerted action by all of the American republics was necessary, since agreements in force among the twenty-one nations called for consultation in the face of any threat to the security of the Western hemisphere. The second meeting of ministers of foreign affairs of the American republics, which gathered at Havana from July 21 to July 30, 1940, therefore took steps to meet this threat of German seizure of the European colonies. Among the public documents representing the decisions reached by this meeting was the Act of Habana, consisting of a declaration and a resolution.[21] The declaration stated that if islands or regions in the possession of non-American nations should be in danger of becoming the subject of barter of territory or change of sovereignty, the American nations, taking into account the imperative need of continental security and the desires of the inhabitants of the islands or possessions, should set up a regime of provisional administration. This would take place under the conditions (a) that as soon as the conditions requiring this measure should cease to exist, and in the event that it would not be prejudicial to the safety of the American republics, such territories should be organized as autonomous states if it should appear that they were able to constitute and maintain themselves, or should be restored to their previous status, whichever alternative should appear to be the most practicable and just; and (b) that the regions should be placed temporarily under the provisional administration of the American republics, which should have the twofold purpose of contributing to the security and defense of the continent, and to the economic, political, and social progress of the regions. The resolution provided for the establishment of an emergency committee composed of a representative of each of the American republics which was to assume the administration of any region in the Western Hemisphere controlled by a European power whenever such assumption of administration should become necessary as an imperative emergency measure to safeguard the peace and security of the continents.

Destroyers for Bases

These arrangements for taking over the administration of the European colonies in the name of the Inter-American system never had to be put into effect, but the Act of Habana had served notice to the world that the fate of these colonies was a matter of international concern. Moreover, the same wartime danger to the security of the hemisphere which inspired the Act of Habana brought about, later in 1940, another international event which was to involve the United States directly in the affairs of the British colonies and which was to lead eventually to the formation of the Anglo-American Caribbean Commission. On September 2, 1940, notes were exchanged between the British ambassador at Washington and the American secretary of state, under which the United States acquired the right to lease for ninety-nine years naval and air bases in Newfoundland, in the islands of Bermuda, the Bahamas, Jamaica, St. Lucia, Trinidad, and Antigua, and in British Guiana. The right to the bases in Newfoundland and Bermuda was a gift of the British government, but the other British bases were acquired in exchange for fifty overage American destroyers.[22] In addition, at the invitation of the Netherlands government, the United States built and manned military, naval, and air installations on the islands of Curacao and Aruba, and in Surinam. In a message to Congress the President cited the agreement with Britain as "an epochal and far-reaching act of preparation for continental defense in the face of grave danger," and added:

This is the most important action in the reinforcement of our national defense that has been taken since the Louisiana Purchase. Then, as now, considerations of safety from overseas attack were fundamental.

The value to the Western Hemisphere of these outposts of security is beyond calculation . . . . They are essential to the protection of our Panama Canal, Central America, the northern portion of South America, the Antilles, Canada, Mexico, and our own eastern and Gulf seaboards.[23]

Taussig Commission

Although considerations of safety from overseas attack may have been the primary motive for the United States to enter into agreement with Britain, it soon became apparent that the actual establishment of the bases would involve the United States in the social and economic problems of the British colonies. Anticipating that erection of the bases might entail considerably more than the mere dispatch of construction materials and personnel, the President appointed a Commission to survey the social and economic problems of some parts of the area. Between November 15, 1940, and January 5, 1941, this Commission, under the chairmanship of Charles W. Taussig, visited Puerto Rico, the Virgin Islands of the United States, and all of the British colonies in the Caribbean area except British Guiana and British Honduras.[24] The Commission's immediate concern was with such matters as the attitude of the people of the Caribbean toward the establishment of the bases in particular and toward the United States in general. But the Taussig Commission also gave consideration, so far as time permitted, to the fundamentals of Caribbean problems.

Members of the Taussig Commission interviewed 150 representative individuals, including the governors of all the colonies, legislators, nearly all of the labor leaders in the area, planters, merchants, educators, medical men, presidents of chambers of commerce, and police officers. The Commission also visited schools, hospitals, churches, work projects, and military installations.

Rexford Tugwell and others credit Mr. Taussig with being the pioneer of the Caribbean Commission concept.* In a dispatch to Sumner Welles, under-secretary of state, from Antigua, on December 4, 1940, when his Commission was barely started on its inspection tour, Taussig reported:

> We put out feelers to ascertain whether the various British Colonies here would look with favor to the setting up of a joint permanent Caribbean social and economic fact-finding and research government organization that would explore our mutual problems. The response to this was always in the affirmative.[25]

On January 7, 1941, the Taussig Commission submitted its report to the President. In this report the Commission stated that it should be most clearly recognized that only if they acted as a regional unit could the Caribbean countries have any considerable influence in world economic deliberations. The report went on to say that the time was propitious for establishing closer relations between the United States and the British West Indies "with a view of finding common ground for a cooperative approach to world economic problems."[26] The report also emphasized the advantages which the Caribbean colonies would derive from working together as a unit both in meeting the war emergency and in carrying out

---

*Charles William Taussig, businessman, for many years head of the American Molasses Company, had long been personally concerned with the social and economic problems of the Caribbean. He is reported to have said once, of the Caribbean, "Here seems to converge the by-products of all the economic and political errors made by man in the past five hundred years." In addition to his business connections, Mr. Taussig had served in government as chairman of the National Advisory Committee, National Youth Administration, and member of the President's Advisory Committee for the Virgin Islands. He died suddenly of a heart attack in 1948.

broad-scale research activities designed to cope with basic problems in agriculture, labor, and social welfare.[27]

While in Barbados on this tour, Taussig discussed his ideas with Sir Frank Stockdale and won the enthusiasm of that official for the idea of an international economic and social organization in the Caribbean. Clearly the foundations were laid for the establishment of the Caribbean Commission.[28]

It is appropriate therefore to end this chapter by citing the first paragraph of the first report of the Anglo-American Caribbean Commission:

It has been no secret that the political, social and economic situation in the Caribbean has left much to be desired. In addition to the attention paid by the United States Government to the problems of Puerto Rico and the Virgin Islands of the United States, the British Government appointed by Royal Commission shortly before the war, namely, in 1938, to investigate conditions in the British West Indies, and the major recommendations of that Commission were accepted early in 1940. In that same year, when the United States acquired 99-year leases of areas for military and naval bases in the British West Indies, the affairs of the United States and Great Britain in the Caribbean became hopefully "intermingled." For practical reasons of security as well as international conscience it became desirable for both countries to cooperate in social and economic development of the area.[29]

2 □ ESTABLISHMENT OF THE ANGLO-AMERICAN CARIBBEAN COMMISSION

Copies of the Taussig Commission report were made available to the British Government early in 1941, and the British in turn furnished to the United States government a copy of the then secret Moyne Commission report. On April 9, 1941, President Roosevelt authorized Under-Secretary of State Sumner Welles to proceed in accordance with the recommendations of the Taussig Commission report looking toward the establishment of some sort of joint agency with the British.[1] Then on October 30, 1941, the President announced the appointment of Taussig, Tugwell, and Coert du Bois as members of a joint Anglo-American committee to consider the problems of mutual interest to both countries in the Caribbean area. Mr. Tugwell was then governor of Puerto Rico, and Mr. du Bois was the officer in charge of the newly formed Caribbean Office of the Department of State.

The American members of this joint committee were instructed to concern themselves primarily with the organization and maintenance of the flow of supplies of food to the West Indies adequate to sustain normal dietary standards. The members were to visit the British Caribbean territories where American bases had been established to ascertain what could be done to raise living standards by means of improving agricultural education; also by the transfer of peoples, the improvement of transportation facilities, and by the development of the Caribbean economy through trade agreements.[2]

Official Documents

Through these committee activities and by personal missionary work on his own, Taussig had succeeded by early 1942 in convincing everyone concerned, including the British Colonial Office, that a joint British-U.S. agency was called for to meet the needs of the war and to plan for the solution of common basic problems. The British government therefore joined with the United States government in the formal establishment of the Anglo-American Caribbean Commission (A.A.C.C.). The new organization was created by means of a joint communiqué released simultaneously in Washington and London on March 9, 1942, by the two governments. The text of the joint communiqué was as follows:

For the purpose of encouraging and strengthening social and economic cooperation between the United States of America and its possessions and bases in the area known geographically and politically as the Caribbean, and the United Kingdom and the British Colonies in the same area, and to avoid unnecessary duplication of research in these fields, a commission to be known as the Anglo-American Caribbean Commission, has been jointly created by the two Governments. The Commission will consist of six members; three from each country, to be appointed respectively by the President of the United States and His Majesty's Government in the United Kingdom—who will designate one member from each country as co-chairman.

Members of the Commission will concern themselves primarily with matters pertaining to labor, agriculture, housing, health, education, social welfare, finance, economics, and related subjects in the territories under the British and United States flags within this territory, and on these matters will advise their respective Governments.

The Anglo-American Caribbean Commission in its studies and in the formulation of its recommendations will necessarily bear in mind the desirability of close cooperation in social and economic matters between all regions adjacent to the Caribbean.

The following appointments of co-chairmen have been made:

For Great Britain:

Sir Frank Stockdale

For the United States:

Charles W. Taussig

The remaining members of the Commission will be named later by the Governments concerned.

The White House press release of March 9, 1942 containing the text of this joint communiqué continued as follows:

In addition to naming Mr. Charles W. Taussig, of New York, as co-chairman for the United States of the Anglo-American Caribbean Commission, the President has selected as the other two American members of the Commission the Honorable Rexford G. Tugwell, Governor of Puerto Rico, and Mr. Coert du Bois, Chief of the Caribbean Office of the Department of State.

He has also named as a Caribbean Advisory Committee Governor Tugwell and the Honorable Martin Travieso, Justice of the Supreme Court of Puerto Rico; Judge William H. Hastie, Civilian Aide to the Secretary of War; and Mr. Carl Robbins of California, formerly President of the Commodity Credit Corporation, together with Mr. Charles W. Taussig, who is also chairman of this Committee.

The study to be undertaken by the Caribbean Advisory Committee relates to the economic and social problems of the very large number of human beings in the British and American islands. The study is intended to improve the standards of living in all of the islands concerned.

It is, of course, clear that neither the Anglo-American Caribbean Commission nor the President's Caribbean Advisory Committee has any authority other than the formulation of recommendations to be submitted in the first instance, to the American and British Governments, and, in the second instance, to the President.[3]

The joint communiqué which served as the original source of authority for the A.A.C.C. was in the form of an executive agreement. Hence the permanence of the new arrangement was not guaranteed as effectively as it might have been by treaty. There was no absolute assurance that the Commission was to be a permanent organization, although there was no indication that its status was to be otherwise. As far as the United States was concerned, the A.A.C.C. was exclusively a creation of the executive branch, financed from the President's emergency fund and accountable directly to the President.[4]

The second annual report of the Anglo-American Caribbean Commission, for the year 1944, had this to say with regard to the original establishment of the Commission:

That the body was established at all was due, in the first place, to the recognition by both Governments that they were confronted with a fundamental problem which may be very briefly and boldly summarized as that of bringing social and economic advancement to a heavily populated region that was largely dependent for its prosperity on the vagaries of a limited number of agricultural crops produced for export, and for its food supplies, largely on imports from outside.

There was nothing new in the recognition of this problem. Many investigating bodies, both American and British, had drawn attention to it for years. Nor did action await the formation of the Anglo-American Caribbean Commission, for much legislation for the betterment of social conditions had been passed and progress had been made, both in the United States territories in the area and in the British West Indies, long before the Commission had even been thought of.

What was entirely new in the Caribbean, and largely new in world history, was that the Governments concerned should have taken the view that international cooperation, on that basis, would provide a powerful auxiliary in the fight for progress; and should have set up the necessary machinery for the purpose.

Through the machinery that was, in fact, set up, the Commission—in itself purely an advisory body—has been brought into the closest possible association with the appropriate agencies of government.[5]

A.A.C.C. Meetings

The A.A.C.C. lost no time in beginning its work. The first full meeting of the Commission took place in Trinidad, March 26–31, 1942, less than a month after the official creation of the new organization. Altogether, during the lifetime of the bipartite Commission, between 1942 and 1945 seven formal meetings were held, plus two conferences under Commission sponsorship.[6]

Regional Coordination

Prior to the establishment of the A.A.C.C. no machinery existed for the interchange of information and experience among the governing authorities of the British and American dependencies. Even the British colonies among themselves had very little direct contact; officially each colonial government or administration could communicate only with the Colonial Office in London. As an example of what was lacking, both Great Britain and the United States maintained agricultural experiment stations in their respective Caribbean territories, and though these British and American stations dealt with agricultural problems common to the entire region they did not exchange information with each other. Neither did the health services of the two powers in the Caribbean consult with each other concerning common health problems. The governor of Jamaica, wanting to find out how some problem was being handled in Puerto Rico, had to go through the British Colonial Office; the British Colonial Office passed the request to the British Foreign Office; the British Foreign Office to the British ambassador in Washington; the British ambassador to the Department of State; the Department of State to the Department of the Interior; and finally through the Interior Department the request could be officially dispatched to the governor of Puerto Rico. The governor's reply would naturally proceed back through the same channels, eventually to reach the governor of Jamaica through the Colonial Office in London.[7]

Caribbean Research Council

To help remedy such obvious deficiencies in communication, the Commission, at its fourth meeting, in August 1943, created the Caribbean Research Council, its first auxiliary body. The Research Council was to act as an advisory body to the Commission and to encourage exchange of information concerning the mutual problems of the two member nations in the Caribbean. It was "to survey needs, determine what research has been done, arrange for dissemination and exchange of the results of research, provide for conferences between research workers or extension workers and recommend what further research and cooperation should be undertaken."[8]

Members of the Council were to be "not less than seven nor more that fifteen persons to represent Great Britain; the Netherlands, and the United States."[9] It is interesting to note from this inclusion of the Netherlands that even in 1943 the A.A.C.C. was looking toward a broader membership. The official document creating the Council went on to state that "provision for the subsequent participation of representatives of other countries in this area is contemplated."[10]

The Commission believed that the problems which had been considered by the recent United Nations Conference on Food and Agriculture (Hot Springs, Virginia, May 1943) were particularly important to the Caribbean area and that the findings of that Conference should be implemented as soon as possible. The Commission therefore set up as the first sectional committee of the Caribbean Research Council a Provisional Committee on Nutrition, Agriculture, Fisheries, and Forestry.[11] Then at its sixth meeting in March 1945, the A.A.C.C. created four additional committees, and the Caribbean Research Council was placed on a permanent basis. The four additional committees were Public Health and Medicine, Industrial Technology, Building and Engineering Technology, and Social Sciences. At the same time the Commission appointed a deputy chairman and a research secretary to serve as the nucleus of the Research Council's organization.[12]

One of the first projects sponsored by the Research Council was the Caribbean Symposium on Land Tenure, which opened at Mayaguez, Puerto Rico, on August 27, 1944. Ralph Bunche reports:

At this symposium on one of the knottiest problems of the region technical papers were presented by representatives from the territories themselves, as well as from the Mother Countries. It is significant that in this symposium delegations were in attendance, for the first time at any function of the AACC, from Cuba, Haiti, and the Dominican Republic. The Netherlands West Indies were also represented. The discussion of the papers presented at this symposium was open to the public, which took advantage of the opportunity to participate. Some groups went so far as to have their interests in the question presented by lawyers.[13]

West Indian Conference

The second auxiliary body set up by the A.A.C.C. was the West Indian Conference. Direct Anglo-American representation having been provided for through membership in the Commission, there remained the problem of devising some sort of a democratic system of conferences and consultations with the inhabitants of the territories themselves. At its third meeting, in 1943, therefore, the Commission recommended to the two member governments that arrangements be made for regular consultation with local representatives of the territories and colonies for the purpose of dealing with common Caribbean problems. Specifically, the Commission recommended:

that a regular system of West Indian Conferences should be inaugurated under the auspices of the Caribbean Commission to discuss such matters. Each territory or group in the Caribbean area should send two delegates. The Conference should meet as and when occasion arises and subjects come up suitable for consideration. It should be a standing body; that is not to say that the representatives at the Conference should always be the same people, but it should have a definite continuity of existence. The Conference should in fact follow on the lines of the Jamaica Conference which met earlier this year under the auspices of the Caribbean Commission. The Secretariat of the Commission, central and regional, would be available to provide assistance. The personnel of the Conference would be varied according to the subject to be discussed. Although the Conference would start only with British and American participation, the possibility is left open of inviting any other countries such as might be interested in particular projects. The Chairman would be the joint Chairman of the Caribbean Commission who is a national of the territory in which the Conference is being held. In the event of the appropriate joint Chairman being absent after the proceedings had been formally opened by his colleague the chair would be taken by another member of the Commission of the same nationality as the absent joint Chairman. Other members of the Caribbean Commission and experts invited by them would have the right of attending all meetings of the Conference.

The Conference should be advisory but it would be hoped that it would attain a really influential position, and it would be open at any time to the interested Governments to agree among themselves to delegate to it any specific powers which they might think desirable.[14]

In January 1944, these recommendations were agreed to by Great Britain and the United States. The joint communiqué issued by the two governments commented on the importance of the recently established Caribbean Research Council and set forth the need for still another means of approach to the amelioration of conditions in the West Indies.

It remained, however, to broaden the base for approach to Caribbean problems to include consultations with local representatives—not necessarily officials—of the territories and colonies concerned. The value of such counsel is recognized and provision has now been made for its expression through a regular system of West Indian Conferences, which, by agreement between His Majesty's Government in the United Kingdom and the United States Government, is to be inaugurated under the auspices of the Anglo-American Caribbean Commission to discuss matters of common interest and especially of social and economic significance to the Caribbean countries.[15]

The first West Indian Conference met in Barbados from March 21 to March 30, 1944. This occasion has been cited by many authors as a historic first in international relations. There were two delegates from each colony or territory, as originally recommended, but only two national sovereignties (British and American) were represented at the Conference, and many of the "delegates" from the British areas were in fact Colonial Service officials stationed in the colonies they were said to represent at the Conference. Charles W. Taussig and others have therefore preferred to regard the second West Indian Conference, of 1946, where many more native leaders were present, and where the Conference was made up of delegations from fifteen territories under four different national sovereignties, as the truly historic and precedent-setting occasion in international relations. In any event, the West Indian Conference sessions, whether the series be regarded as having its true beginning in 1944 or 1946, marked a significant departure from precedent in dealing with the problems of colonial and dependent areas.

It was decided that discussions at the first (Barbados) Conference, 1944, would be confined to matters which were conducive to prompt action, with a number of other important subjects reserved for future sessions. After three days of general and public sessions, the Conference split up into individual committees which considered and reported on the following agenda:

1. Means for raising the nutritional level:
   (a) local food production.
   (b) expansion of fisheries.
2. Reabsorption into civil life of persons engaged in war employment.
3. Planning of public works for the improvement of agriculture, education, housing, and public health.
4. Health protection and quarantine.
5. Industrial development.
6. The Caribbean Research Council—possibilities for expansion.[16]

The reports of the committees on this agenda were submitted to the full Conference, which formally adopted them at the final public session on March 30, and recommended that the "Governments of Great Britain and the United States and the Governments of the territories represented at the Conference should be asked to use their utmost endeavors to give immediate consideration and early effect to such of our recommendations as may be transmitted to them with the support of the Anglo-American Caribbean Commission."[17] To many older Colonial Office officials the tone of this document, issuing from a conference of colonial delegates, came as a distinct shock.

On March 30, 1944, the day the West Indian Conference session ended, the full Anglo-American Caribbean Commission, in its fifth meeting, also in Barbados, agreed to examine the Conference report immediately so as to be able to make prompt recommendations concerning it to the two member governments. This undertaking was amply carried out by the Commission. By means of personal meetings and of a correspondence which soon attained large proportions, it discussed the recommendations of the Conference as a whole and those of each of its committees, with all central and local governments concerned.[18]

The recommendations of the Barbados Conference, as approved by the full Commission, were accepted in principle by the governments of the United States and Great Britain in an exchange of notes dated June 24, 1944, and October 10, 1944. In this correspondence the United States secretary of state informed the British ambassador in Washington that the

United States government endorsed in principle the recommendations made by the West Indian Conference and would give "sympathetic consideration" to any specific proposals based on them that might be submitted by the A.A.C.C. In reply the British ambassador declared that his government regarded the Conference as "marking a notable advance in the development of international cooperation in the Caribbean," and that it equally endorsed the recommendations in principle.[19]

An illustration of the great care with which the recommendations of the Barbados West Indian Conference session were examined, and a remarkable example of the extent to which a colonial power expressed itself as willing to accede to the wishes of its dependent territories, is provided by a look at the action which followed on the part of the British government the adoption by the Conference of Resolution 4. Resolution 4 was as follows:

> Questions of inter-Caribbean trade have been mentioned during our discussions and we recommend that efforts should be made to expand trade within the area and that, as a first step, the various Governments should consider the abolition of import duties on foodstuffs produced within the area.

On October 9, 1944, the British secretary of state for the colonies addressed a circular dispatch to all of the governors of the West Indian colonies. Paragraphs 5 and 6 of that circular are worthy of insertion into the record at this point.

> 5. The only means by which the recommendations of the Conference could be put into operation without giving rise to the infringements of Treaty obligations mentioned above, would be by the establishment of a full Customs Union. Even if this means were adopted, it would presumably be necessary to limit the operation of the resolution to the British Caribbean Colonies, since it is very difficult to see how the establishment of a Customs Union between British and American territories in the Caribbean could be made compatible with existing preferential arrangements applying to the British West Indian Colonies, or, as far as I am able to judge, with the customs arrangements applicable to the U.S. dependencies.
>
> 6. The establishment of a Customs Union embracing the British Colonies in the West Indies would undoubtedly be a matter of difficulty and of far reaching implications such as a restriction on the extent to which legislatures in the separate Colonies could vary tariffs without the concurrence of other Governments within the Union. In spite, however, of the very serious obstacles I am myself inclined to the view that such a Customs Union would have considerable advantages if it could be brought into operation and if it were acceptable to popular opinion in the Colonies concerned. In this latter connection, I have noted with interest that a recent meeting of the Chambers of Commerce of the British West Indies has passed a resolution in favour of the "Economic Federation" of the British West Indies. If therefore, the institution of a Customs Union were acceptable to West Indian public opinion and West Indian legislatures, I should be glad to consider the

possibility of putting the proposal into effect and the measures which would have to be taken to that end.[20]

Surely for 1944 this was a remarkable expression of willingness on the part of a colonial power to adopt far-reaching policies on the basis of their acceptability to colonial public opinion and to the wishes of colonial legislatures. The West Indian Conference was well launched as a body of significant influence. Even the skeptical Governor Tugwell of Puerto Rico was converted to the cause of West Indian Conferences. After expressing at length his disappointment and cynicism over the way—according to him—that the British Colonial Service officials sought to stave off the Barbados Conference or to render it innocuous through the handpicking of "safe" delegates from among the more "responsible" native elements, he records that he was truly surprised at the thorough manner in which the Conference settled down to important business and at the meekness with which the British and American governments received the Conference's far-reaching recommendations. Governor Tugwell was finally moved to remark, "It might be that, after all, a significant piece of international machinery had been created."[21]

Early in 1946 a joint statement was made by the two governments regarding all of the recommendations made by the West Indian Conference session of 1944. This document was published for the information of the second session of the West Indian Conference, which convened at St. Thomas, Virgin Islands of the United States, from February 21 to March 13, 1946. This important paper consisted of thirty-seven detailed "Conclusions" reached jointly by the two governments, accepting with some reservations the recommendations of the first session, and setting forth the policies by which the two governments intended to put the Conference recommendations into effect.[22] This was the first time in history that two metropolitan governments had agreed to base joint policies with respect to their dependent areas upon the recommendations of the territories concerned.[23]

One of the recommendations of the first session was that another meeting of the West Indian Conference should be held within twelve months. The Commission, however, after thoughtful consideration of the matter, came to the reluctant conclusion that it would not be practicable and desirable to hold another West Indian Conference in 1945. Attention had to be given to the comments of certain local governments to the effect that the continuing demands of the war made it impossible for them to devote sufficient time and personnel to ensure the success of another Conference so soon. Furthermore it was realized that several of the recommendations of the first session were still pending because of the continuing shortage of men and materials to put them into effect. Thus it developed that the second session of the West Indian Conference was not held until

1946 (February 21 to March 13), under the sponsorship of the newly created four-power Caribbean Commission. The Barbados Conference was therefore the first and only session of the West Indian Conference held under the auspices of the original Anglo-American Caribbean Commission.

British and U.S. National Sections

Permanent organization in the form of a headquarters and a central secretariat was never fully achieved by the old A.A.C.C. The machinery of the Commission consisted of two national sections, British and United States. The British Section, headed by Sir Frank Stockdale, was in Barbados, where it was virtually a part of the Development and Welfare Organization in the West Indies.* This body had been created in 1940 by the British government to begin the work of improving social and economic conditions in the West Indies, in accordance with the Moyne Commission recommendations. Headquarters of the United States Section of the A.A.C.C. was in Washington; the unit was administratively a part of the Department of State. Coordination between the two sections was provided for by the setting up in Washington of a branch office of the British Section, in quarters adjacent to the United States Section offices. This branch office in Washington of the British Section came under the control of a British resident commissioner, who also held the post of head of the British Colonies Supply Mission in Washington. These two offices of the A.A.C.C. in Washington maintained a small joint secretarial staff, library, and public reading room, at 810 Eighteenth Street, Northwest.[24]

At the second meeting of the full Commission, in Washington, May 26 to June 6, 1942, it was determined that the duties of a permanent secretariat

should be to keep records of the Commission, prepare for and attend meetings, and take such action arising out of conclusions at such meetings as it may be instructed to undertake by the Co-Chairman of the Commission. The secretariat should also have the regular function of keeping in touch with other bodies which may undertake the carrying out of work recommended by the Commission and of receiving and—if necessary—distributing information, e.g., publications and reports dealing with technical subjects and matters of social welfare.[25]

Specifically it was recommended that

*Sir Frank Arthur Stockdale was primarily an eminent agricultural scientist. As early as 1905 he was a lecturer in the Imperial Department of Agriculture for the West Indies. He conducted botanical research in 1908 in British Guiana, and then directed agricultural work in Mauritius in 1912. He also served in Ceylon. Before being sent to the West Indies he served as agricultural adviser to the secretary of state for the colonies, and he edited the journal *Tropical Agriculture* from 1916 to 1928.

British West Indian governments should be encouraged to use the secretariat of the Commission as a channel for inquiries which they may wish to have made in the United States on subjects within the Commission's terms of reference; the governments of American territories similarly to make use of the secretariat whenever convenient for inquiries of a similar character which they may desire to make of British official agencies.[26]

In the absence of a true joint secretariat these functions were carried on separately and not always uniformly by the respective national sections, with some of the burden carried by the jointly operated library. A great deal of the responsibility came to be assumed by the executive secretaries of the two sections in Washington.[27]

Native West Indians Added to Commission

There remains one final development for me to cover before I leave this discussion of the formal structure of the old A.A.C.C. On June 30, 1945, the two member governments issued the following joint communiqué.

For the purpose of associating the peoples of the Caribbean area more closely with the work of the Anglo-American Caribbean Commission and of including in its membership representatives of those peoples, it has been agreed by the Governments of the United States and the United Kingdom to increase the membership of the Commission from three to four members on each side.

This decision modifies the joint communiqué issued in Washington and London on March 9, 1942, when the Anglo-American Caribbean Commission was created.[28]

At the same time as this communiqué was issued the two governments made separate announcements with regard to their future plans for the Commission. The United States announcement said that the additional member of the American Section of the Commission would be nominated from Puerto Rico and appointed by the President. The British statement said that the British Government had full sympathy with the demand which had existed for some time for the appointment of a British West Indian unofficial member to the Commission.* The contemplated expansion of the Commission would permit the appointment of two such commissioners, as Sir Frank Stockdale had retired and one other British commissioner, Mr. A. J. Wakefield, had left his post in the West Indies.

---

*By the word "unofficial" with reference to Commission members or West Indian Conference delegates, the British meant simply individuals who were not themselves British government officials. There was no implication that such persons were in any sense less than full Commission members or delegates. In practice, however, "unofficial" was virtually equivalent to "native" or "Negro."

The British government proposed that the British unofficial delegates to the second West Indian Conference consider and decide upon the method of selection of West Indian representation on the Commission, and if they wished to do so, should themselves proceed to make the selections.[29]

Subsequent developments in 1946 should be reported here to complete the narrative of this change in the composition of the Commission. The British West Indian unofficial delegates to the second session of the West Indian Conference chose Mr. Norman Manley of Jamaica for one of the two British vacancies on the Commission. A tie vote resulted from the balloting for the other vacancy. When efforts failed to break the tie through taking another poll by correspondence, the deadlock was resolved by the secretary of state for the colonies in favor of Mr. Garnet Gordon of the Windward Islands. In a statement announcing his decision, the secretary of state for the colonies declared that he had taken into account the fact that Mr. Gordon was from the eastern Caribbean, while the other candidate was, like Mr. Manley, from the western area of the Caribbean. Mr. Gordon thus provided for representation from as wide an area of the British Caribbean colonies as was possible.

In April 1946, the United States government announced the appointment of Mr. Rafael Pico of Puerto Rico, chairman of the Puerto Rico Planning Board, as the fourth United States commissioner.[30]

In this fashion, therefore, arrangements were made by both member governments to include natives of the West Indies on the governing body of the Commission.

3 □ ACHIEVEMENTS OF THE ANGLO-AMERICAN CARIBBEAN COMMISSION

WARTIME PROJECTS

The creation of the Anglo-American Caribbean Commission in March 1942 coincided with the beginning of the full-scale German submarine campaign in the Caribbean area. Thus to the long-term economic decline of the colonies, aggravated by wartime dislocation of markets and shipping, was added the threat of nearly complete isolation from the rest of the world. Islands which for generations had exchanged sugar and other primary products for foodstuffs and manufactured goods from the outside world faced the prospect of actual starvation, as ship after ship was sent to the bottom by the relentless submarines. Dominica and British Guiana were without bread for more than two weeks, and the American consul at Antigua reported to the Department of State on September 5, 1942:

A small loan of flour from the Army base here was effected through the Consulate yesterday. . . . There is little doubt that a considerable part of the population is now going without food for several days of the week. A large number of laborers, including base workers, have recently left their jobs during the day complaining that they were unable to continue work because of the lack of food.[1]

It is beyond the scope of this book to describe in detail the many substantive projects undertaken by the A.A.C.C. and by the Caribbean Commission over the years, but no account of the Commission's importance and prestige in Caribbean affairs would be complete without a summary of its achievements in meeting the war threat. Although still a new organization, working without effective precedents, the Commission began at once to keep in close touch with war developments in the area. With respect to the emergency problems, it initiated some measures, it contributed guidance to others, and it acted as a "catalytic agent" with respect to still others.[2]

At its very first meeting, in Trinidad, March 26 to 31, 1942, the Commission had to turn its attention to the urgent problems of food. It was imperative to insure food supplies and reserves and to increase local food production. The most pressing immediate task was to arrange for some sort of relatively secure system of inter-island distribution of supplies.

Conference of Supply Officers, 1942

For help in coping with this essential problem the Commission devised the technique of calling in experts on an *ad hoc* basis to advise it on specialized subjects. The commission therefore convened in Jamaica from May 15 to 18, 1942, a Conference of Supply Officers. Comprising officials from the British and American territories come together to cope with a common problem on a mutual basis, this meeting was the early prototype of the future West Indian Conference sessions.

Emergency Land-Water Highway

One of the most striking achievements of this Conference of Supply Officers was the establishment of the Emergency Land-Water Highway. This was an ingenious arrangement designed to escape the menace of the submarines by taking advantage of the comparatively short stretches of open sea between Florida or the Gulf Coast and Cuba, and between the main islands of the West Indies. The first section of the Highway was a shuttle service between Florida and Gulf ports and Havana, Cuba. The other links in the system were a railroad from Havana to Santiago de Cuba, on the eastern end of the island; small boat service across the narrow straits separating Santiago de Cuba and Port-au-Prince, Haiti; a truck service from Port-au-Prince across the island of Santa Domingo to San Pedro de Macoris, Dominican Republic; and another small boat service from San Pedro de Macoris to Mayaguez, Puerto Rico. This arrangement eliminated an 800-mile exposure to the Nazi submarines. Jamaica also participated by operating a shuttle between Santiago de Cuba and Port Antonio, Jamaica, an overwater distance of about 120 miles.[3]

Putting the Highway into operation involved a number of technical and administrative problems. Mr. Taussig, American co-chairman of the Commission, arranged for certain adjustments in railroad rates and services to Florida, for the provision of suitable sea craft, and for the expansion of the necessary port facilities. Then, with the essential cooperation of the governments of Cuba, the Dominican Republic, and Haiti, the United States War Department and the Public Roads Administration rebuilt and maintained the road crossing Santo Domingo and made certain improvements in the railroad across Cuba. Funds were supplied by the Lend-Lease Administration. Truck owners in Haiti and the Dominican Republic entered into contracts to put their trucks exclusively in the service of the Emergency Highway in return for a guarantee of a supply of tires and equipment.[4]

Transport of supplies over the Emergency Land-Water Highway began in October 1942 and continued until August 1943, when a considerable reduction of the submarine menace made it possible to suspend service over this cumbersome and expensive route.

West Indian Schooner Pool

Associated with this rerouting of shipping was another early achievement of the A.A.C.C.—the West Indian Schooner Pool. Unlike the Emergency Highway, which operated for barely a year, the Schooner Pool not only survived the war but continues in operation on a limited scale even today.

The Schooner Pool was organized by the Commission to supplement the Emergency Highway by coordinating inter-Caribbean trade in the eastern area from the Leeward Islands in the north to British Guiana in the south. The purpose was to centralize control over the movement of inter-island sailing vessels so that the most urgent shipping services received priority. The Pool collected a fee for each ton of cargo it carried, and from these funds it defrayed the expenses of keeping the schooners and sloops in operation, it indemnified the owners for loss of vessels sunk by enemy action, and it paid gratuities to the families of crew members lost in action. At the height of its operation about 85 percent of the schooners in the Caribbean area were participating.[5]

The head of the West Indian Schooner Pool was Captain S. H. Trew, an American citizen. He was, however, paid out of British funds and had his headquarters on the British island of Barbados.[6] All in all, the operation of the Schooner Pool was a striking example of a successful international cooperative effort involving a wide range of public and private interests—British colonial administrations, shippers, warehousemen, shipping agents, ship owners, masters, and crews.

The long-range advantages of the Pool quickly became apparent, and after the war it was reorganized under a new name: the Schooner Owners' Association.

Recruitment of Labor for War Work

Another of the early problems faced by the Commission which cut across both the requirements of the war and the long-term needs of the area was that of chronic unemployment and low wages. The Commission quickly perceived that if surplus Caribbean labor could be gotten into work related to the prosecution of the war a dual purpose would be served. Some of the slack of unemployment in the islands was taken up early in the war by construction work on the American bases gained in the destroyer deal with Britain. But by 1942, with the virtual completion of the bases, this source of employment for West Indians was beginning to decline.

The Commission realized that meanwhile, in the United States, the diversion of manpower to war industries and to the armed forces was creating a serious shortage of farm labor, especially in areas requiring a great deal of hand labor in the cultivation and harvesting of seasonal crops. Efforts were therefore begun by the Commission, in cooperation with other interested agencies, to recruit West Indian labor for agricultural work in the United States. On March 16, 1943, an agreement was negotiated by the United States War Food Administration with the government of the Bahamas for the importation of laborers from that colony to the United States. A similar agreement was concluded with Jamaica on April 2, 1943. The A.A.C.C. actively assisted in making these arrangements and in eliminating the various administrative and jurisdictional difficulties which arose. Largely because of the intense work of the Commission in pulling together all of the agencies and facilities involved in the operation, it was only a matter of days between the recruitment of the workers and their arrival at the scene of their new employment in the United States.[7]

In 1944 the United States War Manpower Commission entered the picture by arranging for the transfer of certain West Indian laborers from farm work to war industry. In the fall of 1944 about six thousand workers from Barbados and British Honduras were shifted from farms to industry, in accordance with agreements reached with their respective colonial governments. Other such transfers followed later. In November of the same year, 1944, the British West Indies Central Labor Organization was launched on an unofficial basis to look after the interests of all of the Caribbean workers except those from the Bahamas. The A.A.C.C. kept in close touch with all of these problems and provided the necessary interagency and international coordination.[8]

Cutbacks in industry at the end of the war forced the release of some West Indian laborers but many of them were able to transfer back to agricultural labor in the United States. Altogether, from 1943 to the end of 1947, 116,124 British West Indians were brought to the United States. Their gross earnings were estimated at about one hundred million dollars, of which some forty million was sent back home to the colonies. The quality of the work performed by these West Indians was considered highly satisfactory, and the laborers earned the respect of all concerned for the spirit with which they adjusted themselves to employment in the United States.[9]

Counteracting Enemy Propaganda

Still another urgent wartime problem which had already become acute by the time the A.A.C.C. was established was that of the psychological impact of Axis propaganda. All of the social, economic, and political problems of the area were exploited in enemy radio broadcasts beamed to the Caribbean, and by 1942 the effect on public morale in the West Indies was noticeable. The Nazis broadcasted the gory details of every ship sunk by submarine action, using as their theme the repeated slogan, "He who sails for North America sails certainly to death."

To counter this enemy propaganda, the A.A.C.C. began on December 1, 1942, to transmit from the United States its own radio program for the West Indies, to supplement the BBC coverage of the area. Known as the "West Indian Radio Newspaper," this daily program offered international news and news of the Caribbean region; American popular music; health, home economics, sports, folklore, and history; editorial opinion; interviews; and information about the work of the Commission. The material which was used included recordings made by West Indian officials and by West Indians living and working in the United States. This daily broadcast service continued until 1946.[10]

LONG-RANGE CONSTRUCTION WORK OF THE A.A.C.C.

Many of the other early projects undertaken by the Commission could with justification be cited as ultimately contributing to the war effort. In fact it is probable that in the absence of the war emergency the A.A.C.C. would never have been created. Yet in a larger sense the basic problems of the Caribbean area which the Commission was set up to deal with had a timeless quality which was quite unrelated to the military action then in progress. Owing to the submarine campaign the new Commission was forced to deal at once with the shipping and supply problem and with other war crises as well; but it is noteworthy that in the joint communiqué which set up the A.A.C.C. in 1942 there is not one mention of the war except for a passing reference to the American bases in the area. Taussig, Stockdale, and others involved in the founding of the Commission knew that the problems of the Caribbean were deeper and more permanent than the war and that they would eventually require solution in any case. They wisely took advantage of the immediate crisis to build an organization that looked to the future.

Thus it developed that after the first few months of its existence the Commission found itself dealing almost entirely with essentially peacetime problems. Once the supply situation was under control and the submarine menace had eased, agendas of Commission meetings showed remarkably little connection with the war. In fact, as Tugwell observed, the war might almost not have been going on, for the little attention it received at Commission meetings.[11]

It would therefore be well to conclude this consideration of the A.A.C.C. with a brief survey of some of its efforts toward permanent solution of Caribbean problems.

Public Health: Caribbean Medical Center

Typical of the projects undertaken by the Commission which met both an urgent wartime need and at the same time worked toward solution of a chronic problem of the area was that of the prevention and cure of venereal diseases. This had become a matter of immediate urgency among the armed forces stationed at the military bases in the Caribbean. At its very first meeting, therefore, the Commission decided to attack this age-old health problem, recognizing its dual civilian and military nature. In 1944 the Commission established in Trinidad a Venereal Disease Control Center, later renamed the Caribbean Medical Center. This joint Anglo-American Center carried on mass blood tests and conducted public education by means of films and lectures. It began the training of local doctors, laboratory technicians, nurses, and midwives from Trinidad and the neighboring islands. Representatives of medical services throughout the area were called in for periodic conferences. Results of tests were counterchecked at laboratories in the United States. The Caribbean area thus had access to the most modern techniques of medical science.

After 1945 the Caribbean Medical Center continued to operate, entirely maintained by British and Trinidadian funds. In 1956, for example, its laboratory made a total of 69,688 blood tests. These 1956 tests showed that the positive rate for syphillis and yaws was 4.9 percent, whereas in 1945 the positive rate had been 25.8 percent.[12] The Caribbean Medical Center is thus an outstanding permanent achievement of the A.A.C.C.; it can take credit for very substantial progress in the field of public health.

Ten-Point Program for the Future

The Commission, however, was never conceived of as an agency which in dealing with war problems might make permanent contributions to the well-being of the Caribbean simply as a by-product of its work. From the very beginning of the Commission concept it was planned that the new international agency should engage in long-term planning to meet the basic needs of the Caribbean peoples. As early as 1942 a series of high-level meetings in Washington, London, and in the West Indies resulted in an exchange of notes between the two governments which spelled out a ten-point long-range program for the Caribbean. Note the complete absence of any reference to the war:

1. The economic problems of the Caribbean should be regarded as regional rather than local problems.
2. Generally speaking, a single-crop economy in the West Indies is undesirable. Although the continuation of cash crops must be relied upon to a considerable extent, mixed farming and animal husbandry should be encouraged everywhere, both on a large scale (whether by private enterprise or on a coopera-

tive basis) and by peasant holders. It is undesirable, however, that a closed economy system should be constituted.

3. Inter-island trade throughout the entire Caribbean region should be encouraged.

4. The possibilities of industrial development, although probably limited in the majority of territories, should not be overlooked.

5. Advantage should be taken of fishing grounds in and adjacent to the Caribbean, and local fisheries with facilities for storage and distribution should be developed.

6. While an adequate literary and cultural standard must be maintained, a greater vocational bias should be introduced into the educational system.

7. There is an urgent need for a wide improvement of housing and sanitary conditions and for an extensive school building program.

8. Transportation to and within the Caribbean is inadequate and should be improved. This will need coordination and planning on a broad scale.

9. Tourism intelligently developed can become a substantial source of income to the area. Its potentialities should be carefully studied with a view to action.

10. An immediate and effective approach to the nutritional problem might be met by providing midday meals for children at school. This problem is to be investigated by the Caribbean Commission.[13]

The Commission's terms of reference were therefore broad and included all matters related to labor, housing, health, education, social welfare, and basic economics in the Caribbean. The assumption was always that collaboration among the Caribbean territories and the metropolitan governments in a regional approach offered the best assurance of success in dealing with the common problems.

Local Foodstuff Production

Stimulating local food production was one of the earliest basic projects undertaken by the Commission. The Caribbean area is generally well suited to the cultivation of food crops, but the encouragement of such cultivation entailed the alteration of many established habits. It was necessary to persuade producers to assume heavy financial risks by changing from the cultivation of exportable cash crops to new products the local market for which was highly uncertain. Again it was the war emergency and the resulting shortage of shipping which made action in this area essential.

At its first meeting, in March 1942, the A.A.C.C. recommended that every effort be made to increase local production of foodstuffs, especially those of high protein content. Local governments in the area, with the support and encouragement of the home country authorities, made strenuous efforts to put this recommendation into effect by the use of rewards, incentives, and executive action. Marketing facilities for handling the new food crops were established, and sugar estates were required to allot certain percentages of their lands to the cultivation of foodstuffs. Guaranties were made to purchase the output of producers at prices high enough to compensate for the change of pattern. In addition, the United States Department of the Interior established price support and marketing programs for the American territories in the Caribbean and also guaranteed to purchase the exportable surplus of some of the other islands at fair prices. The Commission kept a close check on all of these activities and it facilitated the making of the necessary arrangements wherever possible.

As a result of these measures food production in the area increased to a measureable extent. In Puerto Rico, for example, in 1943, food production went up 23 percent above the prewar level. Jamaica, by greatly increasing the production of home-grown carbohydrates, was able to eliminate the necessity for importing rice. Trinidad converted fifteen thousand acres to food crops, and 35 percent of the land held by sugar planters in Barbados was turned over to food crops. Additional efforts by the Commission resulted in some increase in the production of livestock and in the regulation of the consumption of meat supplies. This diversion of acreage to food production, and other measures, could have sufficed, in an extreme emergency, to feed the population of the colonies altogether for a short period.[14]

Chronic Sugar Problem

The Anglo-American Caribbean Commission also grappled with the chronic sugar problem. The continuance of large exports of sugar was of course essential to the health of the regional economy. The war caused an increase in the market demand for sugar but at the same time the shortage of shipping and the submarine warfare greatly handicapped the outward shipments. Year-end carryovers threatened to become a serious problem. The Commission was successful, however, in working out production quotas for the territories and marketing agreements with the governments of both the United States and the United Kingdom which kept surpluses to a manageable minimum during the war. However, the Commission and all of those concerned with the affairs of the Caribbean realized that the only permanent solution to the problem of sugar surpluses lay in diversifying the economies of the islands and territories.[15]

Fisheries Development

In dealing with food shortages and the need to increase the local production of foodstuffs, the Commission undertook to investigate the possibility of developing fisheries as a means of supplying additional protein foods. Under the auspices of the Commission, in April 1943 a group of British and American experts conducted a survey of fisheries in the Leeward Islands, the Windward Islands, Barbados, Trinidad, and later in Jamaica and Puerto Rico. This investigation revealed the almost unbelievable fact that it was necessary to *import* nearly one-half of the seafood required to supply the normal needs of the people living in the eastern group of islands. This paradoxical situation was due mainly to the fact that local fishery products had declined to about one-half of the normal level because of the shortage of fishing gear replacement parts. The Commission took immediate steps to supply the necessary gear on a priority basis, so that local production could be swiftly restored to normal levels. Some local price adjustments were also made so as to offer added incentives to local fishermen.

After initial groundwork by the Commission, the governments of the United States and the Bahamas reached an agreement on May 5, 1943, for commercial exploitation of the tuna run passing through the eastern edge of the Gulf Stream between May 1 and July 1 each year. Additional action under Commission sponsorship to increase the local fish supplies included the organization of fisheries cooperatives in Puerto Rico and the rehabilitation of the fisheries industry in Barbados.[16]

In February of 1944, Dr. H. H. Brown, director of fisheries investigations in the British West Indies, and Mr. R. T. Whiteleather, fishery engineer of the United States Fish and Wildlife Service, undertook a comprehensive survey of the fishery resources with the eastern group of the British islands. During the course of this investigation, which lasted nine months, the two experts were able to demonstrate improved techniques in the form of better design and lighter materials in certain fishing nets, the introduction of trammel nets, and the use of multiple trolling lines from small powered vessels.[17] The field work of this survey team was completed in October 1944, and their findings were published as a special bulletin by the A.A.C.C.[18] Following the recommendations of the first session of the West Indian Conference, the Commission also published the *Guide to Commercial Shark Fishing in the Caribbean Area.*[19] This book was written in simple language, with many illustrations, and it was designed for the express use of the fishermen themselves. It was a typical early example of the Commission's efforts to aid the peoples of the area through the dissemination of practical information related to their daily lives.

Tourist Development and Other Work

Mention has already been made of the organization in 1943 of the Caribbean Research Council and of the Symposium on Land Tenure which it sponsored in 1944 (chapter 2, under Caribbean Research Council). Other area-wide conferences were held on the subjects of forestry management, quarantine controls, the development of the tourist trade after the war, and other matters. Some of these meetings were attended by representatives of the independent republics and by experts from the Pan American Union.

The development of the tourist industry, as one means of relieving the economic distress of the region, became one of the first projects of the A.A.C.C. As early as 1943, when the end of the war was not even in sight, the Commission directed Mr. Coert du Bois, one of the American commissioners, to make a field survey for the purpose of bringing within a single comprehensive report an account of the attractions, both actual and potential, of the region. While Mr. du Bois was traveling in the area on this mission in 1943 and 1944 the Commission was engaged in making detailed studies of various aspects of the problem, including the economics of a Caribbean tourist industry, transportation facilities, and types of accommodations required. Representatives of the steamship lines, airlines, hotel companies, and tourist agencies, from the United States, Canada, and the West Indies countries, helped the Commission in its investigation. The conclusions resulting from the field trips of Mr. du Bois, as well as from the independent studies made by the Commission, were published under the title, *Caribbean Tourist Trade: A Regional Approach.*[20]

EVALUATIONS OF THE A.A.C.C.

All of those who took part in the early projects of the A.A.C.C., or who were in a position to observe its work, were very conscious of the fact that they were pioneering new and unprecedented arrangements in international cooperation. Without exception they expressed the hope that the example being set in the Caribbean would prove fruitful for the construction of the future world order. For example, Werner J. Cahnman wrote in 1947:

The Caribbean Commission and the West Indian Conference are generally considered a model effort in international democracy and regional cooperation. One can only express the hope that their example may be heeded in other problem areas upon this globe, notably in South East Asia, in Central Africa, and in the Middle East.[21]

As the years went by it of course became apparent that the Commission concept, as it was embodied in the structure of the Anglo-American Caribbean Commission, was not to become the pattern for international relations in the major underdeveloped areas of the world. The formerly dependent and colonial countries of Africa and Asia preferred to aim for complete sovereign independence. Only among the dependent island territories of the Pacific Ocean was the Commission example followed. There, the South Pacific Commission was formed in

1948, modeled very closely on the structure of the Caribbean Commission. Comprising originally Australia, France, the Netherlands, New Zealand, the United Kingdom, and the United States as members, the South Pacific Commission continues today its constructive work in basic economic and social betterment in the western Pacific.[22]

Because developments in international relations did not occur in the way that enthusiasts of the early Commission idea thought they might, appraisals of the A.A.C.C. written in the early days of its existence are thoroughly outdated. Since this is in essence a case study of the evolution of international institutions, it would be interesting and instructive at this point to recall a very few of the early contemporary judgments of the significance of the Anglo-American Caribbean Commission.

There was first the general recognition that the Commission was evolving valuable techniques for dealing with long-range problems. Speaking in the British House of Commons in March 1943, Colonel Oliver Stanley, secretary of state for colonies, said of the Commission:

In a short year it has made a valuable start, and I hope we shall be able to evolve a technique of international cooperation. The Commission has not started on a high plane of broad theoretical discussions; it has started on a plane of practical solutions to common problems facing both countries, and the sort of problems which will face them in that area after the war, problems of economics, transport, health, and communication which go far beyond the frontiers of one particular unit and can only be solved by common effort. I hope that by means of this Commission we are trying out on a small scale the practical means of solving these problems together.[23]

A few months later, on July 13, 1943, Colonel Stanley told Parliament that it was the wish of the British government to work in close cooperation with neighboring and friendly nations for the solutions of colonial problems of common interest. He concluded:

What they [the government] have in mind is the possibility of establishing Commissions for certain regions. These Commissions would comprise not only the States with Colonial Territories in the region, but also other States which have in the region a major strategic or economic interest. While each State would remain responsible for the administration of its own territory, such a Commission would provide effective and permanent machinery for consultation and collaboration so that the States concerned might work together to promote the well-being of the Colonial Territories . . . . What we have in mind is merely the development of the idea which led to the Anglo-United States Caribbean Commission.[24]

Sir Stafford Cripps is reported to have said in London on New Year's Day, 1943, that the Anglo-American Caribbean Commission was "an important experimental development which may well influence the whole future of the world's colonial policies."[25]

There was universal approval for the concept of international treatment for common regional problems.

Plainly the efforts of each government in its own sphere gradually to further the degree of political independence enjoyed by its territories are in no way connected with any extensions of sovereignty, shuffling of possessions, or initiating of "new" imperialism. Rather it would seem that in recognizing a community of problems in an area where their interests are just about inseparable, Britain and the United States are now more than ever seeing eye to eye and moving in step with each other.

The Caribbean Commission is one of the central elements in this whole process, a deliberate and explicit experiment in cooperation. It does not operate in isolation but against the background of political developments and together with the older and more familiar agencies responsible for Caribbean affairs, often simplifying and uniting their tasks. Its special meaning derives from the fact that it represents a new mode of treating some of the questions raised by individual territories by regarding them as connected parts of a regional problem that can best, or only, be solved by concerted efforts.[26]

There was recognition that the Commission had in effect gone beyond its consultative and advisory role into the realm of actual operations. Ralph Bunche wrote:

The formal powers of the Anglo-American Caribbean Commission appear at first glance to be not great. It is a consultative and advisory body and suffers from the limitations on action and operation inherent in any agency of that quality. But the A.A.C.C., despite this limitation, has demonstrated a remarkable ability to get things done. By a broad interpretation of its function and authority, by presuming on its "squatter's rights" in the field of Caribbean regional cooperation, it has been able to project itself into the realm of operations. It has not been content merely to recommend projects. As in the case of the Schooner Pool, it has undertaken to organize the initiation of projects and has tenaciously followed them up. While not actually undertaking operations, by subtle pressure on local administrations and the home governments, it has been able to accelerate and complete their execution.

It is this dynamic quality of the Commission which is the key to its success. By the terms of the joint communiqué it could have become a purely passive agency, content to rest on its stated function of giving advice and formulating recommendations, leaving the execution of such recommendations to the decision of the governments and to execution, when approved, by other agencies. The A.A.C.C., however, has wisely chosen to follow up and service its recommendations, even though technically it could not undertake their physical execution. This procedure has resulted in closely associating the Commission with jobs actually being done and gives it a much broader significance than it would merit were it to adhere to a narrower conception of its advisory function.

The Commission has demonstrated a useful flexibility and an ability to develop procedures and functions essential to the practical needs of its work. It has constantly expanded its horizon. If it has not always severely confined itself to its terms of reference as defined in the joint communiqué, its activities have never been beyond a reasonable interpretation of those terms.[27]

Some wondered, however, whether the Commission would ever really come to grips with serious basic problems. And, finally, there were fears—fortunately not realized—that the Commission might not survive the end of the war.

No doubt, with the war emergency ended, the tempo of [the Commission's] activity may be in some measure retarded; but to say this is only to enunciate the general truth that it is difficult to carry over into peace the kind of cooperation that exists in an emergency situation. It is not only the work of the Anglo-American Caribbean Commission that stands in danger of being slowed up or even abandoned in the inevitable reaction of a post-war world.[28]

4 □ ESTABLISHMENT AND ORGANIZATION OF THE FOUR-POWER COMMISSION

The work of the Commission was by no means slowed up or abandoned in the postwar world. Instead the Commission was broadened and expanded to include the Netherlands and France, in addition to Great Britain and the United States.

At its seventh meeting, in Washington, July 25, 1945, the A.A.C.C. recommended that invitations be extended to France and the Netherlands to join the Commission, for the purpose of approaching the problems of all of the Caribbean dependencies on a regional and cooperative basis. France and the Netherlands accepted in December 1945, and the Anglo-American Caribbean Commission was thus transformed into a four-power agency renamed simply the Caribbean Commission. The new body met for the first time at St. Thomas, U.S. Virgin Islands, from February 23 to March 13, 1946. The second session of the West Indian Conference also was convened at the same time and place. Transformed like its parent body into a four-power arrangement, the second West Indian Conference was made up of delegates from fifteen different territories under four flags. This was the conference cited by Taussig as being the precedent-making first in international relations.

The first meeting of the full four-power Commission was devoted to the consideration of two main items. The first item concerned preparations for the formal establishment of the expanded Commission, the organization and financing of a central secretariat, and the formulation of rules of procedure for conducting the affairs of the Commission and its auxiliary bodies. The second item before the new Commission involved preliminary consideration of the recommendations of the second session of the West Indian Conference, then in progress, in order to assure their prompt attention by the metropolitan and territorial governments concerned.[1]

To study in detail the problems of formal organization, the new Commission appointed a Working Committee, consisting of the United States Commissioner Ralph J. Bunche as chairman, one commissioner from each of the other three member governments, and three advisers from the United States, the United Kingdom, and France, respectively. The proposals submitted by this Working Committee were unanimously adopted by the Commission as recommendations to the four member governments.

The first group of recommendations had to do with the proposed secretariat:

1. That the Secretariat should have its headquarters in the region, that it should be international in character, and that the Secretary General and the members of the staff should be responsible to the Commission and should not seek or receive instruction from any government or from any other authority external to the Commission.

2. That each member of the Commission should respect the international character of the responsibility of the Secretary General and his staff and should not seek to influence them in the discharge of their responsibility.

3. That the Secretary General should be appointed by the Commission, be its chief administrative official, and be selected on the basis of the highest qualifications for the office.

4. That the personnel of the Secretariat should be selected on the basis of equity representation of the four nations which are members of the Commission, having due regard for the highest standards of efficiency, competence, and integrity, and should be recruited to the greatest extent practicable from the people of the region.[2]

With regard to the West Indian Conference it was agreed that

each Caribbean territory, colony, or group of colonies of the four member nations should be entitled to send two delegates and such advisers as it might consider necessary to each session of the Conference. The Conference should meet biannually, and the location of each session should be based on the principle of rotation of the four member governments of the Commission in the English alphabetical order. The chairman of each session of the Conference should be the co-chairman representing the metropolitan government in the territory in which the session is held.[3]

With respect to the Commission itself, the Committee recommended, and the Commission approved:

1. That the present system of co-chairmen should be retained, and that each co-chairman should preside over Commission meetings according to the English alphabetical order of the Commission, irrespective of where the Commission meeting is held.

2. That the Commission should hold not less than two meetings a year . . . .

3. That during the periods between meetings the Secretary General should obtain approval from the four co-chairmen before taking action on important matters.

4. That the Commission should proceed as far as possible on the basis of unanimous agreement of all of the commissioners present. If this should prove impossible, the decision or recommendations should be by unanimity of the four member nations. Decisions on procedural matters should be considered approved if agreed to by at least three of the four member nations.[4]

With these recommendations before them, the four governments called a special conference to meet in Washington beginning July 8, 1946, consisting of the following representatives of the metropolitan powers: Governor Georges H. Parisot for France; Dr. J. C. Kielstra for the Netherlands; Mr. G. F. Seel, assistant under-secretary of state, for the United Kingdom; and Mr. Charles W. Taussig for the United States. Their agenda was made up of these items: negotiation of a formal agreement for the establishment of the Caribbean Commission; selection of a site for the Central Secretariat; appointment of a secretary general; establishment of a joint operating fund; and the assessment of contributions of the member governments to the fund.[5]

The text of the agreement for the formal establishment of the Caribbean Commission was approved by the members of this special conference and was initialed by them on the last day of their meeting, July 15, 1946. The full text of this agreement and of the rules of procedure for the Caribbean Commission are reproduced in the Appendix. The document was signed in Washington on October 30, 1946, by the ambassadors of three member governments (Great Britain, France, and the Netherlands) and by Mr. Taussig for the United States. Article XXI provided that when notices of approval of all the governments concerned were deposited with the United States government at Washington, the instrument would have legal force. The government of France approved on November 18, 1946; the United Kingdom on March 4, 1947; and the United States on March 4, 1948.[6] The agreement was finally brought into full legal force on August 6, 1948, when the Netherlands deposited its notice of approval.[7]

Purposes and Structure of the Caribbean Commission

In the words of one of the Commission's publicity releases, the aim of the Caribbean Commission was to facilitate and foster the social and economic development of the countries it served. This it did by providing technical assistance either from its Secretariat staff or through experts on loan to it from national or international agencies; by facilitating the flow of information between the countries it served; by organizing regional conferences; and by providing technical advice. The Commission, however, was purely an advisory body. It made recommendations to the governments of the countries it served but could not enforce their acceptance or implementation.[8]

The 1946 agreement which established the Commission was a much more formal and elaborate document than the executive agreement of 1942 which had served as the source of authority for the old Anglo-American Commission. The new agreement described the signatory powers as:

Being desirous of encouraging and strengthening cooperation among themselves and their territories with a view toward improving the economic and social well-being of the people of these territories and

Being desirous of promoting scientific technological, and economic development in the Caribbean area and facilitating the use of resources and concerted treatment of mutual problems, avoiding duplication in the work of existing research agencies, surveying needs, ascertaining what research has been done, facilitating research on a co-operative basis and recommending further research, and

Having decided to associate themselves in the work heretofore undertaken by the Anglo-American Caribbean Commission, and

Having agreed that the objectives herein set forth are in accordance with the principles of the Charter of the United Nations.[9]

The agreement consisted of twenty-one articles establishing and defining the powers, functions, and organizational structure of the Caribbean Commission itself, of the Caribbean Research Council, the West Indian Conference, and the Central Secretariat. The Commission was to consist of not more than sixteen members, four from each national section. It was to act as a "consultative and advisory body" and to "have such legal capacity as may be necessary for the exercise of its functions and the fulfillment of its purposes." Its functions were precisely defined: (1) To concern itself with economic and social matters of common interest to the Caribbean area, particularly agriculture, communications, education, fisheries, health, housing, industry, labor, social welfare and trade; (2) to study, formulate and recommend measures, programs, and policies with respect to social and economic problems designed to contribute to the well-being of the Caribbean area; (3) to assist in coordinating local problems which have regional significance and to provide technical guidance from a wide field not otherwise available; (4) to direct and review the activities of the Research Council; and (5) to convene the sessions of the West Indian Conference.[10]

The two auxiliary bodies which had begun their work under the original A.A.C.C. were thus specifically provided for in the new Agreement. The functions of the Research Council were to recommend to the Commission the number of technical research committees necessary to provide specialized scientific study of special problems; to facilitate and undertake research assignments; to recommend to the Commission the holding of Research Council and committee meetings, as well as conferences of technical experts; and to assist in the interchange of experience among the research workers of the Caribbean.[11]

The objectives of the West Indian Conference were to provide "a regular means of consultation on matters of common interest within the terms of reference of the Commission" and "an opportunity to present to the Commission recommendations on such matters."[12]

The Commission itself had no fixed location since it met twice a year in the various Caribbean countries, but provision was made in the agreement for the establishment of a permanent Central Secretariat, under a secretary general assisted by a deputy secretary general. Headquarters of the Secretariat was to be located within the Caribbean area and its personnel was to be recruited in the West Indies as far as possible. Primary consideration was to be given to the technical qualifications and the personal integrity of candidates for Secretariat posts. Each member government agreed to respect the exclusively international character of the secretary general and his staff.*

It had already been decided by the Special Conference which drew up the agreement that the site for the Central Secretariat should be Trinidad. The first secretary general appointed by the Commission was an American, Mr. Lawrence W. Cramer, who assumed his duties in September 1946. He immediately established headquarters for the Secretariat at Port of Spain, Trinidad. His enthusiasm, energy, and administrative ability attracted a highly competent staff which was representative of most of the races and nationalities of the region. It is interesting to note in this connection that no less than seven hundred applications were received for positions with the Commission Secretariat, mostly from persons in the Caribbean region. Of the first twenty-six appointments made to the staff only four had to be recruited from outside the area.[13] Within four months this multiracial, multilingual group had been welded into an efficient working force.[14] By the mid-1950s, the staff of the Secretariat included a very high proportion of native West Indians: about 50 percent of the administrative staff, 62 percent of the professional staff, and 96 percent of the general service staff.[15]

The second secretary general of the Caribbean Commission was Mr. Everhard Frederik de Vriendt, a native of Holland, who was appointed in January 1952. The third secretary general, a native of the West Indies, was Mr. Clovis F. Beauregard, who was born at Vauclin, Martinique, French West Indies, on May 4, 1907. After completing law studies and obtaining his LL.B. degree he joined the civil service of France and served both in France and in Guadeloupe, where be became head of the Department of Economic Affairs in 1943. He was then appointed special consultant for economic affairs on the staff of the governor of Guadeloupe. In July 1949,

*Article XIV. At this point it should perhaps be emphasized that the Caribbean Commission was not directly related to the various international undertakings of the American republics, such as the Organization of American States. In the words of the Senate report accompanying the resolution which provided for United States membership in the Commission: "With respect to the American Republics, the United States stands as a neighbor among equals. With regard to its commitments in the Caribbean area involved in the work of the Caribbean Commission, however, the United States stands as a possessing Government exercising dominion over non-self-governing areas. The two sets of responsibilities, those of a nation in the inter-American community and those of a nation exercising responsibility for strategically located possessions, should not be confused." (U.S., Congress, Senate, *Report to Accompany H. J. Res. 231, Providing for Membership and Participation by the United States in the Caribbean Commission and Authorizing an Appropriation Therefor,* 80th Cong., 1st Sess., 1947, Report No. 684, p. 4.)

Mr. Beauregard, who was then a senior official of the department of *Enregistrement et Domaines* at Rouen, France, was appointed deputy secretary general of the Caribbean Commission. His association with the Commission, however, dates back to 1946 when he attended the third meeting of the Commission in Curacao as French commissioner. He also attended the fourth meeting, at Jamaica, in the same capacity. In 1955 he was made *Chevalier de la Legion d'Honneur.* Upon the retirement of Mr. de Vriendt in August, 1956, Mr. Beauregard became acting secretary general, and at the twenty-third meeting of the Commission in Barbados, in December 1956, he was unanimously appointed secretary general of the Caribbean Commission.[16] Mr. Beauregard served the Caribbean Commission as secretary general until the transformation to Caribbean Organization in 1961; then, in the same capacity he served the latter organization until its termination in 1965.

Headquarters of the Central Secretariat remained at Kent House, Port of Spain, Trinidad, until mid-1960. At a special session of the West Indian Conference which was held at Charlotte Amalie, St. Thomas, U.S. Virgin Islands, July 28 to August 7, 1959, to arrange for the establishment of a successor organization to the Caribbean Commission, Dr. Arturo Morales Carrion, under-secretary of state of the Commonwealth of Puerto Rico, formally offered on behalf of his government to provide headquarters facilities in Puerto Rico for the new Caribbean Organization. Dr. Morales Carrion further informed the Conference that the government of Puerto Rico, if its offer to become host government to the Caribbean Organization was accepted, would be prepared to make an annual contribution to the Organization of $140,000. The Conference unanimously adopted the recommendation that the offer of the government of Puerto Rico be accepted.[17] In anticipation of the early signing of the agreement for establishment of the Caribbean Organization, the headquarters staff moved to Puerto Rico in June 1960 and set up its offices on the third floor of the Teachers' Association Building, at 452 Avenida Ponce de Leon, Hato Rey, a suburb of San Juan. Only seventeen members of the staff moved from Trinidad to Puerto Rico, for it was the policy of the Commission to employ the majority of the clerical staff in the country in which the headquarters was situated.[18]

The dates of the formal meetings of the Caribbean Commission and its auxiliary bodies are given in Appendix A.

As a sample of the many activities in which the Commission was constantly engaged, the following is a list of the technical conferences and meetings held under the Commission's auspices during a single two-year period, from August 1955 to September 1957:

Meeting of the Preparatory Committee for the Town and Country Development Planning Conference . . . . Trinidad, August 29–31, 1955.

Second Caribbean Fisheries Seminar . . . . Trinidad, September 26–29, 1955.
Second Conference on Cooperatives in the Caribbean (sponsored jointly with
F.A.O.) . . . . British Guiana, January 24–26, 1956.
Meeting of trade promotion liaison officers . . . . Trinidad, February
21–23, 1956.
Meeting of Committee on the Coordination of Disaster Relief Services . . . .
. . . . Trinidad, March 20–21, 1956.
Meeting of the Preparatory Committee for the Conference on the Demo-
graphic Problems of the Area . . . . Trinidad, August 14–16, 1956.
Conference on Town and Country Development Planning . . . . . Trinidad,
November 14–23, 1956.
Conference on the Demographic Problems of the Area . . . . . Trinidad, July
25–August 2, 1957.
Meeting of the Preparatory Committee for the 1958 Conference on the
Financing of Agriculture . . . . Trinidad, September 3–4, 1957.[19]

In addition to sponsoring conferences and meetings, the Commission
also took part in other conferences and seminars at the international level.
In 1957, for example, the Commission was represented at the following
meetings (in parentheses is indicated in each case which official of the
Commission participated):

February 1957: First meeting of the Inter-Governmental Advisory Committee on Extension of Primary Education in Latin America; Cuba (attended
for the Commission by the UNESCO consultant on education).
March 1957: First Caribbean Conference on Mental Health; Aruba (the area
home economist).
July 1957: Meeting of the Regional Committee of the Lisle Fellowship, University of Michigan; Jamaica (the information officer).
August 1957: Study Conference on Economic Development; Jamaica (the
deputy secretary general).
September 1957: Fourth (Geological) Conference of the Guianas; French
Guiana (the deputy secretary general).[20]

One additional organ of the Caribbean Commission was provided for
by the rules of procedure. Between the regular meetings of the Commission the affairs of the organization were directed by a Working Committee, which consisted of one commissioner from each of the four national
sections, or his alternate, as appointed by the co-chairman. The Working
Committee met between sessions of the Commission and advised the secretary general on all matters of policy and administration related to the work
of the Central Secretariat and the auxiliary bodies of the Commission. Its
decisions prevailed until submitted for confirmation to the next regular
meeting of the full Commission.[21]

West Indian Conference

No attempt can be made in a study of this scope to survey in detail the work of each of the various sessions of the West Indian Conference. It is that body, however, which was singled out for more attention than perhaps any other activity of the Commission. All of the literature pertaining to the Caribbean Commission and all of the evaluations of the Commission's significance emphasized the importance of the West Indian Conference as a technique of international cooperation. As has already been indicated, Charles Taussig and others looked upon the West Indian Conference as by far the most important innovation in international affairs which could be attributed to the Commission. For these reasons the West Indian Conference as a functional body deserves at least brief consideration at this point.

The topics taken up by the delegates to these biennial conferences ranged over the entire spectrum of the problems within the scope of the Commission. Detailed recommendations were made by each session, and these recommendations were duly considered by the Commission, and where necessary, were referred by the Commission to member governments and to governments of the area for comment and possible action. The sixth session, for example, made a total of forty-nine recommendations covering such matters as staff appointments; technical assistance; reporting services with regard to animal and plant diseases; education, in relation to economic and community development; the training of leaders; adult literacy and community education; land problems; assistance from UNESCO; organizations of farmers; and so on.[22]

Early sessions of the Conference were marked by extremely crowded agendas covering a very wide range of subjects. In the light of experience, however, the later sessions tended to restrict their attention to one or two principal themes. Elizabeth H. Armstrong, an officer of the Department of State, wrote, after the fourth session, that the first and second sessions, at which many of the delegates were having their first experience with an international meeting, tended to lack focus and be hampered by discursive discussions. The third session, in 1948, concentrated on the subject of "The Industrialization of the Caribbean Area," and the discussions were far more realistic and practical. The fourth session, with carefully prepared documentation, reached "a level of successful application of the conference technique which many other international conferences have not yet achieved."[23]

The sixth session, in 1955, dealt mainly with the questions of education and small-scale farming. The 1957 session took up chiefly the problem of cooperatives in the Caribbean.

The output of the West Indian Conference sessions was, of course, in the form of recommendations only. Participants in these sessions were delegates from nonsovereign territories; these territories were therefore not entirely free to implement or not to implement the various recommendations which their delegates had been instrumental in drawing up.

Conference recommendations required first the concurrence of the Caribbean Commission, but certain of these recommendations were of such nature that they needed the further approval of one or more of the four metropolitan governments. This was particularly true with regard to those which required enabling legislation for their implementation, and especially where in addition funds had to be appropriated from metropolitan government treasuries.

Such was the prestige of the West Indian Conference, however, that a remarkably high percentage of its recommendations were eventually put into practice. The full Caribbean Commission arranged always to meet at the same time and just after each Conference session so that it could give immediate attention to Conference recommendations. Many such recommendations of each session were approved on the spot by the Commission and others were taken up promptly at succeeding meetings of the Commission. Certain recommendations which did not require joint action by the metropolitan governments or which by their very nature could be carried out by territorial officials themselves were quickly put into operation after approval by the Caribbean Commission.

Action on recommendations requiring the approval of home country governments, the passage of legislation, and the appropriation of public funds was naturally slow in coming; but to observers acquainted with the Caribbean area and its problems, there are many evidences of progressive developments which can be traced directly or indirectly to the work of the West Indian Conference.

One rather striking example of exceptionally prompt implementation of a major recommendation of the fourth session occurred in 1948. The Conference recommendation was that existing institutions of higher education in the industrial arts and sciences should arrange to make their facilities available to qualified students from all parts of the area. On December 31, 1948, within little more than two weeks after the close of the Conference session, the University of Puerto Rico announced the establishment of thirty scholarships for students from the West Indian territories, of which ten provided for $300 subsistence in addition to covering the tuition.[24]

5 □ A BRIEF SURVEY OF CARIBBEAN COMMISSION ACHIEVEMENTS

Backed by the authority of a formal four-power agreement, provided with funds and a headquarters staff, and drawing upon the record of solid achievements already obtained in Anglo-American cooperation, the new Caribbean Commission at once settled down to the work for which it was designed. Over a period of fifteen years it did much to enrich the life of the area it served.

Since it is beyond the scope of this study to recount in detail the history of the Caribbean Commission's manifold functional activities, nothing more can be attempted here than a very brief survey of a few of the Commission's more noteworthy accomplishments. For the sake of convenience the work of the Commission will be summarized under seven categories of activities, no one of which is completely exclusive of the others.[1]

1. Agricultural Improvement Activities. Despite the greater prominence given to the story of Caribbean industrial advances (e.g., Puerto Rico's "Operation Bootstrap"), agriculture has been and still is the principal source of income and employment in the region served by the Commission.

One of the most effective of the Commission's programs in this area was its series of field demonstration tours in tropical products. These tours, made up of technical workers, growers, and commercial representatives, provided mutual exchange of data and visual, on-the-spot demonstrations of new or modified practices in agriculture, as well as of specialized procedures which have been developed to meet the needs of the environmental conditions prevailing in the Caribbean area. Thus the knowledge and skills needed to improve crop production in the Caribbean were imparted in the most effective way to people who could most benefit from the experience. Tours were held in cocoa, bananas, coffee, cattle, and grasslands. The Commission organized the tours and supplied technical documents and the necessary administrative services. The local host governments underwrote many of the local costs involved, and the local governments or private industry paid the transportation and other expenses of the tour members.

The demonstration tour itself, however, was merely the beginning of a concerted effort to effect improvement. Each tour was followed up by the establishment of a publications exchange service in the commodity concerned. (Publications exchange services were set up in other subjects as well, and these came to cover fields such as small-scale farming, cocoa, bananas, coffee, nutrition, fisheries, and education.) The tours and the resulting publications exchange services led to an active correspondence between the Secretariat and those engaged in the industries. Each tour and the publicity it generated stimulated additional visits and exchanges by individuals and delegations other than those making the original trip. By these means, therefore, the Commission served to coordinate the efforts of hundreds of planters, scientists, and government officials interested in improving agricultural production.[2]

During the period from May 1955 to August 1957, the Commission's agricultural economist at Kent House received 97 visitors from twenty-seven countries, including eleven countries not served by the Commission, and 112 visitors from Trinidad. During the same period this official conducted 140 persons to plantations, research centers, propagating centers, and other points of agricultural interest in Trinidad. He also served on a number of boards and centers both in Trinidad and overseas.[3]

2. Housing and Technical Assistance Activities. The need for more, better, and cheaper houses is a chronic problem in the Caribbean region. Beginning in 1952 the United States International Cooperation Administration loaned housing technicians to the Caribbean Commission. These technicians helped to build hundreds of low-cost, hurricane- and termite-proof houses by use of the aided self-help technique adopted from Puerto Rico.

Aided self-help housing was started in Puerto Rico in 1935, but no attention was paid to the lessons learned from it in the rest of the Caribbean area until Dr. Pico, a Puerto Rican and one of the United States commissioners of the Caribbean Commission, visited a British island in 1948 and suggested that the experience of Puerto Rico in meeting the need for low-cost housing might be useful elsewhere. The Commission took up the idea, and with the help of the I.C.A. the technique was spread to Trinidad and Tobago, British Guiana, Surinam, British Honduras, Antigua, Barbados, Montserrat, Jamaica, St. Vincent, St. Kitts, Dominica, Grenada, and St. Lucia.

The I.C.A. technicians also advised local governments on problems of construction, on the use of local building materials, on the financing and management of low-cost housing projects, and they trained many local men as supervisors and foremen. This technical guidance project furnished in cooperation with the I.C.A. was one of the Commission's most successful activities.

Housing, however, was but one example of the services rendered by the Commission through its Technical Assistance programs. The Commission provided technical assistance to the countries it served in two ways: (1) through members of the staff of the Central Secretariat and (2) through experts assigned to it by national and international agencies, as in the example cited above of the I.C.A. housing technicians.

The Secretariat of the Commission at Kent House included on its own staff a number of technical experts whose services were available to the governments served by the Commission. The Commission's agricultural economist, for example, worked in St. Lucia, where he advised on the establishment of an Agricultural Credit Bank; in British Guiana, where he made recommendations for land settlement developments; and on Martinique and Guadeloupe, where he advised on the cultivation of cacao. In the same way the services of the Commission's economist, the consultant for industrial development, and the statistician were made available to the governments of the countries served by the Commission.

The number of requests for information and advice addressed to the technical officers of the Commission increased steadily year by year. Service was rendered both by correspondence and by personal visits; in addition, some experts served tours of duty as members of government agencies in the countries served by the Commission, thus making their knowledge and experience directly available.

When the Commission did not have on its staff officers with the qualifications necessary to deal with certain matters which came up, it often engaged well-known experts to assist it. This has been done, for instance, with regard to certain aspects of industrial development, transportation, the utilization of sugarcane by-products, fisheries, and so on.

In addition to the people of its own staff and those experts whom it could hire, the Caribbean Commission had the services of technical experts assigned to it by national and international agencies. Under arrangements made with the United States International Cooperation Administration, the Commission was able to obtain the services of experts in a wide variety of fields. In 1957 alone, experts in education, home economics, agricultural credit, fisheries, and housing were attached to the Commission on loan from other agencies. In addition to providing immediate technical advice, these experts from time to time carried out surveys and wrote reports which have been very valuable to the Caribbean countries in planning their development programs.

Combining its own specialists and those experts whose services were available to it from outside agencies, the Caribbean Commission was able to make available to its constituent countries the best technical guidance the world can offer. This was of particular help to the smaller islands and territories which could by no means themselves have afforded to maintain the technical staff they needed.

In all of these projects the Commission provided administrative, clerical, and translation facilities. In the majority of cases it assumed responsibility for travel costs within the Caribbean area, and on occasion it paid the subsistence expenses of experts as well.[4]

3. Home Economics. This was another broad problem area where technical assistance of the type described above was of great benefit. Under the guidance of a home economist loaned to the Commission staff by the Food and Agriculture Organization of the United Nations, an intensive program for basic improvement in home and family conditions was started. The home economist conducted practical training courses in Martinique, British Honduras, British Guiana, Surinam, Trinidad, St. Lucia, Tobago, Antigua, St. Kitts, and other islands. She was also loaned by the Commission for a time to lead a nine-month course in Jamaica sponsored jointly by the British Development and Welfare Organization and F.A.O.

As a result of these programs home economics departments have been added to many local governments in the area. Training courses in nutrition and other subjects for teachers and family welfare workers were conducted. These were highly practical courses designed to meet the basic needs of the area. Thus, through these efforts of the Commission, home economics has become recognized as a serious subject of study throughout the area—one which can help immeasurably to alleviate the deplorable home and family conditions, where illegitimacy, poverty, and a weak family structure are ever-present problems. A concrete achievement of this program was the development of techniques for making simple household furnishings from scrap and discarded materials.

In 1955 the Food and Agriculture Organization and the Commission concluded that it would be useful to publish a home economics textbook, with adequate teaching materials and a carefully selected bibliography. It was felt that such a book would be a valuable asset to social workers, public health nurses, and extension workers of all types in the area. After further consideration, however, it was agreed that a more useful purpose might be served by printing the textbook in the form of five separate booklets, dealing with subject matter as follows: (1) Nutrition; (2) Textiles and Clothing; (3) Family Relations and Child Development; (4) Housing and Home Improvement; and (5) Family Economics. An additional booklet dealing with Environmental Sanitation was also planned.[5]

4. Education. For several years the Commission assisted in the selection of students from the British, French, and Netherlands areas for the I.C.A. "Caribbean Training Program" scholarships in Puerto Rico. Puerto Rico had for a number of years offered technical fellowships and scholarships to students from Latin American countries, but the privilege was not extended to the Caribbean territories until immediately after action by the fourth session of the West Indian Conference late in 1948. These scholarships were for teacher training in agriculture, vocational education, and home economics, as well as in mechanical and technical trades. By 1961, when the Commission gave way to its successor, more than eleven hundred students from the area served by the Commission had received this specialized training in Puerto Rico.

The Commonwealth of Puerto Rico, and the University of Puerto Rico, in addition to their other educational services to the area, joined with the Commission and with F.A.O. in providing regional training courses in tropical forestry, cooperatives, and home economics; they also aided self-help housing seminars.

5. *Technical Conferences.* In 1946 the Commission began the practice of convening technical conferences which brought together specialists from within the area and from outside as well. Conferences were held on the subjects of forestry, soil science, cooperatives, industrial development, fisheries, home economics and education in nutrition, trade promotion, small-scale farming, town and country development planning, meteorology, tourism, demography, and others. The recommendations made by the delegates at these conferences went to the governments of the area and helped them to plan their development programs with the benefit of the experience of the various countries. According to many observers the rapid strides toward industrialization in the area which took place during the Commission years derived in some measure from the stimulus given by the conference on industrial development which was held in Puerto Rico in 1952.

The technical conference therefore proved to be a most useful technique. Reports coming from these conferences in fact often became guidebooks and manuals for specialists. In at least two cases, too, the conferences resulted in the formation of permanent technical bodies. The Caribbean Tourist Association, which promotes the Caribbean as a year-round regional resort area, for example, grew out of one of these technical conferences. Another conference resulted in the establishment of a uniform hurricane warning system in the eastern Caribbean, in cooperation with the World Meteorological Organization.

Prior to 1949 no organized system for hurricane warnings existed in the Caribbean. For lack of a central administration of the scattered and inadequate warning services which did exist the area was plagued by repeated disasters due to inadequate storm warnings, as well as by unnecessary dislocation of activities caused by false alarms of impending hurricanes. As a result of a conference of area meteorological officials, convened by the Commission in 1949, arrangements were made to set up additional hurricane detecting facilities and to make one central bureau responsible for collecting all data and issuing all official hurricane warnings. As a result of this initiative by the Commission, therefore, all parts of the area now have an adequate storm warning system in which the public can have confidence.

6. *Information and Publications Services.* The Commission headquarters rapidly became a large clearinghouse for information on the

Caribbean area. To it came representatives of governments and industry, as well as private individuals, seeking advice, information, and publications. Every year the Commission answered hundreds of requests for technical information, publications, and pamphlets—even for seeds, cuttings, trees, and roots for experimental planting.

The Commission maintained a Publications Exchange Service, as indicated above in section 1 of this chapter, for service to planters, businessmen, and governments. Publications by the Commission itself, by governments, or by scientists on agricultural or technical subjects were collected by the exchange service, translated by it into French and English, and supplied free to interested inquirers. The booklet on banana growing published by the Commission, for example, was widely circulated in Africa, Australia, Italy, and Hawaii.

Technicians on the staff of the Commission Secretariat carried out research activities on a regular basis. Their findings, when published, have been used as manuals by governments and industry, and some have been translated into many languages for distribution throughout the world.

Some of the most noteworthy major publications by the Commission were: *A Guide to Commercial Shark Fishing in the Caribbean Area*; *Handbook for Cooperative Personnel in the Caribbean* (published jointly with the F.A.O.); *Aspects of Housing in the Caribbean*; *Education in the Caribbean*; *Caribbean Timbers, Their Utilization and Trade within the Area*; *The Industrial Utilization of Sugar-Cane By-Products*; *The Promotion of Industrial Development in the Caribbean*; *Animal Husbandry in the Caribbean*; *Development of Home Economics in the Caribbean*; and many others.

Beginning in August 1947, the Commission published a magazine called *Monthly Information Bulletin*. In January 1955 the name was changed to *The Caribbean*. This publication dealt with the social and economic development of the region served by the Commission, the history and folklore of the various countries, and it served as the official periodical organ of the Commission. Publication of this magazine was suspended temporarily with the issue of April 1960, pending reestablishment of the headquarters Secretariat in Puerto Rico. In November 1960 the Secretariat resumed publication of a six- to eight-page newsletter on a monthly basis.

In addition, the Secretariat distributed a weekly news report for radio broadcast, in four languages, entitled "Caribbean Review." This was a mimeographed document in the format of a prepared radio script, containing short news items of current interest. It was sent to all radio stations, newspapers, and other interested agencies throughout the area. As in the case of the monthly magazine its distribution was suspended in 1960. Other periodical publications of the Commission included the annual *Caribbean Economic Review*, the *Current Caribbean Bibliography*,

Caribbean Statistical Digest, and *Caribbean Technological Abstracts.*

The Commission maintained at Kent House in Trinidad a library which was a very valuable asset to the Commission in its task of disseminating information on Caribbean affairs. The library had an excellent collection of books, documents, periodicals, and films on the Caribbean and on subjects of interest to Caribbean peoples. It was of great help to students, teachers, writers, and journalists. The library was an official depository for United Nations and UNESCO publications, and it received also the publications of other international agencies and of governments. Books were available on loan not only in Trinidad but in any of the countries served by the Commission. The librarian and her staff were always at the disposal of those needing information on the Caribbean area.[6]

The entire library collection was packed and moved to Puerto Rico in 1960 where it was reorganized and turned over in 1961 to the Caribbean Organization.

7. Contributions toward Political Development. This is an achievement of the Commission which, strictly speaking, is not entitled even to mention, for the Commission was of course in terms of its basic document a nonpolitical consultative and advisory body only. The Commission's contributions toward the political awakening of the area therefore cannot be itemized in the same way that some of its more tangible achievements can be described. Nevertheless all competent observers agree that the Commission did a very great deal to enhance the growth toward orderly self-government in the West Indies.

First of all, by the very nature of its principal activities the Commission helped to break the vicious circle imposed by the twin problems of poverty and dependence which have for so many generations plagued the area. Every item of the Commission's work which in any way led to social and economic improvement helped advance political independence. As one writer reported it:

The United States Co-Chairman delineated the Caribbean Commission's field of activity by stating that political developments in the British West Indies were "none of our affair, but our work *is* the affair of those who will guide the political destinies of this area, for idle hands, empty stomachs, and godless hearts can sustain no political system." Indirectly the social and economic measures encouraged by the Commission and undertaken by the governments have important political effects . . . . In varying degrees they tend to change the class structure and to alter the dependence of colonies on the mother countries.[7]

Then, perhaps even more important, the Commission and the West Indian Conference sessions served as training schools in the basic arts of government and administration. The fact that over the years native peoples went to the conferences and served on the Commission was of tremendous psychological importance in the political awakening of the area. At these international gatherings aspiring native leaders met with their counterparts from other islands and territories; they learned about common problems and discussed possible solutions; they learned the fundamentals of parliamentary procedure and the art of negotiation; they learned about the possibilities and the limitations of governmental action; and they became aware of the existence of international agencies and something of the nature of international law. The secretary general told me in 1961 that as he reviewed the political news of the Caribbean area he was struck by the fact that almost without exception the local leaders then in prominence once had sat around the council tables of the Caribbean Commission, and often this had been their introduction to public life.

In her article on the fourth session of the West Indian Conference, Elizabeth H. Armstrong commented on the practical impossibility of keeping "political" questions out of the Conference discussions.

Although the Caribbean Commission and its auxiliary bodies are limited by the terms of the Agreement to consideration of economic and social matters, it would be unrealistic to expect that discussions would not impinge upon political questions from time to time. Political questions were touched upon more than once during the Conference. Such questions could not be stifled in the committees and were handled straightforwardly by the Netherlands co-chairman who was also Chairman of the Conference. Several of the more critically minded delegates tended to stress what they believed to be failures on the part of the metropolitan governments to observe the full letter of the law in such matters as human rights and labor legislation. It was clear, however, that the atmosphere of free discussion, which has developed in the West Indian Conference, has served as an educative medium for many of the delegates, and, together with their experience in connection with local administration in their own territories, has combined to make the Conference a highly responsible body. The general atmosphere tended to become more friendly as the Conference progressed, and there appeared to be, at the close, a greater understanding on the part of the delegates of the problems of other territories.

Although the claim made at the Second Session of the Conference that it was, in fact, a parliament of the region was an exaggeration, the West Indian Conference has become a forum for the discussion of the economic and social problems of the area of high importance to the delegates who attended and to their respective territories. Many delegates at Curacao expressed the opinion that the West Indian Conference constituted the most useful institution for the discussion of problems of the area which has ever existed. Should the West Indian Conference (Fourth Session) be characteristic of those which may follow, the history of the Caribbean Commission will show that regional cooperation in the Caribbean area was not retarded by lack of good will, mutual respect, and understanding among the territorial delegates to the Conference.[8]

In somewhat similar manner the headquarters Secretariat proved to be a training center for native peoples in the basic political arts. Many Secretariat employees, after a tour of duty with the Commission, went back to their home countries much better equipped to take responsible positions in island and territorial governments. From the very beginning the Commission made it the practice to recruit its staff largely from the area it served; this may eventually prove to have been its greatest and most lasting contribution to the well-being of the Caribbean.

6 □ EVALUATIONS OF THE CARIBBEAN COMMISSION

The Caribbean Commission marked its tenth anniversary in 1956. By then its positive contributions to the life of the area, as well as some of its shortcomings, had begun to be assessed. Nearly all of the judgments passed upon the organizaton and its work were largely favorable. Mr. Garnet Gordon put it this way:

The Caribbean Commission is the expression of a lofty concept and plan for regional cooperation between four metropolitan Governments directly interested in Caribbean territories and those territories. Limited in activity to advising in the social and economic field, it has made a handsome contribution to Caribbean progress by marshalling the needs of the area, formulating a massive collection of data on which plans for meeting these needs may be based, and arousing a greater consciousness in all governments concerned and in the United Nations and its specialized agencies as to their opportunities and duties in the area.

The international conferences which it has arranged on governmental, technical, and commercial levels have made very real contributions to progressive thought in the area and have influenced political action. The Commission may justly claim to have made some contribution to British Caribbean federation. It may justly claim to have enriched the life of the area by making it very much more knowledgeable about its several parts. It has not been without criticism; but however valid that criticism may be—and which human organization has done all that it might have done?—it has to its credit solid achievement which the Caribbean area would have been all the poorer without.[1]

The *Caribbean Trade and Industry Annual* of 1956 had this to say about the Commission:

Prior to the coming of the Commission, the inhabitants of the Caribbean lived their lives as complete strangers. Each colony was almost ignorant of the other; life in the area was more on an insular basis with scattered ideals and bewildered objectives. But the Commission's arrival brought the people and their affairs together. The Commission was indeed the harbinger of the Caribbean federation; it showed the inhabitants of the region an example of working together for the common good.[2]

The secretary general, Mr. Clovis F. Beauregard, expressed similar ideas somewhat more fully in his report on the work of the Commission from May 1955 to August 1957:

Men of foresight in the four Governments which shared the responsibility for the welfare and development of the area realized that, in order to avoid wasteful duplication, international cooperation with a view to concerted action in many fields was essential to communities similar in origin, living in scattered under-developed islands and mainland countries, and sharing common problems. . . .

The Caribbean Commission has been able to forge an international link by means of which regional cooperation in the economic and social fields and a good neighbour policy are becoming the common rule throughout the Caribbean. . . .

During the past ten years, West Indian leaders and technicians attending meetings of the West Indian Conference and Technical Conferences and Demonstration Tours convened by the Caribbean Commission have got to know one another and have exchanged views to mutual advantage. By these means they were able to realize that a cooperative approach could help to solve their common problems. These friendly contacts and exchanges have helped to prevent those feelings of frustration and despair so apt to arise when problems are considered in isolation.

A glance at the recommendations made by the seven sessions of the West Indian Conference which have met since 1944 and at the twenty-six technical conferences convened by the Caribbean Commission will show the variety of fields in which delegates felt that the Commission could assist. Indeed, the demands on the Commission have been more than it could meet with its limited means. Nevertheless, the list of its accomplishments is impressive.[3]

Somewhat earlier there was this evaluation of the Commission's work by Arthur Chai Onn, an eighteen-year-old student at St. George's College, Jamaica, winner of an essay contest.

By fulfilling its capacity as an advisory body, the Commission has achieved remarkable success. All territorial governments in the Caribbean will testify to this, and the peoples of the West Indies have observed and are grateful to the Commission for its modest and useful work. The fifteen member territories can be compared to a team of athletes, and the Commission to a coaching body. The members are cooperating and striving to improve its fitness. However, preoccupied with the game, they cannot detect their faults, which the Commission, viewing at a distance, readily sees. By recommendations, hints and expert advice, the Commission helps to train the territories to acquit themselves notably in the marathon existence of today.[4]

There were expressions of somewhat mixed feelings with regard to the Commission's constitutional inability to deal with specifically "political" matters. Some felt that this was the Commission's chief weakness, that the peoples of the region could never give the Commission their whole-hearted support because it was not working to further their political ambitions for greater self-government. Most observers, however, were quick to point out the practical impossibility of trying to separate "political" from social and economic matters. In promoting the general welfare of the peoples of the region the Commission had in effect been engaging, at least indirectly, in political activity of a very basic sort. Also, as was pointed out in chapter 5, the existence of the Commission as a forum and training school for native leaders unquestionably contributed toward the peaceful political evolution of the region.

On the credit side of the ledger it could be argued that its nominally nonpolitical character was one of the greatest sources of the Commission's success.

Because of its informal methods and experimental approach, the Caribbean Commission has been able to avoid many of the usual difficulties with sensitive feelings about colonial affairs. While the Permanent Mandates Commission never did obtain the right of inspection in local territories and this right was secured only with great difficulty and under circumscribed conditions for the Trusteeship Council, the practical equivalent has been practiced in the work of the Caribbean Commission without arousing unfounded suspicions. The Commission has enjoyed good public relations on all sides because it is a service, not a control, agency. In contrast to supervisory organizations, it can devote its energies to taking positive steps toward social and economic development, emphasizing collaboration rather than policing.[5]

Finally, when the Caribbean Organization had been established and was operating, there was this assessment of its predecessor, the Caribbean Commission, in the first edition of the new organization's newsletter.

It is extremely difficult to measure the work of the Commission in terms of concrete achievements. The reason for this difficulty rests in the fact that the Commission, as constituted, was a purely advisory and consultative body with no executive powers and no finances other than for its own administration. The main function of the Commission was to assist those responsible for formulating and implementing the policies of the individual Caribbean Governments, to explore and appreciate the nature, scope and urgency of the problems with which they had to deal and to develop sound programs for their solution. Through the years, the continuous flow of information, recommendations and advice that emanated from the Commission undoubtedly facilitated and contributed to the substantial progress achieved in general, among the countries which it served. The factors underlying many of the basic problems of the Caribbean area were placed in sharp focus at Commission-sponsored technical conferences, at which Caribbean leaders, politicians and technicians met to discuss and work out solutions to their common problems. The Commission was entitled to feel proud of the success it achieved in bringing the peoples of the widely scattered parts of this region into closer relationship with each other and in the desire it stimulated for a greater sharing of knowledge and experience. Further, through its efforts to bring about a closely-knit coordination between the countries it served and because of its international character, the Commission had in no small way served to direct the attention of other international organizations toward the needs and problems of the area.

The countries served by the Commission were in general faced with problems of a magnitude that was out of proportion to their slender financial resources; stiffening competition in markets overseas and rapidly increasing populations at home tended to aggravate the intractibility of many of those problems. Much remained to be accomplished in the fields which the Commission selected for major emphasis, but the Commission had steadily prepared itself for that task by acquiring knowledge of local conditions, practices and requirements; by developing a technique for the regional collection, analysis and dissemination of information; by maintaining close relations with the Governments, agencies and institutions it served; and by convening and servicing technical conferences as well as conferences of policy makers, in which all of the governments of the area were invited to participate.[6]

In short, there was a general belief that through their regional organization the scattered islands and territories of the Caribbean had contributed greatly toward the cooperative solution of their mutual problems. There was also recognition that the Commission had enabled the countries which it served to present a united front to the outside world. Lessons learned in the attempt to solve the basic economic and social problems of the Caribbean benefited other underdeveloped areas of the world through the Commission's publications and through the experience gained in the Caribbean by technicians of international agencies. The Commission also served as the channel through which international assistance could be funneled into the area—assistance which was not only far more effective but far more likely to be given on a regional rather than on an island-by-island, territory-by-territory basis. Just as lessons learned in the Caribbean benefited other depressed areas through the Commission's activities, so likewise the lessons learned elsewhere were applied to the problems of the Caribbean through the coordinating efforts of the Commission. The Commission served therefore not only to convey the lessons of the region's experience to the outside world, but also to focus the attention of the outside world on the problems of the Caribbean and the possibilities of their being solved.

7 □ MOUNTING PRESSURES FOR STRUCTURAL CHANGE

While not in the least wishing to discount the many expressions of praise for the Commission and its work, those who were most closely associated with the day-to-day activities of the organization were nevertheless by the mid-1950s becoming well aware of certain shortcomings. These were first of all shortcomings of a structural nature which were quite apart from the Commission's growing disharmony with the political evolution of the region. Mrs. Frances McReynolds Smith, for example, summarized it this way:

The Commission's shortcomings proceed not only from an unrealistic financial ceiling, which was imposed in its first year, but from certain weaknesses inherent in its very structure. It is merely an advisory and consultative body. It has no executive authority. Three co-chairmen constitute a quorum, only the votes of co-chairmen count, and all substantive matters must be agreed to unanimously. The creation of national sections increases the tendency to think as four national groups rather than as a regional technical body. The appointment of commissioners who have other full-time positions (and sometimes in fields not related to Commission activities) has created less of a technical and more of a political body. While the Commission has recently concentrated its energies in the fields of agricultural and industrial development, housing and basic education, it has on its books a varied assortment of projects which were hastily conceived and hastily approved. Its two meetings a year, of about five or five and a half working days each, usually permit only a superficial analysis of the problems involved. Its staff and funds could more effectively be employed if there were a greater concentration on fewer subjects, and if these were pursued until some practical achievement resulted. At present the Commission attempts to deal with almost all of the subjects handled by the United Nations and all of its specialized agencies. The Research Council has not fulfilled its expectations of being a counselor to the Commission on technical and scientific matters. Its members all have full-time jobs elsewhere; they are scattered throughout the Caribbean and the metropolitan countries and meet at the headquarters of the Commission once every two or three years. The need for the existence of such a body is dubious, especially since the Commission has adopted the system of convening small *ad hoc* groups of specialists to serve as preparatory groups for technical meetings. In addition, the development in the Secretariat of a staff of experts, serviced by a strong statistical unit and a library, has for all practical purposes supplanted the Research Council.[1]

Far more serious, however, for the future of the Commission was the growing spirit of nationalism and pride in self-government which was sweeping the Caribbean area. To the native leaders of this movement the Caribbean Commission with its four national sections representing the metropolitan powers seemed more and more anachronistic—a nagging reminder of the colonialism which they were so eagerly putting behind them.

These matters will be explored at greater length in the next chapter, but to give an example of the sort of difficulties the Commission was experiencing in accommodating itself to the political evolution of the Caribbean, let us consider for a moment the question of voting in Commission meetings. Article VI of the 1946 agreement, as supplemented by the rules of procedure, gave the vote only to the co-chairmen, three of whom had to concur for procedural matters and all four for substantive questions. Other commissioners were entitled to speak and have their views recorded in the minutes, but not to vote. This in effect meant that decisions with regard to Commission activities were taken by representatives of the metropolitan governments, not by natives of the area. There is reason to believe that leaders of the British islands might have been satisfied with a change in Commission operations which would have permitted their own native commissioners to vote at Commission meetings.[2] But others, notably the leaders from Puerto Rico and the Netherlands Antilles, were willing to agree to nothing less than a revision which would remove from the Commission altogether representatives of the metropolitan powers and substitute instead commissioners from the islands and territories only.*

As early as 1952 the matter of fundamental revision of the Caribbean Commission structure to reflect changing constitutional relationships in the Caribbean was brought up for serious public discussion. At the fifth session of the West Indian Conference, which met at Montego Bay, Jamaica, from November 24 to December 3, 1952, the delegates agreed to add to their provisional agenda the following items:

(a) a draft resolution presented by Mr. I. C. Debrot (Netherlands Antilles) requesting the Member Governments to take early action with a view to the revision of the Agreement for the Establishment of the Caribbean Commission in the light of the new constitutional relationships with the Caribbean area which have developed since the establishment of the Commission:

(b) a draft resolution presented by Mr. R. L. Bradshaw (Leeward Islands) recommending to the Member Governments' consideration the revision of the Agreement so as to enlarge the national section (at present, the four Co-Chairmen

---

*A former official of the United States Section told the writer that the American co-chairmen were well aware of Caribbean sensitivity on this matter of voting. Whenever it was the American's turn to preside at Commission meetings he always took pains to canvass systematically the views of all of the commissioners, in order to disguise as much as possible the fact that only the co-chairmen could actually vote.

constitute a quorum), and to give Commissioners equal voting status with the Co-Chairmen.[3]

In presenting his draft resolution to the Conference, Mr. Debrot pointed out that his country had gained full control of its economic, financial, social, and educational affairs. He therefore expressed the feeling of his delegation that the 1946 agreement, which had been drawn up and ratified before this constitutional development had taken place, was not sufficiently in keeping with the relationship then existing between the metropolitan country and the Netherlands Antilles.

Mr. Debrot pointed out that the term *gebiedsdeel*, "territories," in the Dutch-language version of the agreement, was suggestive of "colony," which the Netherlands Antilles no longer was. By Article II, he said, commissioners are appointed by the signatory governments; the Netherlands Antilles, however, would like appointments to take place with the concurrence of the local governments. Article VI, concerning the veto power of the co-chairmen, gives far too much power to appointees of the metropolitan governments, he asserted.

Mr. Bradshaw, from the Leeward Islands, also in his turn spoke of the need for revision of the 1946 agreement. He stated that he considered Article V, under which the four co-chairmen of the Commission constituted a quorum, inconsistent with the aim of the Commission to encourage and strengthen cooperation among the member governments and their Caribbean territories. Article VI, he said, giving the veto power to the co-chairmen, was undemocratic as well as inconsistent with the objectives for which the Commission was established. Rule V of the Commission's rules of procedure, under which any commissioner who differed from his co-chairman on any matter either of substance or procedure was entitled only to have his views recorded in the minutes, was also undemocratic. In Mr. Bradshaw's view the co-chairman was only first among equals, and no commissioner should be in an inferior position with regard to voting.[4]

Mr. Bradshaw, however, eventually agreed to the withdrawal of his draft resolution in order that the Conference might concentrate on Mr. Debrot's proposal. After endorsing two amendments to Mr. Debrot's draft, the Conference unanimously adopted the following statement:

WHEREAS it is agreed that the social, economic and cultural cooperation within the Caribbean area as commenced in the Anglo-American Caribbean Commission and carried on in the Caribbean Commission has proved to be of great benefit,

WHEREAS uninterrupted continuation of the cooperation within the Caribbean and with respective Metropolitan Countries is necessary to facilitate the interchange of information and to prevent the duplication of research for which the Commission was established,

WHEREAS since the establishment of the Commission the constitutional relations of the territories in the Caribbean area and their respective Metropolitan Countries have been altered in such manner that the Caribbean Commission in its present form no longer reflects the new relations between the Member Governments and the Caribbean countries,

WHEREAS the experience of the Caribbean Commission and of its auxiliary bodies has shown a growing interest on the part of the people of the region, as expressed through their governments, in the general problems of the region and their solution,

WHEREAS, therefore, it is advisable to submit the revision of the Agreement for the Establishment of the Caribbean Commission as from now to a thorough study;

The West Indian Conference refers the present statement to the Caribbean Commission for transmission to Member Governments of the Caribbean Commission for early action with a view to the revision of the Agreement establishing the Caribbean Commission and its auxiliary bodies, in the light of the new constitutional relationships with the Caribbean area, and in the light of the demonstrated desire and ability of the peoples of the area to accept increased responsibility in solving the problems of the region.[5]

Three years later, at the sixth session of the West Indian Conference, meeting in Puerto Rico, a statement was adopted which, after referring to the recommendation of the fifth session, noted that "further significant changes increasing the political and economic autonomy of the area, including the achievement by some of our countries of a full measure of self-government, have taken place since the last Session of this Conference, and others are being contemplated." The statement then went on to put the Conference on record as recommending prompt completion of the work of revision of the agreement for the establishment of the Caribbean Commission "in a manner faithfully reflecting the new constitutional realities in the Caribbean area and facilitating the continuance of needed social, economic and cultural cooperation in this region."[6]

Constitutional changes in the direction of greater self-government in the Caribbean continued to take place in the years following the fifth and sixth sessions of the West Indian Conference. It became increasingly apparent that the survival of an international organization in the Caribbean depended on the reaching of agreement with respect to the fundamental revision of the Commission's structure. In December 1956, in conjunction with the celebration of the tenth anniversary of the Commission, the four member governments issued a joint statement which read in part:

The four Governments consider that the purposes and objectives as set out in the present Agreement should continue to be the basis of any new organization resulting from such revision; that is to say, it would be an advisory and consultative body set up for the purposes of studying specific economic and social problems common to the Caribbean area and making proposals thereon to the various

Governments concerned for consideration in accordance with their respective constitutional powers and processes. It should however reflect appropriately the new responsibilities which the Governments of the area have undertaken since 1946 as well as those which some of them are about to assume.

In order to ensure the greatest possible expression of opinion by the Caribbean peoples, the four Governments invite the Governments of the area now served by the Caribbean Commission, to meet at the earliest practicable date and to discuss the formulation of a new Agreement. The draft of such an agreement would be submitted to the Governments signatory to the 1946 Agreement as well as to the Governments participating in the special conference for consideration and approval in accordance with their respective constitutional processes and responsibilities.

In the meantime the Caribbean Commission, as presently constituted, will continue to serve the area in the best tradition of the Commission.[7]

In February of 1956 the United States government had proposed to the governments of Great Britain, France, and the Netherlands that the Commission be reorganized under a new name, such as "Caribbean Conference." All of the local governments served by the Commission would become participating members of the new organization. The four metropolitan powers would be entitled to send two observers each with the right to participate in discussion but not to vote. The United States government suggested further that the existing machinery of the West Indian Conference be utilized to serve as a revision conference.[8]

Such a revision conference finally took place in 1959. From July 28 to August 7 of that year, the West Indian Conference met in special session at Charlotte Amalie, St. Thomas, U.S. Virgin Islands, for the purpose of arranging for the establishment of a successor organization to the Caribbean Commission.

The procedure for revision of the Commission structure had been suggested by the seventh session of the West Indian Conference, which met at Curacao in November of 1957. With the approval of the Commission an Ad Hoc Committee was appointed at that time

to consider the problems relating to the functions, structure and working method of a successor organisation to the Caribbean Commission;

to prepare a preliminary draft of an Agreement setting up such a successor organisation; and

to propose Budget Estimates and Apportionment of Budget.[9]

The Ad Hoc Committee met at the Commission's headquarters from July 24 to August 4, 1958, and again from April 2 to April 10, 1959. At its second meeting, the Ad Hoc Committee recommended, and the Commission agreed, that a special session of the West Indian Conference should take place in July 1959 to arrange for the establishment of a successor organization to the Caribbean Commission. On the invitation of the government of the Virgin Islands it was agreed that the session should be held in that country.[10]

Thus, at last, a plenary international gathering was assembled with its sole item of business the revision of the Caribbean Commission to reflect the changed constitutional relationships in the Caribbean. Once again the Caribbean Commission was pioneering unprecedented arrangements in international relations, for here were four metropolitan powers saying in effect that a formal agreement among them should be revised and supplanted, not by themselves, but by delegates of their dependent or associated territories.

The special session set the stage for its work by adopting as a general policy recommendation:

> That the Caribbean Organization should be a consultative and advisory body which should concern itself with social, cultural and economic matters of common interest to the Caribbean area, particularly agriculture, communications, education, fisheries, health, housing, industry, labour, music, the arts, social welfare and trade.[11]

Then the Conference proceeded to adopt recommendations with regard to various administrative and procedural matters pertaining to the transition from Caribbean Commission to Caribbean Organization. It accepted the offer of the government of Puerto Rico to become the host country for the new Organization; it adopted recommendations with regard to the apportionment of the budget; and it called for the appointment of a Working Group of experts, representing each of the governments participating in the Conference, which would help facilitate the transition from Caribbean Commission to Caribbean Organization. This it would do by giving consideration to all matters connected with the setting up of the Commission in Puerto Rico and by undertaking to frame guiding principles for the work of the new Organization.[12] Finally, the special session of the West Indian Conference, acting in its assigned capacity as constituent assembly for the new Caribbean Organization, adopted a draft agreement for the establishment of the Caribbean Organization and a draft statute of the Caribbean Organization, and recommended acceptance of these instruments by the four metropolitan governments.

The four governments did accept the documents substantially as they were drafted by the special session. The agreement for the establishment of the Caribbean Organization was signed in Washington on June 21, 1960, by the ambassador of France, the ambassador of the Netherlands to the United States, by the British ambassador, by Secretary of State Christian Herter, and by the American co-chairman of the Commission, Mr. Roderick O'Connor. The full text of the agreement and of the statute of the Caribbean Organization are set forth in the Appendix.

It would be fitting to close this chapter by citing a portion of an eloquent statement looking to the future which was made at the special session by the Honorable Robert L. Bradshaw, a delegate from the (British) West Indies:

The new organisation which we will create shall be our forum for peaceful cooperation and constructive work rather than a place from which threats are hurled and recriminations made—a forum in which we will attack our problems instead of attacking each other. We have no territorial designs upon each other. We live in an under-developed area whose people are striving for the sun, as it were, seeking for education, striving to be in a position where their next meal was not problematic, where their housing was decent, where their culture was established and where their countries had status and standing in the world. It is my fervent hope and the fervent hope of the Government of the West Indies on whose behalf I have the honour to speak, that success will crown our labours, resulting in the creation of an organisation which within its powers will well serve certain stated needs of our countries and peoples.[13]

8 □ CONSTITUTIONAL DEVELOPMENTS DURING THE CARIBBEAN COMMISSION YEARS, 1946 TO 1961

Of all the factors which can be identified as having prompted the successive changes in the structures and activities of the agencies for regional cooperation in the Caribbean, one stands out as absolutely fundamental to the whole process—namely, the constitutional growth of the territories in the direction of increasing self-government and independence. As we have already seen, those adjustments in the governmental relationships between the metropolitan powers and their former dependent territories in the Caribbean which occurred during the Caribbean Commission years tended to make the four-power Commission appear more and more anachronistic. This was a plain fact which was clearly recognized not only by ambitious local politicians eager to throw off the lingering vestiges of colonialism but by dispassionate observers of the Caribbean scene as well. As early as 1952 people concerned with the affairs of the Caribbean Commission had begun to realize that changes would eventually have to be made in the Commission agreement in order to reflect the emerging political realities in the West Indies. In other words, such was the degree to which most of the Caribbean territories had become self-governing that if the Caribbean Commission or any other international body in the Caribbean concerned with social and economic problems were to continue to exist it would have to be an organization governed and directed by the leaders of the Caribbean territories themselves.

It is appropriate, therefore, to give attention at this point to some of the formal constitutional changes which took place in the major territories of the Caribbean up to 1961. Only in the light of these developments can it be fully understood why the Caribbean Commission had to give way to the Caribbean Organization.

In chapter 12 the political evolution subsequent to 1961, including the political disintegration of the West Indies Federation, will be discussed as a major factor contributing to the failure of the Caribbean Organization, with the resulting shift in 1965 to the informal pattern of cooperation represented by Puerto Rico's CODECA.

Primary attention here will be given to Puerto Rico, the British West Indies Federation, the Netherlands Antilles and Surinam, and the French *départements*, since these were the territories which represented the leaders in the political evolution which occurred in the region during the Commission years.

66

The political evolution of Puerto Rico will be considered first, and with considerable background material in view of the fact that Puerto Rico has emerged as the prime mover in both of the recent shifts in level of regional cooperation in the Caribbean, namely, the change from Caribbean Commission to Caribbean Organization, and from Caribbean Organization to CODECA.

PUERTO RICO

Curiously enough Puerto Rico was granted virtual self-government in 1897 while it was still under Spanish rule. On November 25 of that year the Spanish crown issued decrees authorizing the establishment of a legislative assembly and the formation of a quasi-autonomous government under universal manhood suffrage.[1] Before these reforms could take full effect in Puerto Rico, however, the Spanish-American War broke out. American troops occupied the island, and by the Treaty of Paris, signed in December 1898, sovereignty over Puerto Rico passed to the United States. Not until 1952, according to Puerto Ricans, did the island—under the American flag—regain the level of political autonomy to which it would have been entitled under Spanish rule after 1897.

During the years between 1898 and 1952 Puerto Rico was an "unincorporated territory" of the United States and made only gradual progress toward self-government. Under the terms of an Organic Act (the Foraker Act) passed by Congress in 1900, the governor, the heads of the six executive departments, the upper house of the legislature, and the justices of the Supreme Court were all appointed by the President of the United States. The people of the island could elect only the members of the lower house of the legislature, the officers of the municipal governments, and a resident commissioner in Washington who was given a seat in the House of Representatives and the right to speak, but no power to vote.[2]

Through the early years of the twentieth century American generosity toward Puerto Rico took the form of economic, rather than political, concessions to the people of the island. Puerto Rican products, notably sugar, were admitted to the United States markets free of duty. The people of Puerto Rico were not required to pay United States taxes or otherwise contribute to the support of the federal government. All United States customs duties collected in Puerto Rico on foreign goods brought into the island, and all federal excise taxes due on Puerto Rican products sold in the United States were paid into the treasury of the island government rather than into the federal treasury in Washington.[3] These provisions of course had the effect of subsidizing the insular government. Also, another provision of the 1900 Organic Act (Section 14) made inapplicable in Puerto Rico all United States internal revenue laws.

Generous as the 1900 law may have been from an economic and fiscal standpoint, however, it was viewed as a complete failure by the politically sophisticated elements of the Puerto Rican community. The act said nothing about the granting of United States citizenship to the people of Puerto Rico. In effect it created a body politic styled "The People of Puerto Rico," composed of citizens of Puerto Rico who were entitled to the protection of the United States but who in reality had very limited political rights.[4] The United States Supreme Court, when asked in 1901 for an interpretation of Puerto Rico's political status, ruled:

> that whilst in an international sense Puerto Rico was not a foreign country, since it was subject to the sovereignty of and was owned by the United States, it was foreign to the United States in a domestic sense because the island had not been incorporated into the United States, but was merely appurtenant thereto as a possession.[5]

It is thus no wonder that the people of Puerto Rico and their political parties were inspired to engage in unceasing agitation for a more liberal political regime for their island. It was not until 1917, however, that Puerto Rican demands for more self-government were even partially met.

In the Organic Act of 1917 Congress granted United States citizenship to the people of Puerto Rico. The act also established an elective upper house and authorized the governor to appoint all of the department heads of the island government except the attorney general and the commissioner of education. These two officers, the auditor, the justices of the supreme court, as well as the governor himself, remained presidential appointees.[6]

Though bills which would have made further changes in Puerto Rico's status were frequently introduced into Congress in the years following 1917, no real change in the island's governmental structure was made until after World War II. The first step was the appointment by the President in 1946 of Jesús T. Pinero as governor of Puerto Rico, to succeed Rexford G. Tugwell. Pinero was not only the first native Puerto Rican governor, but in addition he had been elected by the people to the post of resident commissioner in Washington in 1944.[7]

The next step, an entirely logical one, came in the form of the Jones Act of 1947. This amended the Organic Act to permit the people of Puerto Rico to choose their own governor, and it made the heads of all Puerto Rican cabinet departments appointees of the governor, with the advice and consent of the Puerto Rican Senate.[8] Luis Muñoz Marín became in 1948 the first popularly elected governor of Puerto Rico. In 1960 he was reelected for his fourth term.

Even under the Jones Act, however, Puerto Rico retained virtually a colonial administration. The President of the United States still appointed the auditor and the justices of the Puerto Rican Supreme Court. The President also retained the power to give finality to gubernatorial vetoes of bills passed by the Puerto Rican legislature. Congress retained the power to revoke Puerto Rican legislation, and of course Congress could at any time amend unilaterally the basic structure of government for Puerto Rico as embodied in the Organic Act.[9]

The breakthrough to the present Commonwealth status for Puerto Rico came with Public Law 600 of the Eighty-first Congress, drafted in Puerto Rico and introduced into Congress by Resident Commissioner Antonio Fernos Isern. The law was passed by Congress and signed by the President on July 3, 1950. Its first article stated "that, fully recognizing the principle of consent, this Act is now adopted in the nature of a compact so that the people of Puerto Rico may organize a government pursuant to a constitution of their own adoption."

This, then, was no ordinary act of Congress. In effect it provided for the drawing up and the sealing of a compact between the people of the United States and the people of Puerto Rico. The first step was the holding of a referendum in Puerto Rico, for Public Law 600 provided that only if its provisions were accepted by the electorate of Puerto Rico could it come into full effect. The referendum was held on June 4, 1951; 65 percent of the 777,675 qualified voters of Puerto Rico participated and 76.5 percent of those voting approved the act.[10]

Public Law 600 next provided that the legislature of Puerto Rico was to call a constitutional convention to draft a constitution for Puerto Rico. According to the law the constitution would have to provide for a republican form of government and include a bill of rights.[11]

Thus in August of 1951 another election was held in Puerto Rico, as a result of which ninety-two delegates were chosen for the Constitutional Convention. The Convention met in September 1951 and concluded its work of drafting a constitution for Puerto Rico in February of 1952. On March 3, 1952, the draft constitution was accepted overwhelmingly by voters of the island in still another special election.[12]

President Truman transmitted the draft constitution to Congress for approval, as required by Public Law 600, and Congress signified its acceptance of the new Puerto Rican constitution in July 1952, by enacting Public Law 447, Eighty-second Congress. This act, however, made final congressional approval of the constitution contingent upon the acceptance of three changes in the document as it was originally drafted: the addition of a clarifying clause in one section of the bill of rights; the elimination of another section of the bill of rights, which seemed to some members of Congress to be socialistic; and the addition of certain provisions with regard to future amendments of the constitution. The Puerto Rican Constitutional Convention reassembled hastily, and, regarding the congressional conditions as reasonable, it amended the document to conform to the wishes of Congress. On July 25, 1952, the new Constitution was proclaimed to be in effect and the Commonwealth of Puerto Rico came into being.[13]

The people of Puerto Rico have since 1952 been fully self-governing except that as citizens of the United States they are subject to federal laws of general applicability passed by Congress, and to the executive acts of the federal government in such fields as defense and foreign affairs. Section 19 of Public Law 447, Eighty-second Congress, provides: "The statutory laws of the United States not locally inapplicable . . . shall have the same force and effect in Puerto Rico as in the United States, except the internal revenue laws." This means, of course, that Congress still can and does legislate for Puerto Rico in all matters of general concern within the competence of the federal government. Thus, Puerto Rico is governed by United States federal legislation in such matters as the control of immigration, the maintenance and regulation of the monetary and postal systems, pure food and drug standards, and customs tariffs; Puerto Rico also comes under the entire body of social security, public welfare, and financial assistance legislation which has accumulated over the years for the aid of veterans, farmers, schoolchildren, retired persons, and so on.[14]

Within the framework of general federal legislation, therefore, Puerto Ricans exercise basically the same rights of self-government as those enjoyed by other citizens of the United States. Puerto Rican young men, like their fellow citizens in the States, are subject to compulsory military service.

The basic charter of the Puerto Rican government is of course the Constitution adopted by the Constitutional Convention in 1952. The bill of rights, which heads this document, not only protects the traditional civil rights of the individual but also imposes upon the Commonwealth the obligation to guarantee, by positive governmental action, certain economic and social rights. Articles III through VI establish a government divided into legislative, executive, and judicial branches, with appropriate and traditional American devices for a system of checks and balances. Article VII provides that the Constitution can be amended only by the Puerto Rican people and their representatives. In other words, the United States Congress can no longer alter the governmental structure of Puerto Rico at will through the passage and amendment of Organic Acts.

The Commonwealth legislature is divided into two chambers, a Senate and a House of Representatives. The members are elected by universal suffrage for four-year terms. The governor, who is also popularly elected for four-year terms, is the only elected official in the executive branch of the government. Subject to the approval of the Puerto Rican Senate he appoints all department heads and other high-ranking executive and administrative officers.

The judicial branch of the Puerto Rican government is called the

General Court of Justice. It is divided into three operational levels, consisting of a Supreme Court, a Superior Court (which holds sessions in the nine major cities of the island), and a District Court (which holds sessions in all Puerto Rican municipalities). All of the judges are appointed by the governor, with the advice and consent of the Senate.[15]

The framers of the Puerto Rican Constitution adopted the term "Commonwealth" primarily to avoid the confusion that might arise in the American federal system if Puerto Rico were to be called some form of "state." But since in Spanish there is no equivalent of "commonwealth" Puerto Rico was designated formally and legally as *Estado Libre Associado de Puerto Rico*. This title translated into English literally as "Associated Free State of Puerto Rico," or, as it is usually rendered in English, "Free and Associated State of Puerto Rico."

The status of Puerto Rico vis-à-vis the outside world is in some ways as much of a puzzle as was the island's relationship to the United States in the years following the conquest of 1898. Oxford University's monthly journal of international affairs, *The World Today*, made this comment about Puerto Rico's status:

> Since 25 July 1952, its political status is called "Commonwealth" in English and "Free and Associated State" (*Estado Libre Associado*) in Spanish. Chief Justice Warren called Puerto Rico's new position vis-à-vis the United States the most remarkable constitutional development of the twentieth century. A political opponent of the Governor, Miguel Angel Garcia Mendez, referring to the rather indeterminate and floating nature of the arrangement, called it "a political sputnik." Students of the British Commonwealth will, of course, detect a similarity to Dominion Status.[16]

Governor Muñoz Marín wrote in 1954:

> The most significant aspect of the new status lies in the recognition that the arrangement is indeed founded on the principle of consent, expressed by a compact in the form of an Act of Congress subject to the approval of the people of Puerto Rico at the polls. Another basic characteristic is the concept of association as distinguished from the historical idea of union, so far as states are concerned, and of possession, so far as unincorporated territories are concerned. It embodies association with the United States, not union among the States. These are the characteristics that clear the status of the former colonial character of "territory" or "possession."[17]

The external status of Puerto Rico was tested in a long debate at the United Nations in 1953. The United Nations had to resolve whether Puerto Rico in its new governmental garb was a self-governing political entity, or whether despite the changes it remained a non-self-governing territory. If it remained non-self-governing then the United States would have to continue reporting on the island to the United Nations under Article 73(e) of the Charter.*

The outcome of the debate in the United Nations was a victory for the liberal interpretation of Commonwealth status. In November 1953, the General Assembly adopted a resolution in which the opinion was expressed "that it stems from the documentation provided that the association of the Commonwealth of Puerto Rico with the United States of America has been established as a mutually agreed association." The General Assembly resolution went on to declare that "the people of the Commonwealth of Puerto Rico have been invested with attributes of political sovereignty which clearly identify the status of self-government attained by the Puerto Rican people as an autonomous political entity."[18]

While the General Assembly debate on the status of Puerto Rico was in progress, President Eisenhower instructed Ambassador Henry Cabot Lodge to address a message on the subject to the United Nations:

I am authorized to say on behalf of the President that if, at any time, the Legislature of Puerto Rico adopts a resolution in favor of more complete or even absolute independence he will immediately thereafter recommend to Congress that such independence be granted. The President also wishes me to say that, in this event, he would welcome Puerto Rico's adherence to the Rio Pact and the United Nations Charter.[19]

Within the politics of Puerto Rico there has been a very small minority which seeks complete independence for the island. Extremist adherents of this faction were responsible for the attempted assassination of President Truman in 1950 and for the shooting of several members of the House of Representatives in 1953. Another somewhat larger minority would have Puerto Rico join the federal Union as the fifty-first state. Most of the island's political leaders, however, advocated continued evolution of the unique Commonwealth status which Puerto Rico had worked out for itself, at least until the 1968 election. The people of the island likewise appear to approve of their Commonwealth status, as was demonstrated in the referendum of July 23, 1967 (see chapter 12).

*Article 73 of the United Nations Charter reads in part as follows: "Members of the United Nations which have or assume responsibilities for the administration of territories whose peoples have not yet attained a full measure of self-government recognize the principle that the interests of the inhabitants of these territories are paramount, and accept as a sacred trust the obligation to promote to the utmost, within the system of international peace and security established by the present Charter, the well-being of the inhabitants of those territories, and, to this end: . . . (e) to transmit regularly to the Secretary-General for information purposes, subject to such limitations as security and constitutional considerations may require, statistical and other information of a technical nature relating to economic, social, and educational conditions in the territories for which they are respectively responsible."

THE (BRITISH) WEST INDIES FEDERATION

It would be tempting to pass lightly over the constitutional evolution of the West Indies Federation in view of the known fact that this political entity did not survive beyond 1962. Yet the story of the Federation's founding must be told, for in it are elements which typify the overall problems of integration in the Caribbean.

What complicates the picture in the British West Indies is that the units of the former Federation are islands—small, poor, and widely scattered. The units which joined to form federal unions in the United States, Canada, Australia, and Nigeria were large contiguous land units, with much actual and potential wealth. By contrast, Jamaica, which was the largest island in the West Indies Federation (4,411 square miles in area), is smaller than the state of Connecticut (5,009 square miles); Trinidad (1,980 square miles) is barely larger than Rhode Island (1,124 square miles); and the total area of the entire Federation of ten units (8,005 square miles) was less than that of the state of Maryland (10,577 square miles). Moreover, these islands were and are for the most part underdeveloped and overpopulated, and their basically agricultural economies tend to be competitive with each other. Because of the many mountains and steep hillsides, nearly half of the Federation land area was unfit for cultivation. The transportation and communications network among the islands was inadequate; both airline fares and ocean freight rates were frequently cited as being among the highest in the world. And, finally to add to all of the other difficulties, the region was and is beset by frequent hurricanes which in a few hours can destroy the slowly accumulated assets of years.

The idea of federal union, the concept of nationhood, was slow in forming and quick to dissolve. Each of these islands had its own history, its own more or less independent development. The people are Jamaicans, Trinidadians, or Barbadians first and foremost, and there was little or no sense of West Indian nationality, except perhaps among the articulate leaders of the Federation movement.

Politically the Federation structure was largely imposed from above and from without. All the while, despite the advent of federation, each island was steadily undergoing its own independent political and constitutional evolution. Jamaica, and to a slightly lesser degree Trinidad and Barbados, had attained individual self-governing status. Other islands still displayed lingering traces of the old colonial status vis-à-vis the United Kingdom. Furthermore, each island or group of islands within the Federation retained its governor appointed by the Queen, in addition to the governor-general of the whole Federation. Thus each island in the Federation occupied in effect two political roles: one within the Federation and one within the wider British Commonwealth. Even two years and more after the Federation came into being it was a matter of acts of Parliament in London or of Orders in Council of the United Kingdom government to revise and amend the constitutions of the islands in the Federation. Each of the islands had been pursuing its own economic development projects, some with grants-in-aid directly from London, and as late as 1961 there was no unrestricted freedom of movement for either people or goods within the Federation. It was a strange, patchwork arrangement which came into being on January 3, 1958.

The West Indies consisted of ten units embracing altogether thirteen islands: Antigua, Barbados, Dominica, Grenada, Jamaica, Montserrat, St. Kitts-Nevis-Anguilla, St. Lucia, St. Vincent, and Trinidad and Tobago. Jamaica is the largest, with 4,411 square miles and a population in 1960 of 1,606,546. The smallest is Montserrat, with 32 square miles and a population of around 14,000. Jamaica and Trinidad together contained 83 percent of the total federal land area and 77 percent of the Federation's population of slightly more than 3,000,000. The seat of the federal government was at Port of Spain, Trinidad.

The mainland colonies of British Honduras and British Guiana remained outside the Federation. Their failure to unite with the islands meant that the Federation government controlled only 7 percent of the total land area of the British Caribbean.[20]

Generally speaking each of the island territories emerged from World War II still governed by some variation of the crown colony system. The basic feature of this system was the strict separation of powers. The governor, appointed by the crown, was in complete charge of the executive branch of the government. He exercised power with the advice—and sometimes the consent—of a council which he had himself appointed. Legislative authority was vested in an assembly, generally elected on a very restricted franchise, but holding nevertheless the exclusive right to initiate or to amend money bills. The flaw in this system of government was that there was no link between the executive and the legislative branches. The governor, as head of the executive, was a representative of the Colonial Office and responsible to the United Kingdom for policy positions. The views held in London with respect to colonial matters were frequently at complete odds with those of the leading groups that in each colony had effective control of the legislative assembly.[21]

The break with the past began with the various war-inspired declarations of policy with respect to the future of the British Empire. It was proclaimed that colonies were to advance as rapidly as possible toward autonomy and self-rule within the Commonwealth. In the West Indies Jamaica was selected for the first experiment in a gradual political evolution. In 1944 that island was given a new constitution. It provided that the policy-making body, to be known as the Executive Committee, should consist of ten members, five of whom were to be elected by—and thus responsible to—the colonial legislature. Three of the remaining five members were to be Colonial Service officials, and the other two were to be nominated by the governor from among the members of the legislature. This was an important step toward self-government because it meant that the initiation of public policy virtually passed into the hands of the elected legislature. Other constitutional reforms for Jamaica followed in later years, and comparable changes were initiated at varying rates in the other islands.

Meanwhile the British government was studying the problems that would arise with the multiplication of small, independent communities in the West Indies. Federation appeared to be an obvious solution. In March 1945, therefore, Colonel Oliver Stanley, secretary of state for the colonies, sent a dispatch to the governments of the West Indian colonies in which he pointed out that "the aim of British policy should be the development of federation in the Caribbean at such time as the balance of opinion in the various colonies is in favour of a change, and when the development of communications makes it administratively practicable. The ultimate aim of any federation which may be established would be full internal self-government within the British Commonwealth." He suggested that the proposal be debated in the legislatures of all of the colonies concerned, and that, if they agreed in principle to the idea of federation, a conference should be called to discuss definite proposals for closer political association.[22]

The colonial legislatures agreed to Colonel Stanley's proposal, and in 1947 Mr. Creech Jones, Colonel Stanley's successor at the Colonial Office, proposed that a conference be held later that year to discuss the question of federation. In his message the colonial secretary said: "It is clearly impossible in the modern world for the present separate communities, small or isolated as most of them are, to achieve and maintain full self-government on their own . . . . On the other hand, a community of well over two million people in the Caribbean area, with much that is homogeneous in their culture, could reasonably hope to achieve real self-government and to be strong enough to stand against economic and cultural pressure and to formulate and carry through a policy and way of life of its own."[23]

Prodded on in this fashion by London, the Conference on Closer Association of the British West Indian Colonies was convened at Montego Bay, Jamaica, in September 1947. It was presided over by Creech Jones, and it was attended by delegates nominated by the legislatures of the island territories and of British Honduras and British Guiana as well. All of the delegates at this Conference, except those from British Guiana and British Honduras, accepted the principle of a federation in which the constituent units would retain complete control over all matters except those specifically assigned to the federal government.

The Montego Bay Conference of 1947 recommended the appointment of a committee to work out in detail a federal constitution. This committee, called the Standing Closer Association Committee, met the following year under the chairmanship of Sir Hubert Rance, then governor of Trinidad. All of the other members of the Committee were West Indians chosen by the territorial legislatures.

In 1950 the Standing Closer Association Committee published its report, outlining proposals for a federal constitution. There would be a bicameral legislature, with a popularly elected House of Assembly and a Senate nominated by the governor-general; the executive would consist of the governor-general, assisted by a State Council with a majority of members from the House of Assembly, one of whom was to be designated prime minister.[24]

From this point on the negotiations over federal proposals become too complex to describe in detail here. Suffice it to say that faced with the actual prospect of a federal government the leaders and the people of each of the units began to have serious second thoughts. There were earnest discussions over the exact composition and powers of the Federation government, over the sources of the federal revenue, over the nature and jurisdiction of the federal judiciary, over the recruitment of the federal civil service, and over the question of the degree to which internal migration would be permitted within the proposed federation.

In 1953 the secretary of state for the colonies called a conference in London of representatives of all of the territories which had agreed to be included in the federation. This conference finally reached agreement on a federal plan which the delegates felt they could present to their territorial legislatures.

By 1955 these 1953 federal proposals had been accepted in principle by all of the legislatures. Barbados and Trinidad, however, were at odds on the question of internal migration. With its dense population pressing hard on meager resources, Barbados insisted on complete freedom of migration within the territory of the federation. Trinidad, on the other hand, with the richest and most diversified economy at that time, feared that it might be submerged by a stream of immigrants from Barbados and from some of the other poor and overcrowded islands if freedom of migration became the rule.

Another conference was therefore called by the British government to deal with this thorny problem of migration within the federation. Meeting in Trinidad in March 1955, this conference finally worked out a compromise formula which was acceptable to all of the islands and which could be incorporated in the federal constitution.[25]

Further progress was made in 1955 with the appointment of three commissions to study and report on the controversial issues of the fiscal, civil service, and judicial arrangements, respectively, of the proposed federation.

In 1956, once again, a conference was called in London to deal with the major unresolved issues in connection with the formation of the Federation. Meeting from February 7 to 23 under the chairmanship of Mr. Lennox Boyd, the new colonial secretary, the 1956 London Conference was attended, as in 1953, by delegates from all of the West Indian governments which had agreed to the principle of federation. The conference dealt with the reports of the three commissions set up the year before and with other outstanding issues. The delegates agreed that the federal plan put forward at the London Conference of 1953 and subsequently endorsed by the territorial legislatures should, with certain modifications, be the basis for a federation constitution which should be drafted by the end of 1956. Federal elections should be held as soon as possible after January 1, 1958, and in any event not later than March 31, 1958. Realizing that much detailed work still remained to be done, the delegates agreed to constitute themselves a Standing Federation Committee to carry out the necessary preparatory constitutional and administrative arrangements until the appointment of the Federation's first governor-general, and after that to serve in an advisory capacity until the first federal elections.

On August 2, 1956, Parliament enacted the British Caribbean Federation Bill, which provided for the eventual establishment of the British Caribbean Federation by Order-in-Council and for the establishment of a federal government, a federal legislature, and a federal Supreme Court. The enactment of this bill was celebrated throughout the British West Indies as a public holiday, although legally the Federation still could not come into existence until after the Federation Constitution had been adopted and a governor-general appointed.[26]

In July 1957, Parliament approved the West Indies (Federation) Order in Council, providing for the establishment of the Federation of the West Indies. The Constitution of the West Indies, comprising 118 articles, was published as an annex to the Order-in-Council. Shortly before, in May, it had been announced in London that the Queen had appointed Lord Hailes (formerly Mr. Patrick Buchan-Hepburn, minister of works in the Anthony Eden government) as the first governor-general of the West Indies.

The Federation, then, finally came into formal existence on January 3, 1958, when Lord Hailes was sworn in as governor-general of the West Indies at Port of Spain, Trinidad.

The first item of business for the new nation was to choose members of the federal House of Representatives. Elections were held on March 25, 1958. Chief contenders were the Federal Labour Party, whose leaders included Norman Manley, chief minister of Jamaica, Dr. Eric Williams, chief minister of Trinidad, and Sir Grantley Adams, premier of Barbados; and the Democratic Labour Party, whose leaders included Sir Alexander Bustamante and Mr. Albert Gomes, leaders of the opposition in Jamaica and Trinidad, respectively.

The Federal Labour Party won twenty-five seats, the Democratic Labour Party, nineteen, and the Barbados National Party, one seat. Sir Grantley Adams of Barbados was elected the first prime minister of the Federation when the new federal House of Representatives met for the first time on April 18, 1958, at Port of Spain.

In accordance with the new Constitution, the governor-general appointed the nineteen-member Senate and the ten-member Council of State.

The first Parliament of the West Indies Federation was officially inaugurated at Port of Spain on April 20, 1958, by Princess Margaret. The princess read a message from the Queen expressing warm greetings to the West Indian people and congratulating them on "the achievement of closer association with each other on which they have decided, and which holds so much promise for their future." In reply Sir Grantley Adams reaffirmed the loyalty of the West Indian people to the throne and stressed that the Federation would need the help and encouragement of Great Britain in its further progress toward full nationhood.

The Constitution of the West Indies, which was approved by the United Kingdom Parliament in July 1957, provided for a bicameral legislature, consisting of a Senate of nineteen members appointed by the governor-general (two representing each territory except Montserrat, which had one), and a House of Representatives of forty-five members (seventeen from Jamaica, ten from Trinidad, five from Barbados, one from Montserrat, and two from each of the six other units), elected by adult suffrage. Both chambers normally were to have a life of five years, but the House of Representatives could be dissolved earlier. Any bill except a money bill could be introduced into either house; money bills had to originate in the House of Representatives only. Money bills could be presented to the governor-general for assent regardless of the action of the Senate; with regard to other bills the Senate had a delaying power of one year.

The executive authority of the Federation was vested in the Queen, but subject to the provisions of the Constitution the authority could be exercised on her behalf by the governor-general. A Council of State, consisting of the prime minister and ten other ministers, normally presided over by the governor-general, was the principal instrument of policy formulation for the Federation. The prime minister was elected in the House of Representatives from among its members, and the other ministers were appointed by the governor-general on the advice of the prime minister, not less than three being members of the Senate and the rest members of the House.[27] The governor-general was required to act in accordance with the advice of the Council of State except in certain specific instances. In matters concerning defense, external relations, or the financial stability of the Federation, he was required to obtain the approval of the United Kingdom government if he acted contrary to the advice of the Council of State.

There was a federal Supreme Court, presided over by a chief justice and three federal justices, each appointed by the governor-general after consultation with the prime minister. The federal Supreme Court had original jurisdiction in proceedings concerning the Federation as a whole or involving more than one unit. It was also the court of appeal from the highest courts of all of the unit territories. Within the territories federal laws could be enforced only by territorial courts.

For the first five years the Federation was to derive its revenue from a mandatory levy on the territorial governments. Under the schedule set forth in the Constitution, Jamaica was to pay 43 percent; Trinidad, 39 percent; Barbados, 9 percent; and the rest ranged from 1.74 percent for St. Lucia down to 0.27 percent for Montserrat.

Subjects for legislative enactment in the Federation were set forth in an Exclusive List and a Concurrent List, as provided for in a schedule appended to the Constitution. The federal legislature had the power to legislate with respect to any matter on either list, federal law prevailing in the event of inconsistency with the law of a territory. The unit legislative assemblies could legislate on subjects in the Concurrent List. Legislation on matters not covered in either list was reserved for the units.

The Exclusive List covered such subjects as defense, exchange control, immigration and emigration, the public service of the Federation, and matters having to do with the University College of the West Indies (located in Jamaica). The Concurrent List covered legislation on such matters as civil aviation and shipping, banks and banking, industrial arbitration, currency, customs and excise duties, industrial development, postal services, higher education (except for the University College of the West Indies), research and surveys, telegraph and telephone communications, trade and commerce, and trade union matters.

Legislation by Order-in-Council of the United Kingdom government in London could be enacted for the Federation in matters pertaining to defense, external relations, or the maintenance of the financial stability of the Federation.

The Constitution provided that not less than five years after it came into force a conference should be convened for the purpose of reviewing and possibly amending the Constitution. The conference should consist of delegates from each of the units and from the United Kingdom government. Among other things the revision conference was supposed to consider the adequacy of powers conferred on the federal government to raise revenue.[28]

The West Indies in 1961 was still a long way from being a nation in the ordinary sense of the word. There was, for example, still no common currency. Jamaica employed a monetary unit called the Jamaica pound, which was kept at par with the British pound. The other islands of the Federation, however, together with British Honduras and British Guiana which were not in the Federation, used the British West Indies dollar, which in 1961 was worth U.S. $0.58. There was no Federation postal system. There was, as mentioned before, no absolute freedom of movement of persons and no customs union. A citizen of one island who wished to travel to another had to secure a British passport and submit to whatever documentary requirements might be imposed by the government of the unit territory he wished to visit. There were no federal taxes and no federal laws directly binding upon individuals, except for members of the federal civil service.

West Indian leaders were so reluctant to yield power to a federal legislature that many crucial matters which in Canada and Australia came under the jurisdiction of the national parliament almost from the start were by the Constitution of the West Indies left for concurrent enactment. Many observers at the time believed that the concessions of power to the central government in the West Indies were much too niggardly and that the resulting impotence would jeopardize the success of the federal experiment. Norman Manley, chief minister of Jamaica, was moved to remark, "We have been willing to enter matrimony, but we have hedged the contract around with so many stipulations and safeguards that I can only pray that by some Divine Providence it will produce offspring in due course."[29]

Within the Federation the two largest units, Jamaica and Trinidad, were continually at odds over Federation issues. Jamaica, with industrial development well under way, was opposed to a customs union and held that the power of taxation should remain with the local unit governments. Trinidad, on the other hand, favored a customs union and greater powers for the federal government, including the power to impose income and excise taxes.

Relations between Jamaica and the Federation became strained almost from the start. In October of 1958 Sir Grantley Adams of Barbados, the federal prime minister, stated that a federal income tax should be introduced as soon as possible and made retroactive to the date of federation. On November 1, 1958, Norman Manley, chief minister of Jamaica, issued a statement saying that concessions with regard to income taxes (individual and corporate) were an established part of his government's policies for the stimulation of economic development, and that if the

Federation government contemplated measures which would limit Jamaica's freedom in these matters, "Jamaica would be forced to reconsider her position in regard to federation itself."

On September 28, 1959, a conference of the federal government and all of the unit governments was convened at Trinidad. This was a preliminary conference under the constitutional provision for revision of the Constitution after five years. The Conference made little progress toward revision of the Constitution. While reaching no final decision with regard to the items on its agenda, the Conference did agree in principle that representation in the federal legislature should be on the basis of population, but without diminution in the number of seats currently held by each unit. The delegates failed, however, to agree on a formula for redistributing the seats, or on the matter of the revision of the powers of the Federation government. No other item on the agenda was reached.

The Conference adjourned *sine die* on October 8, 1959, but the delegates set up two intergovernmental committees, made up of federal and territorial representatives, one to consider the constitutional and political issues, the other to deal with the question of a customs union, financial policy, and concessions and incentives to industry.

On January 11, 1960, during a visit to London, Norman Manley, chief minister of Jamaica, said that Jamaica must insist on a form of federation which would not disrupt the area as a whole or her own economic development, otherwise "Jamaica will have to get out." He would not accept under any circumstances the continuation of the Federation without adequate Jamaican representation, and he would never agree to federal control over every aspect of economic development. He added that Jamaica would seek independence for herself if these problems could not be solved, though he would "prefer Jamaica in an independent Federation if that can be achieved on what would be a sensible basis."

On June 2, 1960, Manley announced that a popular referendum would be held in Jamaica in 1961 to decide whether the island should secede from the Federation. He explained that this decision had been forced upon his government by a change in the policy of the opposition Jamaica Labour Party, which had just announced that it was now opposed to Jamaica's continued membership in the Federation. Manley went on to say that from 1949 to 1960 both parties had joined in working toward federation; in fact the basic decisions with regard to federation had been made while the Jamaica Labour Party was in power. But now that that party had resolved to oppose federation, it was right that this great issue should be decided by the people.

All the while that Jamaica was making these threatening gestures, Her Majesty's government in London continued to press the West Indians toward eventual independence. In a statement to the House of Commons on June 21, 1960, Ian Macleod, colonial secretary, reported on the results of a recent two-week tour of the West Indies, during which he had conferred with government officials at all levels.

I made it clear that the shape of the Federation and the pace at which it should advance to independence were essentially matters for the West Indians to settle, but that Her Majesty's Government remained convinced that federation offered the best solution for the problems of this area, and that, as soon as West Indians had made up their minds on these questions, and provided that the essential attributes of sovereignty were satisfied, Her Majesty's Government would be ready and anxious to help them achieve independence at the earliest possible date, and would be proud to sponsor for full membership of the Commonwealth a country which, I am convinced, has much to teach the world—not least the way in which people of many varying racial origins can live together in friendship and cooperation.

In anticipation of eventual sovereign independence for the West Indies, the British government also took steps to tidy up the constitutional evolution of the unit territories. In June 1959, a conference held in London reached agreement on important constitutional changes for the Leeward and Windward Islands, to take effect on January 1, 1960. The report of this conference stated that as the West Indies Federation as a whole became a sovereign member of the Commonwealth, it was desirable that the constitution of each of its component units should be brought on to the same basis and that this required an extension of the powers of the legislative and executive councils of each territory. Meanwhile full self-government had been conferred upon Jamaica by an Order-in-Council approved by the Queen on May 13, 1959. In 1960 constitutional reforms were approved for Trinidad by which it, too, became in effect a self-governing territory.

Finally, on August 16, 1960, the Queen signed an Order-in-Council conferring full self-government upon the Federation. This development left the Federation only one constitutional step short of full sovereignty; defense and foreign affairs still remained in British hands. Under the terms of the Order, the Constitution of the West Indies was amended so that the semi-appointed Council of State was replaced as the policy-making body in favor of a cabinet made up of members of the ruling majority in the House of Representatives. The prime minister would henceforth be named by the governor-general, not elected by the House, and he would choose his own cabinet.[30]

In October of 1960 fifteen recruits for the future West Indies diplomatic service left Trinidad for training at the London School of Economics and at the British Foreign Office. At the end of their training in England they were to be attached to various United Kingdom embassies and high commissionerships for further training and experience.[31]

Also in October 1960, the deputy prime minister of the Federation, Carl La Corbiniere, attended the Bogota meeting of the Organization of American States as a guest observer. He indicated that upon reaching sovereign independence the West Indies Federation would seek full membership in the Organization of American States.[32]

At this high-water mark in the life of the West Indies Federation we leave the story for the time being. In 1961 the Federation took its place as one of the charter members of the Caribbean Organization, no thought having been given, apparently, to what would be the position of the islands vis-à-vis the Organization should the Federation dissolve—as it did all too soon.

THE NETHERLANDS ANTILLES AND SURINAM

On December 7, 1942, the first anniversary of Pearl Harbor, Queen Wilhelmina of the Netherlands, in exile with her government in London, addressed all of the peoples of the Dutch kingdom in a radio talk. With the full consent of her cabinet, the Queen said:

> I am convinced, and history as well as reports from the occupied territories confirm me in this, that after the war it will be possible to reconstruct the Kingdom on the solid foundation of complete partnership, which will mean the consummation of all that has developed in the past. I know that no political unity nor national cohesion can continue to exist, which are not supported by the voluntary acceptance and the faith of the great majority of the citizenry.[33]

The Queen also pledged the Netherlands government to confer on the populations of the overseas territories at the end of the war a greater independence and a greater share in the administration, and to call a round table conference for this purpose as soon as possible after the war. The Queen then added, "I visualize, without anticipating the recommendations of the future conference, that they will be directed toward a Commonwealth in which the Netherlands, Indonesia, Surinam, and Curacao will take part, with complete freedom of conduct for each part regarding its internal affairs."[34] From this radio address by the Queen in 1942 dates the modern constitutional evolution of the Netherlands Antilles and Surinam.

The kingdom of the Netherlands in the Caribbean region consists of one mainland country in South America (Surinam), plus the Netherlands Antilles, which comprises five small islands and a part of a sixth in the Caribbean Sea. Surinam (or Dutch Guiana) has a population of about 250,000 and an area of 54,000 square miles, much of which is uncharted jungle. Its capital is the city of Paramaribo.

The islands which make up the Netherlands Antilles are clustered in two groups, widely separated. In the extreme southern Caribbean, just off the coast of Venezuela, lie the so-called "ABC" islands, Aruba, Bonaire, and Curacao. Aruba has a population of about 57,000 on 69 square miles. Bonaire has 5,500 people on 112 square miles. Curacao, the largest and most important island, seat of the capital of the Netherlands Antilles, has a population of 114,000 living on 173 square miles.

The Netherlands Antilles also includes three tiny islands which form part of the long chain of islands extending east and south from Puerto Rico to Trinidad. Saba and St. Eustatius are wholly Dutch; St. Martin is half Dutch and half French (Department of Guadeloupe). The total Netherlands area of these three outer islands is only 29.8 square miles, with a combined population of only 35,000.

Before World War II both Surinam and the Netherlands Antilles were governed in much the same way as the crown colonies in the British empire. In both colonies the executive authority was vested in a governor appointed by the crown. He was assisted by an advisory council, also appointed by the crown and usually consisting for the most part of administrative officials of the colonial service. There was also in each colony a legislative council which shared legislative and budgetary powers with the governor. In Surinam, which had been founded originally as a plantation colony, the colonists had lived under a special charter since 1682. As a heritage of this system the members of the legislative council there were elected, but under a highly limited franchise. In the Netherlands Antilles the members of the legislative council were until 1936 simply appointed by the crown from among the leading citizens of the colony.[35]

The postwar negotiations over the forging of a new constitutional order for the Netherlands Antilles and Surinam were in many ways as protracted and complex as were the steps leading to the creation of the West Indies Federation. The main difference between the two situations was that whereas the British islands had to be prodded and pushed by London into forming their federation and agreeing on its structure, the Netherlands areas in the Caribbean registered impatience and frustration over the length of time which it took to satisfy their demands for autonomy. On the side of the home-country government in Holland, the negotiations were held up and made more controversial and difficult because of the long and bitter struggle over Indonesia. In the Netherlands it was also necessary to amend the Constitution of the kingdom in order to grant full self-government to the colonies; this was a procedural step which it was never necessary for the British to take.

In 1948 a new regulation was promulgated for the Netherlands Antilles and Surinam which established institutions of self-government in the colonies as much as the existing prewar Constitution of the kingdom would allow. This Regulation, for example, instituted universal franchise; it abolished the system whereby certain members of the legislatures were appointed by the crown; it greatly increased the legislative authority of the new locally elected legislatures; and it instituted in each colony a provisional Governing Council which was intended eventually to become a cabinet. The Regulation also provided that the governments of Surinam and of the Netherlands Antilles should each appoint a representative to be stationed in Holland, to maintain contact with the authorities of the Netherlands.[36]

In the same year, 1948, the first Round Table Conference was held at The Hague to consider the enlargement of self-government beyond the limits of the old Constitution. The Conference unanimously adopted seventeen resolutions under which the existing relations between the Netherlands, Surinam, and the Netherlands Antilles were to be replaced by a new constitutional order, uniting the three areas in a new "Kingdom of the Netherlands" under the House of Orange-Nassau. It was also decided that a new overall charter should be worked out to delineate the precise structure of the new kingdom arrangements.[37]

Again in 1948 the Parliament of the Netherlands accepted certain transitory constitutional amendments by which the old Constitution was "forced open" to allow for further changes in the internal political structures of the Netherlands Antilles and Surinam. According to one of these provisions "a new constitutional order based upon the results of the consultations held and to be held with and between the representatives of the peoples should be established with respect to the territories concerned, in pursuance whereof these territories would, as united, co-equal partners, foster their common interests and assist each other, all of these conditions to be fulfilled under the guarantee of the rule of law, fundamental human rights and freedoms, and sound government." Another of these transitory provisions stipulated that the new constitutional order "must be established by its voluntary acceptance through democratic procedure in each of the territories." Finally, additional provisions made it legal to depart from the basic text of the old Constitution to whatever extent the changeover might require, without awaiting the final, formal amendment of the whole Constitution.[38]

In 1949 and 1950 the Regulation of 1948 was revised to provide complete internal self-government for Surinam and the Netherlands Antilles respectively, as allowed by the transitory constitutional amendments of 1948. These new provisions necessarily had an interim character, inasmuch as the discussions between the mother country and the overseas territories had not been completed. Under this Interim Order, in any case, it was provided that the territories should manage their own internal affairs completely. The parliamentary system was introduced, with politically responsible ministers. The territories were to have their own treasuries and a separate currency, and all internal legislation was to be freed of any influence from the mother country. A limited list of non-internal affairs was agreed upon, the most important being defense and foreign affairs. With respect to these matters the representatives of the territories in The Hague were to assist the responsible ministers of the Netherlands government in reaching decisions for the whole kingdom.[39]

The Interim Order became effective for Surinam on January 20, 1950 and in the Netherlands Antilles on February 7, 1951. Under this new order of affairs the Netherlands government ceased making reports to the United Nations regarding Surinam and the Netherlands Antilles under Article 73 (e) of the Charter.

In 1952 a new amendment to the Netherlands Constitution provided that the relations between the Netherlands, Surinam, and the Netherlands Antilles should in the future be governed by a Charter, on which the three countries as equal partners should agree, and which should be incorporated into the constitutional law of the kingdom.[40]

The second Round Table Conference, which hammered out the sixty-one articles of the new Kingdom Charter, assembled at The Hague on April 3, 1952, and completed its work on June 3, 1954. The parliaments of the three countries passed separate bills of ratification, and the new Charter was promulgated officially on December 15, 1954. Fourteen days later, on December 29, 1954, in a solemn ceremony participated in by the Queen and the three prime ministers, the reconstructed kingdom was declared to be in existence.[41]

The most important provision in the Charter of the Kingdom of the Netherlands is the simple rule that the three partners "manage their own affairs autonomously." With that, self-government for the overseas territories became a part of Netherlands constitutional law.

The three countries themselves have the right to determine their own constitutions. This includes the right to revise and amend them, subject only to the condition that they not impair the general principles of respect for human rights and fundamental freedoms which are common to the kingdom as a whole.

A number of matters, which are of equal concern to all parts of the kingdom and which require therefore to be administered in a uniform manner by organs of the kingdom, are described in the Charter as "Kingdom Matters." The most important of these are again defense (although military service is a matter of concern for each individual country) and foreign affairs (although Surinam and the Netherlands Antilles have far-reaching powers which in some instances amount to a veto). Apart from these kingdom affairs Surinam and the Netherlands Antilles have complete autonomy.[42]

Like the Constitution of Holland, the constitutions of the Netherlands Antilles and of Surinam are based on the principle of a constitutional monarchy. The constitutions of both territories stipulate that the ruler of the Netherlands is also the head of government in these countries. Surinam and the Netherlands Antilles are thus kingdoms in their own right.[43]

The King (actually, at present the Queen) of the Netherlands is represented in each of the two overseas countries by an appointed governor, who has the same position in the territories as the Queen does in Holland. He has no power without the consent of the local parliament and the signature of the responsible local ministers. He has no responsibility toward the parliament.

In the Netherlands Antilles legislative power is vested in a one-chamber parliament of twenty-two members, elected on a basis of universal suffrage. The members are elected on party lists under a system of proportional representation modified to the extent that each island is entitled to a stipulated number of members. Curacao elects twelve members; Aruba, eight members; Bonaire, one member; and the three outer or Windward Islands together elect one member. This legislative body has all the usual attributes of parliamentary supremacy. It has the power to vote the budget and to enact every law. Any member may introduce bills and submit cabinet ministers to questioning.

The cabinet consists of five or six ministers and is headed by a prime minister. The ministers are responsible not to the governor but to parliament. The ministers are nominated by the governor on the advice of the parliament.

Because of the long-standing rivalry among the islands, especially between Curacao and Aruba, it was necessary for each of the islands to have its own separate government. Each of the "ABC" islands therefore has its own legislative body and its own executive council, headed by a local lieutenant governor appointed by the Queen. The three outer islands (Saba, St. Eustatius, and St. Martin) were bound together in one administrative unit with one local government. Administrative and financial matters were divided between the central government in Curacao and the four separate island governments; actually more than half of the administrative functions of government were assigned to the islands.[44]

In Surinam the constitution provides for an election system by administrative districts; it grants ten out of the total of twenty-one seats in the parliament to the capital city, Paramaribo. The constitution provides for eventual establishment of local government bodies, but only limited use has yet been made of this opportunity. Administration and finance in Surinam therefore remain largely centralized.[45]

As equal partners of the realm, the Netherlands Antilles and Surinam share in the governing of the kingdom as a whole. Complex and detailed articles of the Kingdom Charter provide that whenever the Council of Ministers of the Netherlands government at The Hague is dealing with kingdom affairs, as defined in the document, the resident ministers from the Netherlands Antilles and Surinam must be present with full powers of discussion and vote. When kingdom affairs require the enactment of a statute by the States-General of the Netherlands, the Charter provides for a simultaneous debate and vote on the draft bill by the parliaments of Surinam and of the Netherlands Antilles. These latter legislative bodies have the power to voice objections, offer amendments, and under certain stipulated conditions to impose a suspensive veto on the measure in the States-General.

Thus, like Puerto Rico but unlike the West Indies Federation, the Netherlands Antilles and Surinam appeared to have reached an equilibrium point with regard to their political status, on the eve of the inauguration of the Caribbean Organization. Again like the Puerto Ricans, the leaders of the Netherlands Antilles were fiercely proud of their new autonomous status and were eager to display it and to defend it before the world. All of the people who had any connection with the affairs of the Caribbean Commission during the transition years beginning in 1952 testify to the almost fanatical determination of the Netherlands Antilles delegates to reconstruct the organization in such a way as to eliminate the metropolitan powers from governing control.* It was I. C. Debrot, who in 1952, at the fifth session of the West Indian Conference, presented the first resolution adopted by the Conference on the subject of revision of the Commission structure. Over the ensuing years the Netherlands Antilles representatives, perhaps more than the Puerto Ricans, pushed for the end of the Commission and the creation of the Caribbean Organization. There was, therefore, every reason to believe that the Netherlands Antilles would be one of the most interested and active participants in the affairs of the new Caribbean Organization.

THE FRENCH DEPARTMENTS OF GUADELOUPE, MARTINIQUE, AND FRENCH GUIANA

The story of constitutional developments in the French Caribbean areas during the Caribbean Commission years can quickly be told, for essentially there is only one occurence to record. On March 19, 1946, Guadeloupe, Martinique, and French Guiana became, by law, departments of France proper, integrated into the political and administrative life of the metropolitan country. This final, decisive development in the status of these territories took place in the same year that the four-power

---

*This was the observation, for example, of Mr. David Maas, one of the United States Commissioners to the Caribbean Commission, whom I interviewed in his office in St. Thomas, Virgin Islands, on March 9, 1961. Mr. Maas and others observed that whereas the Puerto Ricans were embarrassed by the structure and wished to see it changed because it represented bad publicity both for themselves and for their friends in continental United States, the Netherlands Antilles leaders displayed outright anger and bitterness over this lingering reminder of a colonial status which they had thrown off. I can testify from my more than two years of residence in Aruba that there was among the leaders of the Netherlands Antilles a degree of bitterness toward the home country government which was markedly absent in Puerto Rico.

Caribbean Commission came into being. Thus while all of the other countries served by the Commission were struggling to achieve a status of self-governing autonomy, the French areas, their goal with respect to status reached, settled into the routine of life as a part of the French community.

The colonial administration of these French territories had been somewhat more liberal than that of the crown colonies in the British empire. Universal suffrage for all males, regardless of race or color, became a fact after about 1870, for example. Then, beginning in 1871 the colonies were regularly represented in the French parliament in Paris by locally elected deputies.[46]

There was a governor in each colony, appointed by the government in Paris, who was in charge of the executive administration of the colony. He was assisted by a "privy council" (Conseil Privé), a body which was a direct heritage of the Ancien Régime. The general council (Conseil Général) acted as a sort of local parliament, voting the budget for local government services (except for the army and navy) and fixing taxes, under the supervision of the governor. These colonies thus had a large measure of local autonomy, and the political parties contested fiercely for seats in the Conseil Général.[47]

The law of March 19, 1946, was short, simple, and to the point:

1. The Colonies of Guadeloupe, Martinique, Reunion, and French Guiana are elevated to departments of France.
2. The laws and decrees in effect in metropolitan France which have not yet been applied to these colonies, will be promulgated in these new departments.
3. From the time of the promulgation of this law, all laws and decrees applicable in the metropole will automatically be applied in these new departments unless express provisions to the contrary are inserted in their texts.[48]

For reasons which seem somewhat obscure there developed within France some controversy over the exact meaning of article 3 of the law quoted above. Thus when the Constitution of the Fourth Republic was adopted in October 1946, an attempt was made in that document to spell out more carefully the applicability of French legislation to the overseas departments. Article 73 of the Constitution specified that "the legislative regime of the overseas departments is the same as that of the metropolitan departments, save for exceptions as determined by law." Under the terms of this provision it was ruled that when a legislator wished to exclude the overseas departments from the application of a law he had to say so expressly in the text of the bill, unless the subject matter being dealt with made such an express reservation unnecessary.

A number of decrees promulgated on March 30, 1948, brought into force in the Caribbean departments a whole series of legislative arrangements which were in effect in France, thus inaugurating for these departments a complete legal community with continental France.[49]

The new Constitution of the Fifth Republic, adopted in 1958, made no ostensible change in the status of the French overseas departments, but it did leave a small crack in the door for possible future adjustments in the status of these areas. Article 73 of the new Constitution made provision for the possibility of a new organic law to modify the legislative regime and administrative organization of these three overseas departments in view of their peculiar situation vis-à-vis the rest of France.[50]

Voting in the referendum of September 28, 1958, with regard to the acceptance of the new Fifth Republic Constitution was as follows in the French Caribbean departments.[51]

	Yes	No
French Guiana	7,595	400
Guadeloupe	93,945	14,422
Martinique	73,580	4,975

With the change in 1946 to departmental status, the governor, responsible to the Ministry of Colonies, was replaced by the prefect, responsible to the Ministry of the Interior. The Conseil Général in each department votes the budget; it also organizes and administers the departmental services of government, such as highways, public health, and so on. It is assisted by a departmental commission, consisting of seven members of the Conseil Général, which meets once a month between sessions of the Conseil Général to supervise the administrative affairs of the department and to act as liaison between the prefect and the larger body. In all of these arrangements the overseas departments are administered or governed in the same way as the departments of continental France.[52]

Martinique and Guadeloupe each have three deputies in the National Assembly and two senators. French Guiana has one deputy and one senator.[53]

All of the French citizens from the overseas departments with whom I talked in 1961 (including the secretary general of the Caribbean Commission) expressed complete satisfaction with the status of their homelands as departments of France. They emphasized that the aim of French colonial policy had always been in the direction of social and cultural assimilation. The residents of the colonies (at least, most of them) therefore came to want nothing more than to be integrated with the metropolitan country in every way. Petitions for the elevation of the colonies to departments of France began to circulate before the turn of the century, and the goal of integration which was finally realized in 1946 was almost reached in 1909 and again in 1923.

Frenchmen from the Caribbean departments point out that they enjoy all of the benefits of the advanced social legislation of France, including health services, family allowances, old-age pensions, unemployment insurance, veterans' benefits, and all the rest. True, they have to pay taxes on the same scale as do residents of France proper, but the tax laws are sufficiently progressive that the burden is not great on people of low income. The Caribbean departments calculate that they receive two francs or more in benefits from the French treasury for every one franc of taxes they pay, just as does any department of the country where the level of income is considerably below the national average.

From the point of view of the typical Caribbean French citizens, therefore, what had been taking place in the constitutional evolution of Puerto Rico, the West Indies Federation, and the Netherlands territories in the Commission years was all but incomprehensible. They could not understand why the residents of any colonial or dependent area would want deliberately to pull away from the mother country. For the French Caribbean citizen the highest possible status and honor he could conceive for his home island or territory was its political integration with the mother country, not the creation of a separate national identity for it.

Caribbean Commissioners who were at the special session of the West Indian Conference in 1959, and others who attended as delegates, informed me that hopes for the Caribbean Organization were almost dashed by the seeming intransigence of the French delegation. The French appeared almost willfully determined not to understand why any change in the structure of the organization was necessary.

Yet there were hints which were significant to outside observers, and of which the special provision in the Constitution for the Fifth Republic was only one indication, that the attempt at thorough political and administrative integration had not been a complete success. In the years after 1946 there were recorded countless cases of local governmental or administrative matters which could have and should have been settled on the local level but which had to be referred to Paris for decision.* Also there was the feeling that while the individual citizens of the French Caribbean departments had benefited economically from the assimilation of 1946, the islands themselves (and French Guiana) had lagged seriously in economic development behind their neighbors in the Caribbean—this for the lack of capacity to plan on the local, territorial scale for means of attracting developmental capital (to construct tropical tourist resort facilities, for example).

---

*For example, according to a case described to me, a resident of Martinique who wished to buy baby chicks from a hatchery in Puerto Rico which was prepared to offer air delivery, had to apply for a foreign exchange license and also for a license to import live animals into France. Both applications had to go by mail to Paris, there to be included with the tens of thousands of other such applications from all over France, to be acted upon finally by a minor official who probably had no knowledge of local conditions and special economic needs in far-off Martinique.

Officials of the Caribbean Commission Secretariat reported that in the early years after 1946 the French participated rather grudgingly in most of the Commission's activities. Their attitude was such that Commission officials seriously wondered why France had accepted the invitation of Great Britain and the United States to join the Commission in 1946. They often failed to attend technical conferences and other special events, and they seemed to take little interest in technical assistance and self-help schemes. Their point of view was that since these islands and French Guiana were now departments of France they should learn to look to Paris for assistance in meeting their needs, not to their neighbors or to a regional organization in the Caribbean. A growing undercurrent of dissatisfaction in the Caribbean departments with this attitude of France, however, gradually produced a change of policy in Paris. Certain leaders of Guadeloupe and Martinique knew, for example, that the aided self-help housing program which originated in Puerto Rico and which the Commission was offering to help start in other islands would have been of enormous benefit to their islands; but the attitude in Paris was that the French government had adequate technical assistance facilities and that in due course French housing technicians would be sent to the Caribbean.

In any event, during the late 1950s people associated with the Commission noted some change in the attitude of the French government toward the Caribbean Commission. In the summer of 1960, at the thirtieth meeting of the Commission, for the first time three out of the four French commissioners were deputies and senators, men who had been elected by the people of the Caribbean departments to represent them in Paris, whereas in previous years the men from the islands and from French Guiana chosen to be French commissioners were usually civil servants or local businessmen.

Groundwork for Transition to Caribbean Organization

Thus in the major territories served by the Commission the stage had been set by 1961 for the transition from Caribbean Commission to Caribbean Organization. With the ever-increasing responsibility for managing their own affairs which these peoples had assumed in the preceding years (except, of course, for the French) it had come to seem only logical and just that the Caribbean Commission should indeed give way to the Caribbean Organization, managed and directed by the local peoples themselves.

Yet, what those who pressed for the end of the Commission and the birth of the Caribbean Organization often tended to overlook was that the Caribbean Commission resulted from a solemn agreement entered into by four countries, the United States, the United Kingdom, France, and the Netherlands. The constitutional relationships in and among those four countries which constituted the Commission had *not* changed. What *had* changed, of course, was the extent to which most of the Caribbean territories had assumed governmental control over many of the affairs with which the Caribbean Commission was originally established to concern itself.

The fact remained, however, that as of 1961 the three metropolitan powers (the United States, the United Kingdom, and the Netherlands), despite their ejection from formal membership in the international organization of the Caribbean, would continue to have interest in and certain responsibilities for the Caribbean area. Moreover, their continued assistance to the Caribbean territories—economic and otherwise—would be essential to most of the projects which the new Caribbean Organization would undertake.

Viewed in this light, the insistent demands on the part of delegates to West Indian Conference sessions—demands arising from below, so to speak—that the Caribbean Commission (the organization of the metropolitan powers) had to be changed in order to reflect changing constitutional realities in the Caribbean appeared somewhat illogical. Not only that, but the proposal seemed to have inherent in it the danger that in effecting the desired change in the structure of the organization the Caribbean countries might be cutting themselves off from the very sources of assistance which they would need to carry on their cooperative projects, namely, the metropolitan powers. As we shall see in chapter 13, problems of this nature did enter into the ultimate failure of the Caribbean Organization in 1964.

No one could deny, however, that indeed the political realities had changed, and this is what made the transition to Caribbean Organization inevitable. Furthermore, it could be said, on the side of those who insisted on the alteration of the Commission structure, that if political realities in the Caribbean had changed it was the Commission itself which had done a great deal to further those changes. From its very beginning the Commission had sought more and more to involve the local peoples and their governments in its work. The West Indian Conference was encouraged to grow in stature and prestige, so that the continuing work of the four-power Commission consisted to a large extent in dealing with the stream of recommendations produced in West Indian Conference sessions by delegates from the Caribbean territories. Also, it had become the firm practice that two to three out of the four commissioners in each national section should be natives of the Caribbean area. The four powers, and through them the Caribbean Commission, thus could blame no one but themselves if the Caribbean peoples had gained the impression that the Caribbean Commission was *their* organization and that it should be more completely managed and directed by them. It was to the credit of the metropolitan powers that they encouraged this growth of self-government and that they yielded gracefully and peacefully to the inevitable change in the pattern of international organization in the Caribbean.

9 □ THE DEPARTURE OF THE COMMISSION SECRETARIAT FROM TRINIDAD

The constitutional developments in the Caribbean which were examined in the last chapter were the manifestations in the West Indies of the same political forces which were sweeping away formerly colonial and dependent regimes throughout Africa and Asia. These forces made the change in structure from Caribbean Commission to Caribbean Organization inevitable, but the actual process of change is no less interesting for that reason. This chapter then will begin a somewhat detailed examination of the fortunes of the Commission during the difficult transition period which began in 1958 or 1959.

In chapter 4 it was noted that the special session of the West Indian Conference, meeting in St. Thomas in July 1959 to draw up the charter for the Caribbean Organization, accepted the generous offer of Puerto Rico for the establishment of the headquarters of the new organization in San Juan. Puerto Rico's interest in attracting the Secretariat to San Juan will be explored in a later chapter, but first there should be some explanation of why the Commission left Trinidad.

On the face of it there would appear to be no logical explanation of the move away from Port of Spain. Trinidad, as one of the units of the West Indies Federation, and the seat of the federal capital as well, might be expected not only to continue its participation in the work of the organization but even to take an added interest in its affairs with the changeover to Caribbean Organization. The Commission was permanently established at Kent House, and over the years it had gathered and trained a competent and hard-working local staff. The Commission could have gone out of existence and the Caribbean Organization come into being with no physical dislocation of the headquarters and with most of the staff remaining in the same jobs, at least initially. In fact, according to the testimony of those few staff members who made the move to Puerto Rico, the removal of the Commission from Trinidad set the work of the Secretariat back for nearly a year and caused dislocations in its administration from which it did not recover for a long time. Why, then, was this burden of an international move placed upon the Commission Secretariat in addition to the strain arising from the structural transformation of the parent body?

The Commission's decision to abandon Trinidad was reached ostensibly because of the unwillingness of the Trinidad government to undertake the financial burden of being host to an international organization.

Behind this attitude of the Trinidad government, however, was the real root cause of the Commission's difficulties on that island, namely the unrelenting hostility toward the Commission on the part of Dr. Eric Williams, chief minister of the government of Trinidad and Tobago. Some members of the Secretariat staff were even willing to say that Dr. Williams drove the Caribbean Commission off of the island of Trinidad.

Dr. Williams's hostility toward the Commission was particularly ironical because he, like so many of the other native West Indian political leaders, had been at one time closely associated with the Commission. In fact, Dr. Williams was for some seven years the third-ranking official of the Secretariat staff.

Born in Trinidad in 1911, Eric Eustace Williams received his doctorate at Oxford University, and in 1939 he was named professor of social and political science at Howard University in Washington, D.C. He wrote a number of scholarly books on West Indian affairs, including *The Negro in the Caribbean* (1942), *Capitalism and Slavery* (1944), and *Education in the West Indies* (1950). He gained the reputation for being thoroughly anticolonial and single-mindedly devoted to the economic and social development of the West Indies islands. He was an enthusiastic supporter of the West Indies Federation movement.

After holding several posts, both in the British Section of the old Anglo-American Caribbean Commission and in the four-power Commission, Dr. Williams was named in 1948 deputy chairman of the Caribbean Research Council and head of the Research Branch of the Secretariat. In this post he ranked just after the secretary general and the deputy secretary general.

According to staff members who were with the Commission at the time, Dr. Williams devoted tremendous vigor and enthusiasm to his work, driving himself and his immediate associates to the point of exhaustion. Williams singlehandedly wrote many of the Commission's technical and research papers. So forceful indeed was his application to his work that, according to one long-time staff officer, the entire Secretariat came to be polarized around the Research Branch and its dynamic chief. The rest of the Secretariat, in other words, became little more than a service and administrative appendage to the Research Branch.

After Williams left the Commission in 1955 the Caribbean Research Council never met again, though it remained technically one of the auxiliary bodies of the Commission. No one else was ever named head of the Research Branch to replace Williams, and in due time the Secretariat was reorganized in such fashion that responsibility for the research work was decentralized to the other operating branches.

It has of course never been publicly revealed why Dr. Williams's association with the Commission was terminated in 1955. Officers of the Secretariat were understandably quite reluctant to discuss the matter. All that they could say officially was that in 1955 the Commission saw fit not to renew its contract with Williams. There is no question, however, that his departure from the Commission was accompanied by considerable bitterness. It is known that prior to the break in 1955 Williams had severe disagreements with the then secretary general, de Vriendt, and with others in the Commission.

According to one former staff member, Williams had begun to dabble in Trinidad politics while still a staff officer, in strict violation of staff rules and of Article XIV, paragraph 5 of the Commission agreement, which stated that the staff "shall refrain from any action which might reflect on their position as international officials responsible only to the Commission." It was primarily for this reason, according to this informant, that Williams was fired by the Commission in 1955.

In any event, Williams left the Commission in anger, and he devoted his first public appearance following the break to a rousing attack on the Commission. This took the form of a public speech which was subsequently printed in booklet form and widely distributed in Trinidad. (Eric Williams, *My Relations with the Caribbean Commission, 1943-1955* [A public lecture, given under the auspices of the People's Educational Movement of the Teachers' Economic and Cultural Association, in Woodford Square, Port of Spain, Trinidad, June 21, 1955] [Trinidad: Published by Eric Williams, 1955]).

This little booklet sets forth in detail—from the author's point of view—the troubles which Eric Williams had with the Commission from the very beginning of his association with it. It reveals an angry man with a chip-on-the-shoulder attitude, eager to interpret every criticism of himself as a thinly veiled attack on the West Indian people and the whole Negro race, struggling to emancipate itself from economic slavery and political imperialism. His chief substantive criticism of the Commission's work is that the Commission engaged in all sorts of frivolous activities which merely skirted the edges of the region's basic problems. He complains, for instance, that on one occasion the Commission sent experts out to a poverty-stricken island to teach community singing; on another occasion experts were sent out to teach the West Indian people how to candle their eggs, when, according to Williams, the people had little or no means to produce eggs in the first place.

He also complains bitterly that the Commission sought always to keep incompetent non-West Indians (i.e., white citizens from the metropolitan countries) in positions of responsibility whereas highly qualified native (Negro) West Indians—with himself as the prime example of course —were shunted off to lower jobs, their work criticized unfairly and their recommendations ignored. He found continual evidence that the Commissioners (even some of the West Indian appointees) and the high officials of the Secretariat were lackeys of the vested interests. Consequently the survey teams saw only what their hosts wanted them to see, recommended only what their hosts deemed safe and reasonable to recommend.

With regard to his dismissal from the Commission Secretariat, Dr. Williams has this to say, after a long exposition of his struggles with worthless, incompetent staff members whose only claim to the jobs they held, according to Williams, was that they were white non-West Indians:

That is the Caribbean Commission. The four governments vote about half a million dollars a year for its upkeep, and in return the jobs go to imported officials. In my Washington branch office I got sick and tired of calls from Congressmen as to the number of Americans employed at the Commission; in Trinidad I got sick and tired of hearing Americans talk about the amount of money voted by the U.S. taxpayers for the Commission. As more and more Colonial areas shake off imperialist control, the pressure is increased on the remaining areas of imperialist influence to provide jobs for outsiders. Not the least significant feature of the Commission's decision not to renew my contract for another five years is that in 1956 the contract of the present Secretary General expires. According to the rules of rotation, the next Secretary General must be British or French. *My claims to the post would have been difficult to resist if my contract as Deputy Chairman had been renewed.* [pages 48–49. Italics added.]

Dr. Williams had apparently never forgiven the Commission for crossing him. In 1959, when the future status of the Commission was somewhat uncertain, Williams let it be known in the course of several radio talks and press conferences that in his opinion the Caribbean Commission had been of no value to Trinidad and that Trinidad was not interested in having the successor body make its headquarters on that island.[1]

Following his departure from the Commission, Dr. Williams took up politics and founded a new political party, the People's National Movement. This party won a majority of seats in the legislative council in the Trinidad general elections of September 1956, and Dr. Williams, as the party leader, became chief minister and minister of finance, planning and development of the government of Trinidad and Tobago. With the achievement of independence in 1962, Dr. Williams became prime minister, a post which he has held ever since.

Williams rapidly gained international notoriety for his violent campaign against continued occupation by the United States of the naval base at Chaguaramas. Although the base was supposedly secured by the United States for ninety-nine years in the destroyers for bases deal of 1940 with Great Britain, Williams maintained that the agreement was no longer valid since it was made without the advice and consent of the Trinidad government. He also insisted, along with officials of the Federation government, despite several studies to the contrary,[2] that Chaguaramas was needed for the capital of the Federation government. Williams proceeded to make Chaguaramus the rallying cry for a long and heated Yankee-go-home movement in Trinidad, a campaign which often took bizarre forms.

When plans for the transformation of the Caribbean Commission into the Caribbean Organization were still in the formative stage, the four member governments of the Commission decided that if the Caribbean territories were determined to take over the Commission as full members in their own right, then one of them should also agree to accept the normal responsibilities for the privilege of being host government to an international organization. That is, whichever country was to be the seat of the new Caribbean Organization, the government of that country should, in line with normal international practice, agree to furnish the headquarters building and possibly also the residence of the secretary general without charge to the organization. This would be in addition to the country's normal contribution as a member to the operating budget of the organization.[3]

This matter of the responsibility of the host government did not arise in the time that the Commission Secretariat was at Port of Spain. The members of the Commission were at that time of course the four metropolitan powers; thus, technically speaking, the Secretariat was not in the territory of any of the members, since Trinidad (or the West Indies Federation) was not then a member of the Commission. In any event the government of Trinidad never subsidized the Commission in any way. The rent for Kent House and all other expenses incident to the operation of the Secretariat were paid in a routine manner out of the funds received by the Commission as contributions from the member governments. It is conceivable that the Secretariat of the Caribbean Organization could have stayed on in Port of Spain on this same basis, that is, paying its expenses out of its operating funds with no assistance from the host government. But, as noted above, there was a definite feeling on the part of the Commission members that if the Caribbean countries were to insist on forming their own international organization they should be initiated into the responsibilities which accompany that privilege.

The British Section of the Commission therefore approached the West Indies Federation government and asked whether it would accept the normal financial responsibilities in connection with having the seat of the Caribbean Organization in its territory, presumably at Port of Spain, Trinidad. (As indicated before, this was quite apart from the matter of normal contributions to the organization's working budget, an additional complicating factor for the British territories which will be explored in chapter 10.) The West Indies Federation government replied that it could not itself accept this additional financial burden. It went on to state that the government of the island where the Secretariat was to be located would have to appropriate the necessary funds, either directly to the Caribbean

Organization or by payment through the Federation government. These payments would of course be in addition to that island's normal contribution to the federal budget. The Federation government accordingly asked the government of Trinidad whether the latter would assume certain expenses to be incurred in connection with having the Secretariat of the Caribbean Organization in Port of Spain. The negative response of the government of Trinidad, headed as it was by Eric Williams, was a foregone conclusion. Thus it began to appear inevitable that the Secretariat of the Caribbean Organization would not be in Port of Spain, Trinidad. The Federation government could at any time have changed its policy and agreed to accept the headquarters expenses itself, thus in effect allowing the Secretariat to remain at Port of Spain. In and of itself the Trinidad government probably could not have forced the Secretariat to leave Port of Spain, but it was taken for granted by nearly all of the people who had any responsibility for the Commission's affairs that in the hostile atmosphere of Trinidad the new organization would be subject to harassments which would surely impair its effectiveness.

Thus when the special session of the West Indian Conference met at St. Thomas in July 1959, the matter of a site for the new organization was up for decision, even though the question did not appear as a formal item on the agenda. At this point, then, the West Indies Federation could have come forward with a bid for the headquarters site, either at Port of Spain or on some other island of the Federation. It did not do so, however. Puerto Rico, on the other hand, *did* make an offer, a very generous offer, for the headquarters site, and that offer was accepted by the West Indian Conference. Thus it came about that the seat of the Caribbean Organization was to be in San Juan, Puerto Rico.

Some people in Trinidad were distressed to see the Secretariat leave Port of Spain even if the chief minister of the island's government was not. The decision to set up the headquarters of the new Caribbean Organization in Puerto Rico received considerable newspaper coverage in Trinidad and throughout the British West Indies.

There was, first of all, criticism of Williams for his personal spite in the matter. On April 26, 1959, the *Trinidad Guardian* carried an article by Albert Gomes, a member of the Federation Parliament from one of the electoral districts of Trinidad (and also, it should be noted, a leader of the political party in opposition to Dr. Williams).

Of all the strange and surprising things done by this Trinidad Government since its assumption of office, its refusal to support the plans to retain the services of the Caribbean Commission as an organization of the territories is certainly the most shocking.

Is there no limit to this projection of personal pique into the public affairs of our island? I ask this question because it is manifest to me, as it must be indeed to countless others, that the objective reasons for Trinidad's participation in the new Caribbean Organization are unequivocal and compelling.

Trinidad more than any other territory has very substantial and selfish reasons for wanting the Commission to survive; but these obviously do not override the vigorous subjective pressures to which, apparently, the members of the present Government become susceptible when they attempt to treat the question of the Commission's future as a strictly public matter—which it in fact is.

My own astonishment is boundless, especially when I recall the many occasions in the past when Dr. Williams, then an employee of the Commission, bitterly complained to me about the apparent indifference of West Indian legislators to the existence and work of the Commission. No one did more than he to persuade me of the immeasurable importance of the Commission to the West Indies. And now his Government, which more than any other should welcome the democratisation of the Commission, is seeking instead to make its new emergence a still birth.

Is this another symptom of the dictatorial trend which is causing widespread alarm throughout the island? Dr. Williams reenforces the suspicion that in his determination to have everything his way he is seeking to cut us adrift from every other anchorage except that of his arrogant over-assertion.

Editorially, the *Trinidad Guardian* took the government to task for an error of judgment, without mentioning the chief minister by name.

The Trinidad Government has unfortunately decided not to subscribe to the new organization, as it considers the Caribbean Commission to be of no value to Trinidad. The Commission has in fact done useful service in its advisory and information services, and in the field of research and technical assistance, and the Trinidad Government in our opinion has been guilty of an error of judgement in not agreeing to support the new group. We welcome the plan to create a new organization constituted by the Caribbean territories themselves and under their full control and trust that all will work smoothly at the July conference and that a way will be found to strengthen the practical side of the work.[4]

But most criticism of Trinidad's stand in the matter focused on the direct material and financial loss to be suffered by the island through the removal of the Secretariat. On April 18, 1959, the *Guardian* said editorially:

If the Caribbean Commission leaves Trinidad, the territory would lose not only the annual budget (just under $400,000) which maintains the central secretariat in Port of Spain, but also the valuable prestige of being host country to an international organization linked to France, the Netherlands, the United Kingdom, and the United States.

The Trinidad Government, which has never paid any money towards the maintenance of the Commission established by the four metropolitan governments in 1946, has refused to contribute to the Commission under the new agreement now being formulated.

The Trinidad Government has indicated it had no use for the Commission. Dr. Eric Williams, Chief Minister, was a former deputy chairman of the Commission's Research Council and was relieved of his post when his contract was not renewed.

The Central Secretariat at Kent House will consequently be removed from Trinidad, most likely next year, to one of the many other Caribbean territories which have already offered to provide headquarters.

Kent House staff, from the Secretary General to gardeners, numbers 77, of which 50 per cent are Trinidadians. When the Central Secretariat moves out, local staff members—mostly typists, clerks, and employees on a low-scale—will lose their jobs because of deep-rooted family ties in Trinidad.

Last year the Minister of Housing, Mr. Gerard Montano, in a public speech, thanked the Commission for making available to the Trinidad Government the services of aided self-help housing experts from I.C.A., to whom most of the credit for the housing schemes in Trinidad has been acknowledged.

The services of these experts were obtained at the request of the Trinidad Government.

The Caribbean Commission was also the channel through which the $19,000,000 Grace Fertiliser Plant came to Trinidad.

It started in 1955 when a large American organization wrote to the Commission expressing an interest in establishing a factory within the British West Indies, in view of the industrial incentive legislation being enacted in the various territories.

The Commission not only sent this company copies of the relevant legislation but also drew its attention to the presence of natural gas on one of these islands— Trinidad.

Additional significant details were added in an editorial on April 22, 1959:

Aside from staff salaries and wages the Commission arranges conferences of one kind and another (two were held in Trinidad during the past month) which bring considerable "tourist" money to the island. Taking one thing with another the Commission probably puts between $700,000 and $800,000 in local circulation in the course of a year. The Trinidad Government could help to ensure its stay here by contributing through the Federal Government to the cost of operating the Commission under the new arrangements.[5]

So well aware, in fact, were the people of the West Indies of the concrete financial advantages accruing to any island which was the seat of an agency such as the Caribbean Commission, that the delegates to the special session of the West Indian Conference in 1959 took steps to have the matter spread on the official record of the proceedings.

The Conference requested the Secretary General to inform it of the extent to which the national income of Trinidad and Tobago had benefitted from the presence of the Central Secretariat in that country in terms of local staff employed and money spent. The Secretary General informed the Conference that the present establishment of the Central Secretariat is 77, of whom 52 are Trinidadians. From a study recently made in the Central Secretariat, it is estimated that an amount equivalent to approximately 84 per cent of the Commission's present budget of U.S. $368,000 is being spent yearly in Trinidad. This figure represents staff salaries, local expenditures by the Commission itself, and local expenditure by technical experts and participants in various conferences, seminars, etc., sponsored by the Commission and held in Trinidad.[6]

Any listing of the various meetings, seminars, conferences, and other gatherings held under the auspices of the Commission will reveal that Trinidad was chosen as the location more than any other single place in the area (see, for example, the list on pages 42–43). The reason for this was obvious. By meeting at the Secretariat headquarters the group in question could have the advantage of all of the administrative, technical, and information services which the Commission's staff had to offer. Moreover, and again for obvious reasons, a check of the activities of any of the technical officers of the Commission would show the heaviest concentration of services in the immediate area surrounding the Secretariat. As it was noted on page 47, during the period from May 1955 to August 1957, the agricultural economist at Kent House received 97 visitors from twenty-seven countries other than Trinidad, but during the same period he received 112 visitors from Trinidad alone.

All of this concentration of activity, attention, revenue, and prestige which surrounded the Secretariat was shifted to Puerto Rico in 1960. Trinidad's loss of benefits could be attributed almost entirely to the intransigence of the island's chief minister, Eric Williams.

10 □ THE END OF AN ERA: TERMINATION OF THE CARIBBEAN COMMISSION

If we seek an answer to the question of what finally set in motion the actual process of transforming the Caribbean Commission into the Caribbean Organization, after years of apparent procrastination by the four metropolitan governments, Puerto Rico is the key country, just as it was to be the key country in the next shift of pattern in 1965.

At the seventh session of the West Indian Conference, meeting in Curacao in late 1957, the Puerto Rican delegation delivered what was hailed in the newspapers of the West Indies as an "ultimatum," in the form of a threat to boycott future sessions of the West Indian Conference until the Commission structure should be reorganized in accordance with the wishes of the Caribbean territories.

According to *El Mundo*, the leading daily newspaper of Puerto Rico, in a dispatch from Curacao dated November 27, 1957, Mr. Ramos Antonini delivered the following statement to the West Indian Conference, at the instruction of the secretary of state of Puerto Rico:

The Government of the Free and Associated State of Puerto Rico has consistently endorsed the activities of the Caribbean Commission and its auxiliary bodies in spite of the fact that since 1952 Puerto Rico has ceased to be a dependent territory and that its status of self-government as a Free and Associated State, recognized as such by the United Nations, is incompatible with the continued participation of Puerto Rico in the current structure of the Caribbean Commission.

The Government of the Free and Associated State nevertheless has continued to offer its cooperation and has participated in the work of the Commission. This continued participation, however, necessarily must have a time limit. The Government of the Free and Associated State sincerely hopes that no later than November, 1958, a revision conference will be held as per the resolution submitted to our consideration.

The Government of Puerto Rico, however, does not believe it proper to attend other future sessions of the West Indian Conference until the revision has been accomplished in line with the constitutional changes which have occurred in Puerto Rico and in the region. This decision should not be interpreted in any way as a denial of our wish to cooperate with the peoples of the area. The Government of Puerto Rico is prepared to extend its program of technical assistance in the Caribbean and to foster a series of workshops, seminars, and international conferences in the fields of principal interest for the economic, social, and cultural development of the Caribbean region.

In this task the Government of the Free and Associated State is certain that it will obtain the cooperation of all of the governments and public and private institutions dedicated to the welfare of the area and to a firm and constructive international understanding.[1]

Antonini, when questioned about the nature of this statement to the seventh session, replied that despite its diplomatic language the statement was indeed intended to be an ultimatum to the Caribbean Commission. All of the delegates were well aware that that was what the statement meant. The Puerto Ricans, he said, were quite annoyed over the way the four powers were, as he put it, dragging their feet on the revision of the Caribbean Commission charter. It was therefore decided that Puerto Rico would make this dramatic gesture at the seventh session in order to force action in the matter.[2]

The seventh session thereupon recommended that an Ad Hoc Committee be appointed to begin at once the necessary preliminary work in connection with the transformation of the Commission into the Caribbean Organization. The Commission adopted this recommendation. The Ad Hoc Committee began to function in 1958. The machinery thus appeared to be set in motion for the reformation of the Caribbean Commission.

To Puerto Rico, then, goes the credit for giving the necessary push to get action started on the technical process of transforming the Caribbean Commission. But to the United Kingdom, in company with the West Indies Federation, must be given the credit for action of an entirely different kind—that of very nearly destroying the Caribbean Commission, as well as the Caribbean Organization, before the new organization could even come into being.

Financial Crisis

"It may be that the West Indian Conference would not have passed its 1952 resolution about 'constitutional realities' if it had thought a little more about financial realities."[3] With that wry comment the *Trinidad Guardian* captured the essence of the crisis which beset the Caribbean Commission in 1958 and 1959.

Beginning in 1957 the United Kingdom government polled the governments of its territories in the Caribbean to inquire whether, in view of the impending revision of the Caribbean Commission agreement, they would be willing to assume the financial burden of contributing to the new organization. One by one the territorial governments replied in the negative. Based on certain statements by British government leaders in London and on other evidence, the belief began to spread that the United Kingdom would soon announce its intention of withdrawing financial support from the Commission and its successor. Thus if the organization were to continue to exist the monetary contribution which formerly had been paid by the United Kingdom government would in the future have to be paid by the West Indies Federation, in as much as the individual unit governments had declined to do so. Moreover, since it was taken for granted by most observers that the federal government likewise would be too poor to assume the burden of paying for membership in the Caribbean Commission or its successor, the days of the Commission were thought to be numbered. "In the Commission itself the betting is two to one that the Commission will fold up at the end of 1958," reported the Jamaica *Sunday Gleaner* on July 21, 1957.[4]

Even though for the time being these fears for the life of the Commission were all based on supposition, the threat was sufficient to provoke a considerable amount of editorial comment deploring the anticipated early demise of the Commission.

In an editorial entitled "Well Done," for example, the *Trinidad Chronicle* on June 19, 1958 said, in part:

Few will dispute that the Caribbean Commission has done an excellent job of collecting and collating information over the past eleven years or so of its existence.

It has served as a vast research agency in undertaking investigation in practically every field and placing the results at the disposal of the various Caribbean governments.

There is little to indicate that the best or much use has been made by governments of this wealth of data with which they were so gratuitously presented by the Commission.

This may account in part for the sneering question asked from time to time by the cynics: "Does the Caribbean Commission justify its existence?"

The question seems to have been changed within recent months to: "Will the Caribbean Commission continue to exist, and, if so, how long and in what form?"

This question has been, to a vast extent, prompted by the advent of Federation and by the belief that sooner or later the British would withdraw their financial support to the maintenance of the Commission, thus placing the onus on the Federal Government to accept or reject the committment.

So far there is no evidence, at least no public evidence, of the British intention to adopt such a policy. But there is ample evidence that changes of some form are contemplated, changes which are designed to give expression to the new and forward face of the Caribbean since the Agreement setting up the Commission was signed in 1946.

On November 24, 1958, the British confirmed the Caribbean region's worst fears by dropping its long expected "bombshell." At the opening session of the twenty-seventh meeting of the Caribbean Commission, in Trinidad, Mr. Douglas Williams, acting British co-chairman, announced that the British government was considering whether it would be possible to ensure participation of its territories in the work of a successor body to the Caribbean Commission because they had not found it possible to agree to contribute to it. The United Kingdom government, he added, had given the most careful consideration to the Ad Hoc Committee's proposals on the setting up of a successor body. On the constitutional side the issue was clear, he said. But on the financial side "the British Government has always made its policy clear that if its territories assume full membership of bodies of this kind then they must also accept responsibility for ensuring the financial burden."

"To put not too fine a point on it," Mr. Williams remarked, "he who calls the tune must also pay the piper."[5]

The crisis was now full blown, and prospects for the new organization were thought to hang in the balance. In his welcoming address to the twenty-seventh meeting, Sir Grantley Adams, the federal prime minister, remarked that "in principle we welcome the new arrangements that are now envisaged," but he added: "I would, however, be lacking in candor if I failed to observe that the new arrangements will pose a very serious financial problem for the West Indies and the other British territories in the Caribbean."[6]

The *Trinidad Guardian* maintained editorially that although the Caribbean territories had been seeking since 1952 to take over control of the Commission the idea that they might also have to pay for its upkeep was new and unfair.

It will be a tremendous pity if the Caribbean Commission is brought to a standstill because of the inability of the West Indies and other British Territories of the Caribbean to contribute adequately to its financial support. Yet this is the prospect which the bombshell dropped at the recent meeting of the Commission in Port of Spain by the British Co-Chairman unmistakably holds out . . . . The desire of the Territorial Governments served by the Commission to take over effective operating control of the organization was first made known in 1952 at a meeting of the West Indian Conference in Jamaica, and has been under more or less continuous study ever since. Yet the United Kingdom Government chose the present moment to announce for the first time that if the Territories wish to assume full membership they must accept full financial responsibility.[7]

Albert Gomes, member of the Federation Parliament, whose attack the following year on Eric Williams for his stand with regard to having the headquarters Secretariat located at Port of Spain, has already been cited, criticized the British government in colorful language for its refusal to help pay for the new organization's upkeep.

The speech made by Mr. Douglas Williams, at the formal opening of the recent Caribbean Conference in Port of Spain, deserves stern reprobation for the ungracious spirit which it exemplified.

As British spokesman on the occasion, Mr. Williams was obviously speaking officially, when he avowed that West Indian Governments would have to share the cost of maintaining the Caribbean Commission, if they wished more popular representation in that body.

Under ordinary circumstances, it would perhaps be no more than fair to remind the West Indies that if they wish more power and influence they must find the additional money to pay for these things.

In the present context, such a statement from an official U.K. spokesman does no more than stoke the fires which are threatening to destroy the frail structure of the West Indian nationhood, which Her Majesty's Government have always appeared so anxious to preserve and improve.

We, in those parts, have every reason to be angry at this statement, seeing that in the light of Caribbean Commission history, it now begins to seem that the Commission was created merely to provide a convenient forum for the metropolitan governments to settle their disputes during the war, and immediately afterwards, and is no longer necessary, now that it is possible for it to serve the interests of the nascent West Indian nation . . . .

For it is now that the Caribbean Commission can serve the West Indies in a way its architects, I'm sure, never anticipated in their wildest dreams.

The Commission has, during its comparatively short life, become the repository of a wealth of information of all sorts and fashions that the Federal Government of the West Indies desperately needs.

But apparently the British Government would prefer its death rather than its democratisation.

Surely the British Government are aware of the grave financial problems that face the new nation. They must be aware also of the extent to which they compromise their friends in these parts and please their enemies, when they act in this matter. . . .

They obviously know that it would be extremely difficult and politically very dangerous for the Federal Government to assume any increased financial burdens at this time. . . .

Now that by one of those curious twists of history, what began as a wartime expedient has become of inestimable value to the Government of the peoples of the West Indies, H. M. Government present us with the choice of finding money which we have not got, or of facing the loss of something we really need.[8]

There were, however, those who were willing to dispute this contention that the West Indies Federation government did not have the money to contribute to the Commission's upkeep. It is significant that one of the most effective presentations of the opposite point of view was written by a resident of Trinidad's rival island, Jamaica. In a column entitled "The Commission and the Federation," in the Jamaica *Daily Gleaner* of November 29, 1958, Percy Miller wrote:

According to the statement by Mr. Douglas Williams at the opening of the Caribbean Commission conference in Port of Spain last Monday, the British Government is now considering the question of West Indian participation in the financing of the Commission in view of the fact that the proposed new constitution will place that body more under the direction of the Caribbean countries than the four metropolitan powers. . . .

It appears, from Mr. Williams' remarks and from the hint of "problems" given by the Prime Minister, Sir Grantley Adams, that while the other participating territories in the work of the Caribbean Commission are able and willing to carry their part of the finances, the West Indian Federation finds itself in a different position altogether. After all the proud and public talk of the West Indian people becoming a nation and having a heritage and taking a place beside the other independent nations of the world, the Federation (of which Jamaica is now claiming loudly to be the biggest and most well-to-do part) is privately having to nudge the British Government and say that now the question arises of shouldering obligations, it is the British Government's turn to step forward on behalf of the West Indian responsibilities.

The reason for this is not really that the West Indian territories as a whole are unable to afford the money it would take to help keep the Commission in operation. The Commission costs under half a million pounds per annum to maintain, and since this is to be distributed amongst five or six member groups, the sum the West Indies will be called upon to pay is trifling in proportion to the size of the Jamaica budget, for example.

It couldn't be either, that the work the Commission has done in the past and its potential for the future is of no recognised significance. The direction small-scale farming development is taking in this island at the moment owes a great deal to the exploratory work of the Commission; and the oil-spraying of bananas here and the revolutionary thinking about coffee yields can both be accurately stated as having originated with the Commission's operations.

What lies at the root of this embarrassing situation for the West Indies is the extremely shabby politics being played in this island in particular with the question of Federation: people are being flagrantly misled into thinking that the unification means only added burden, and the benefits to come and which will prove paramount to the future are being accounted as meaning nothing at all.

This writer hopes that for the initial years of the new role of the Caribbean Commission, the British Government will be able to evolve some formula to keep the Federation in the Commission framework.

Without going into unnecessary detail with regard to the subsequent negotiations on both sides, suffice it to report here that the United Kingdom government did retreat somewhat from its position announced in 1958. In April 1959, it was agreed that by means of a grant-in-aid to the Federation government, the British government would cover one-half of the Federation's membership dues to the Caribbean Organization for a period of three years.

The transition period in the life of the organization presented additional complications, however. The Caribbean Organization was originally scheduled to come into being in September 1960. When it did not, largely because of the inability of the United States Congress to approve the new arrangement on behalf of the United States before it adjourned for the

1960 election campaign, the problem of keeping the Commission afloat financially for perhaps another full year was at hand. Although Britain had given the required one year's notice of her intention to withdraw from membership in the Commission, to take effect at the end of 1960, she agreed to extend her membership in the Commission until the new Caribbean Organization could take over. Unlike the United States, France, and the Netherlands, which continued to pay dues to the Commission without assistance from their associated territories,[9] Britain required both the West Indies Federation and British Guiana to share the interim costs of her membership in the Commission. Moreover, this combined British contribution for 1961 totaled only $70,000, in contrast to the previous normal United Kingdom contribution to the budget of the Caribbean Commission of $125,477. By operation of the percentage formula under which the contributions to the Commission were calculated, this unilateral British decrease from $125,477 to $70,000 resulted automatically in a scaling down of the contributions due from the other three members. For the fiscal year October 1, 1960, to September 30, 1961, therefore, the Caribbean Commission had to operate on a budget of $215,913 instead of its normal $365,823.

Budget Formula of the Commission

At this point it might be well to describe the formula under which contributions from the members were assessed during the years that the Commission was in normal operation.

The method of calculation which was agreed upon by the Commission in 1946 was as follows: (1) one-third was to be assessed equally among the four members; (2) one-third was to be assessed according to the populations of the Caribbean national groups; and (3) one-third was based on the national income of the metropolitan governments. On the basis of this formula, as it was worked out in 1946, the contributions were stated to be as follows:

France	16.0%
Netherlands	11.3
United Kingdom	34.3
United States	38.4
	100.0

These proportionate shares of the total budget of the Commission remained unvaried. In 1958 and 1959 the budget of the Commission was $365,823, based on the following individual contributions from the members:

France	$ 58,531.68
Netherlands	41,388.00
United Kingdom	125,477.29
United States	140,476.03
	$385,823.00

In anticipation that the Caribbean Organization would come into being in September 1960, Great Britain agreed to contribute only $70,000 for 1960, representing roughly the amount due for that two-thirds of the calendar year during which the Caribbean Commission would still be in existence. In September 1960, with the Caribbean Organization still not ready to be born, the Commission was forced to request additional contributions from the four members, and a fiscal year October 1, 1960 to September 30, 1961 was arbitrarily projected. The British countries (United Kingdom, West Indies, and British Guiana) would not agree, however, to any increase in their combined contribution of $70,000, so that amount had to be accepted from them as their contribution for an entire fiscal year. By operation of the percentage formula this forced a scaling down of the amounts due from the other three members. For that last fiscal year, then, the Commission operated on the following scale of contributions:

France	$32,653.06
Netherlands	23,061.22
United Kingdom	70,000.00
United States	78,367.35
	$204,081.63

That is, by pegging its 34.3 percent at $70,000, Britain caused a corresponding reduction in the amounts due from the other three. Adding $11,831.37 from surplus funds, the Caribbean Commission was forced to operate on a budget of $215,913.

The Ad Hoc Committee and the special session of the West Indian Conference struggled with the problem of allocating the costs of membership among the prospective members of the Caribbean Organization. The Ad Hoc Committee, after attempting unsuccessfully to apply several proposed formulas for calculating the fair amount due from each member, finally recommended the adoption of the following percentages:

British Guiana	7.5%
West Indies	28.0
French Guiana	4.0
Guadeloupe	5.5

Martinique	6.0
Netherlands Antilles	7.5
Surinam	6.0
Puerto Rico	31.0
U.S. Virgin Islands	4.5
	100.0%[10]

The Ad Hoc Committee had been proceeding on the assumption that the budget of the new organization would be approximately $316,000 per year, a decline of about $50,000 from the normal Caribbean Commission budget. Then, at the special session the Puerto Rican delegation announced that if Puerto Rico's invitation to be host to the new organization were accepted Puerto Rico was prepared to contribute $140,000 annually to the Caribbean Organization. This generous offer immediately changed the financial picture, for $140,000 is considerably more than 31 percent of $316,000.

With the Puerto Rican offer in hand, the Conference proceeded to draw up a new table of the percentages and amounts which would be paid by the prospective member governments:

	Percentage	Amount (U.S.$)
France	16.00	$ 50,560
Netherlands Antilles	7.75	24,490
Surinam	6.25	19,750
British Guiana	3.721518	11,780
West Indies	14.00	44,240
Puerto Rico	44.303797	140,000
U.S. Virgin Islands	7.974685	25,200
	100.00	316,000[11]

The two most important changes in this table, as compared with the one proposed by the Ad Hoc Committee, are first, the greatly increased Puerto Rican share of the total and, second, the fact that the contribution due from the West Indies was cut in half, from 28 percent to 14 percent. There is reason to believe that Puerto Rico's generosity in offering $140,000 was due in part to her desire to salvage hopes for the new organization. Fearing that the West Indies Federation might decline to participate, pleading inability to pay 28 percent of the proposed budget, Puerto Rico, by offering $140,000, made possible a great reduction in the amount to be required from the Federation. This was taken as further evidence of Puerto Rico's sincere interest in, and enthusiasm for, the work to be undertaken by the Commissioner's successor.

As was widely anticipated, the delegations of the West Indies and of

British Guiana informed the special session that because of their governments' restricted budgetary situations they could pay no more than 14 percent and 3.7 percent, respectively, toward the support of the new organization. Their delegations presented to the Conference a lengthy memorandum of their views on the desirable scope of the proposed Caribbean Organization. As described in this memorandum the Caribbean Organization would have a staff of only eighteen employees and a budget of $136,600 per year.[12]

The Caribbean Organization was thus to begin life with an annual budget of $316,000, or roughly $50,000 less than the Caribbean Commission used to have for its yearly support. But this was by no means the full story of the organization's reduced budget.

In Trinidad the annual rent for Kent House, plus certain other items of overhead expense, had amounted to approximately $7,000 (U.S.$). In Puerto Rico, by contrast, the comparable items would total around $35,000 ($30,000 rent for the office quarters, plus about $5,000 rent for the secretary general's residence). A cost of $35,000 in Puerto Rico as against $7,000 in Trinidad meant an added financial burden of $28,000. This on top of the overall budget cut of $50,000 meant that the new Caribbean Organization would initially have some $78,000 less for its programs and activities than the Commission did.[13]

Nor was this all; for the cost of every possible service and facility which the Caribbean Organization had to purchase in Puerto Rico— utilities, office supplies, repair services, printing costs, general service staff, etc.—was much higher than in Trinidad. The Secretariat calculated that its operating expenses in these areas would run anywhere from 30 percent to 50 percent more than in Trinidad. Taken all in all, therefore, the Caribbean Organization would at the start have somewhere in the neighborhood of $100,000 *less* than the Caribbean Commission to devote to those activities for which the organization was designed.[14]

As one indication of the organization's straitened financial status, a Secretariat staff of only thirty-six persons was projected for Puerto Rico, as contrasted with the seventy-five or more employed in Trinidad.

Staff Changes in the Transition

What do these figures mean if we look at the human beings involved in this transition from Caribbean Commission to Caribbean Organization? Any international agency is more than a charter or statute, a budget, and a list of program goals. It is always a group of people—the Secretariat officials and employees—who carry the major responsibility for its life and work. No international organization, even one as small as the Caribbean Commission, could move its headquarters from one country to another without causing profound changes in the lives of the people involved.

Drastic reductions in the staff were necessary on the eve of the move from Trinidad to Puerto Rico. In fact the Secretariat began its work in San Juan with only fifteen holdovers from Trinidad. Reasons for this great cut in personnel were, first, the Commission's policy—in line with the general practice of international organizations—of hiring the bulk of its general service staff in the host country. This meant the automatic discharge of some thirty to forty persons in this category who had been employed in Trinidad. Then there was the quite obvious fact that many of the employees at Kent House simply would not agree to move to Puerto Rico. Married women, for example, or other employees with ties of family or sentiment in Trinidad would not have moved even if they had been asked. Finally, there was the hard fact that the member governments of the Commission offered no increased contributions to the budget to cover the expenses of the move. Thus the Secretariat could pay for the move to Puerto Rico only by effecting great economies in the personnel and program budgets. In short, the Commission had to discharge its employees and virtually cease its activities so that the money thereby saved in salaries and expenses could be used to transport the archives, furniture, and other physical equipment from Trinidad to Puerto Rico.

At its twenty-eighth meeting, in St. Thomas, August 10–15, 1959, the Caribbean Commission authorized the secretary general to retain the services of those members of the staff who would be required by the Secretariat after the transfer of the headquarters and for whom replacements would not readily be available in Puerto Rico. Based on this original policy a tentative list of twenty-four persons, in addition to the secretary general, was drawn up, constituting a hard-core group of employees to be moved to Puerto Rico.[15]

Each succeeding meeting of the Commission and of the Working Committee resulted in further reductions in the hard-core group, due to budgetary limitations. In addition several of the employees originally tagged for transfer decided to decline the honor. The secretary general had to inform the Working Committee in April 1960 that of twenty-five members of the Secretariat originally to be taken to Puerto Rico, the statistician, two technical officers, one office assistant, two stenographers, and one typist had decided not to go.

Meanwhile retrenchments in the staff at Kent House began in earnest late in 1959. In November 1959, two employees were terminated; in December, seven; in January 1960, five; in February, two; in March, three; in April, eight; in May, sixteen; and in June 1960, one.

Officials of the Secretariat took great pains, by means of group meetings and personal interviews, to impress upon the people slated for transfer to Puerto Rico some of the changes in their lives that would result from the move. They were told that the cost of living was much higher in Puerto Rico than in Trinidad; especially was this the case with respect to housing and food. Many of them had been used to driving cars in Trinidad; but they were told that with the higher costs of gasoline, service, and insurance in Puerto Rico they might not be able to afford cars any longer. Many of them also had servants in Trinidad; they had to be told that servants were virtually unobtainable in Puerto Rico at any price.

The group was reminded that their status was indefinite at best since the United States Congress was not likely to act in 1960 upon the matter of Puerto Rican participation in the new Organization. Furthermore they were reminded that if and when the Caribbean Organization came into being, its Council would have the responsibility for staff and personnel policy matters. No firm promises could therefore be given that all or any of them would be retained by the Caribbean Organization, once the programs and activities of the new organization had been projected. No commitments could be given whether the new organization would agree to allow them the privilege of periodic home leave. And so on.

In view of the way in which the matter was reportedly presented to them, it is a tribute to the human sense of adventure that any of the Secretariat staff, much less seventeen, actually agreed to the change.

How did the group which moved to Puerto Rico make out? Not too well, from what I observed during my visit to the Commission Secretariat in 1961. Of the seventeen former staff from Kent House who actually landed in Puerto Rico, two gave notice almost at once and returned to Trinidad. Several of the remaining fifteen were talking of returning or were in various stages of negotiation with prospective new employers in Trinidad or in their home islands.

Morale among the fifteen was not good. The universal complaint was that the cost of living in Puerto Rico was far higher than any of them could possibly have imagined. Every one of them complained that he was paying at least twice as much for rent and that even at such prices the houses and apartments were not as spacious or as comfortable as in Trinidad.

The fifteen transferred employees were given a straight 10 percent increase in pay. But they were quick to point out that according to conservative government surveys the cost of living in Puerto Rico at the time of the move was 45 percent higher than in Trinidad and that there had been since then further increases in the cost of living in Puerto Rico.

While I was visiting the Commission Secretariat early in 1961, the long-time employees were continually holding meetings, circulating petitions, and drawing up statistics, in order to bring their plight to the attention of the Secretariat officials and through them to the Working Committee and the Commission itself. Their attitude was that they, as faithful employees of the Commission, should not be expected to suffer a drastic reduction in their standards of living simply because the Secretariat was moved from one island to another. They requested an additional raise in pay plus the grant of cost-of-living and rental allowances.

Effect of the Move on the Work of the Commission

By early 1960 the substantive work of the Secretariat had come to a virtual halt, as all efforts were concentrated on preparations for the move. Meetings of the Commission and of the Working Committee dealt almost exclusively with arrangements for the move of the Secretariat and for the transition from Caribbean Commission to Caribbean Organization. One by one the technical sections of the Secretariat were closed and their correspondents were informed that the activities had been suspended.

The only major outside activity of the Caribbean Commission during 1960 was representation at the third meeting on Cooperatives in the Caribbean Area, held in Grenada from July 5 to 8. Apart from the F.A.O. cooperatives expert and the Commission's cooperatives officer, who continued to travel about the area as usual, all traveling in 1960 by staff officials was strictly confined to attendance by the secretary general and the administrative secretary at Caribbean Commission and Working Committee meetings.

There were several reasons why, out of all of the manifold activities normally participated in by the Commission, only the cooperatives project kept going at about its normal pace during the confusion of 1960. First, the Commission's two cooperatives officials were both on loan to the Commission (or "seconded" to the Commission, to use the term current at the Secretariat) by outside agencies, one by F.A.O. and the other by the government of Trinidad. They were both about in the middle of their tours of duty with the Commission at the beginning of 1960. Thus to have let their work collapse along with the rest of the technical work of the Secretariat would have been a waste of skill and talent which the Commission could not always count on having.

Second, the nature of the cooperatives project requires the technical officers to do most of their work by traveling around the area, for the purpose of lecturing, conducting short-term training courses, consulting, answering questions, and assisting in the setting up and managing of cooperative units. This part of their work the cooperatives officers could continue to do in 1960 despite the turmoil existing at the Secretariat.

Finally, there was a feeling in the Commission that the cooperatives work was one of the most basic keys to the problem of economic development in the West Indies. Apart from the sugar culture and some new industries, virtually all of the economic production in the area served by the Commission was small-scale farming. For these small producers cooperatives have been found to be essential to the orderly and economical marketing of their output. Following the basic groundwork on cooperatives in the Commission countries by W. J. W. Cheesman (whose book, *Handbook for Cooperative Personnel in the Caribbean*, published in 1956 by the Caribbean Commission and the F.A.O. jointly, became an instant success not only in the Caribbean but also in Africa, the Pacific, and other underdeveloped areas), the cooperatives idea had taken root in the West Indies. The whole movement at the beginning of 1960 was thought to be at a critical stage of evolution. Thus the Commission decided that the cooperatives work had to go on at all costs in 1960; it was too important to the well-being of the area to let slide while the Secretariat was in the throes of moving.*

Departure from Trinidad

The story of the actual move of the Secretariat from Trinidad to Puerto Rico has an almost pathetic quality. For here was an international organization which, small though it was and meager its budget, had over the period of some fourteen years contributed immeasurably to the well-being of the area it served; yet in 1960 it found itself unwanted by the government of Trinidad. It had to discharge the majority of its faithful employees, virtually cease its good work, and then—without any sort of help—it had to auction off its surplus goods, pack its remaining possessions, and leave.

The secretary general's residence in Port of Spain, which the Caribbean Commission owned, was sold to the highest bidder, the Bank of London and Montreal, Ltd., for $52,200, less legal costs. Surplus property, including the Commission's right-hand drive vehicles, was disposed of by means of a public auction, for around $5,100.

The lease of Kent House, where the Secretariat had its offices in Trinidad, required that upon termination the Commission had to restore the building to its original condition by removing any additions or alterations which the Commission had made, by making any repairs required, and by replacing all window hangings and balcony awnings. Fortunately the Commission had on hand an amortization fund which could be used for this work.

In anticipation of the move the Commission had asked the member governments and the governments of the countries served by it whether they had any ships or airplanes that could be put at the Commission's disposal for use in moving the physical equipment and archives. Receiving no response the Commission made arrangements with the owners of a small freighter to transport its property from Trinidad to Puerto Rico during the last week of May 1960. A few days before this ship was due to load, however, the owners informed the Secretariat that it had broken down in a South American port. Fortunately there was a Japanese freighter sailing from Trinidad to Puerto Rico about the same time, and

---

*But one employee who had been with the Secretariat since 1946 told me that over the years the Commission had first one pet project, then another. In 1960 cooperatives was "the blue-eyed, fair-haired child." In another year it would have been some other project which would have been kept going at all costs.

the Commission's property was shipped on that vessel. The lowest price which could be negotiated with the Japanese company, however, was three dollars a ton more than would have been paid to the owners of the other freighter. This, plus the fact that the bulk of the shipment proved to be greater than the shippers had estimated, increased the cost to a figure considerably higher than had been anticipated.

When the decision was made to move the Secretariat to Puerto Rico in May or June 1960, it was clearly understood that the new building would be ready for occupancy by the fifteenth of May and that the interior partitions for the Secretariat could be built within three to four weeks after that date.

Unfortunately the new building was not ready when promised. Completion dates were changed several times, and it was well into August before the Commission could actually move into the building, which even then was not entirely finished. Meanwhile the owners of the new building, the Teachers' Association of Puerto Rico, were kind enough to provide a few desks in their old and crowded quarters for the Secretariat's use, but during that time the Commission's files and equipment sent from Trinidad remained in storage and inaccessible. This not only added to the cost of the move but delayed the Secretariat still further in hiring new employees and resuming its normal work.

These administrative and housekeeping details are put on record at this point simply because of the need to emphasize by the concrete example of the Commission's experience how utterly dependent the work of an international organization is upon its staff, its physical setting, and its accessibility to services and equipment. It is doubtful that any of the delegates to the special session of the West Indian Conference stopped to think that in voting to accept Puerto Rico's offer of headquarters facilities for the new Caribbean Organization they were also voting to bring the work of the Secretariat to a virtual halt for a year, that they were voting to change completely the lives of all of the people associated with the Commission, and that they were voting to introduce certain subtle changes in the character of the Secretariat made inevitable by virtue of its resettlement in a location so utterly different from its previous surroundings. In other words, there is more to this story of the changing patterns of international relations in the Caribbean than an account of the changing constitutional realities or a description of the formal structure of the Caribbean Organization or its successor.

Settled in Puerto Rico

By March 1961, there was a general feeling in the Secretariat of the Caribbean Commission that the worst was over. The difficult period of transition which began in 1958 or even earlier was believed at last to be drawing to a close. Although the new Caribbean Organization still had not come into being, there were no longer fears, as there had been many times during the previous years, that the Commission would go out of existence altogether through the failure of the Caribbean countries to agree on the structure and financing of the new body.

The confusion of the move from Trinidad, as well as the agonizing loss of more than fifty members of the Secretariat, was beginning to recede into the distance. Settled finally in their comfortable new office quarters, with furniture in place and files accessible, the Commission staff concentrated on establishing new routines of activity.

There was evidence that certain changes in the character of the Secretariat and its work by virtue of its relocation in a new setting—which the British West Indian newspapers had predicted—were indeed beginning to occur. Of the first sixteen new employees hired after the move all but three were Puerto Ricans. They had no knowledge of the way things had been done in Trinidad. For them it was a matter of a new job with a new organization, or at least one new to Puerto Rico. They had no personal experience of the difficult years when the future of the organization seemed so in doubt. They knew nothing of the fifty-odd staff members who were left behind when the Commission moved, nothing of the countless ways in which by their habits and the force of their personalities those people had shaped the nature and scope of the Secretariat's activities. In short, the habits and traditions of the Secretariat as a going concern in Trinidad were all but wiped out. In time, of course, the Secretariat acquired a new orientation to life in Puerto Rico, but with the old-timers from Trinidad quickly outnumbered by the new employees it was quite apparent that the pace would soon come to be set by the newcomers.

Spanish, for example, became a language of current usage in the Secretariat. The Puerto Ricans who were hired, at least those above the level of custodial help, had a working knowledge of English, but their everyday conduct of business in the office among themselves was all in Spanish. The officials of the Commission reported that they had to begin to deal continually with papers and documents in Spanish. The typists and the proofreader reported that whereas in Trinidad they rarely had to deal with a paper in Spanish, in Puerto Rico more than half of their work was in that language. Among the fifteen who transferred from Trinidad, those who had little or no knowledge of Spanish to begin with had to take lessons or otherwise make earnest efforts to learn the language.

Bit by bit the tempo of the Secretariat's substantive activities was beginning to increase by early 1961, although many plans for the future had to remain highly tentative until the new organization could approve of projects and assign priorities.

The first new official recruited by the Secretariat on the executive level after the move to Puerto Rico was Mr. G. C. L. Gordon, to be executive secretary in charge of the Social Affairs Branch. His responsibilities were to include the Commission's work in cooperatives, nutrition, home economics, community development, education, health, demography, and so on. Before joining the staff of the Secretariat Mr. Gordon, who is a Jamaican, worked for two years in British Guiana on cooperatives and community development projects for the government of that country. In January and February 1961, Gordon made a tour of the countries served by the Commission in order to familarize himself with the area's problems and to plan the future activities of the Commission and of the Caribbean Organization.

The number of outside visitors calling at the offices of the Secretariat was still quite small, early in 1961. The Secretariat had lost its public relations and information section in the course of the move from Trinidad, and consequently little or no attention had been given in the press to the arrival of the Commission in Puerto Rico. Moreover the officials of the Secretariat quite understandably felt that deliberate efforts to publicize the organization's existence and its work should wait until the new Caribbean Organization could assume charge and determine the major policies to be pursued.

Looking toward the Future

Fortunately for the future of international cooperation in the Caribbean there was, as of early 1961, a general feeling of optimism in the Secretariat of the Commission. There was a feeling that the crisis was past—a crisis during which at times it looked as though, with much work remaining to be done, there might soon be no international agency to carry it on. Now, with the future structure of the organization assured, it was thought to be a time for reassessing progress, surveying needs, and making preliminary plans for future projects.

With regard to the meager budget for the support of the new Caribbean Organization, there was a general belief that once the Caribbean territories had assumed responsibility themselves for the direction of the organization's good work in their midst, they would find some way to increase the budget to a more adequate level.

By the spring of 1961, then, the curve which represented the vitality of the Caribbean's international organization had already passed its lowest point and was well into the upturn. One era—represented by the Commission's fourteen years at Kent House—had ended, and a new era was beginning. The Secretariat had survived the transition period and was ready to move ahead with its work. The Secretariat had, in effect, shifted to the new pattern of international organization even if technically the Caribbean

Commission still was not dead. Thus when the new Caribbean Organization came into formal existence, in September of 1961, it had an advantage which was not enjoyed by the Anglo-American Caribbean Commission in 1942 or by the four-power Caribbean Commission in 1946, that is, it inherited a headquarters organization which was already a going concern.

11 □ THE CARIBBEAN ORGANIZATION CARRIES ON THE GOOD WORK

Inauguration of the Caribbean Organization

On September 5, 1961, the Caribbean Commission assembled for its thirty-first and last meeting at the San Juan Intercontinental Hotel in Puerto Rico. At 4 P.M. on the following day, September 6, 1961, the final session of the Commission was called to order by its chairman, the Netherlands representative. His Excellency Governor Luis Muñoz Marín arrived and was escorted to the meeting room by the four co-chairmen of the Caribbean Commission and by the secretary general. The national anthems of the four Commission members were played, together with the traditional anthem of the host island, Puerto Rico.[1]

The chairman welcomed the governor and called on the three other co-chairmen to make their closing remarks. He then made his final address, after which he closed this last meeting of the Caribbean Commission. The four former co-chairmen stepped down from the meeting table and took their places in the room as observers.[2]

At 5 P.M. the Joint Declaration specifying September 6, 1961, as the effective date for the establishment of the Caribbean Organization was signed by representatives of the four powers. The pen used for signing the Joint Declaration which brought the Caribbean Organization into being was presented to Governor Muñoz.[3] In the years during which the Caribbean Organization served, efforts were made to publicize September 6 as Caribbean Day (Día del Caribe), in honor of the inauguration of the Caribbean Organization on that date in 1961.

The first formal session of the Caribbean Council convened at 5:15 P.M. on September 6, 1961. The delegate of the Commonwealth of Puerto Rico, Mr. Mariano Villaronga, was unanimously elected chairman.[4]

At the invitation of the chairman, the governor of Puerto Rico addressed the meeting and formally declared the session open. In his address the governor stated that it was a great honor for Puerto Rico to be host not only to such a distinguished group of visitors but to the Caribbean Organization itself. He reviewed the constitutional changes which had taken place in the Caribbean area and which had led to the creation of the Caribbean Organization. "Here in the Caribbean," he said, "new forms of political freedom of association between nations are being worked out. Here freedom is promoted by friendship." He added that it was appropriate that the governments of France, Great Britain, the Netherlands, and the United States should be thanked for having created the Caribbean Commission which preceded the new Organization. In closing, he renewed the pledge of the Commonwealth government to cooperate fully with the Organization in all its endeavors.[5]

The chairman thanked the governor for his greeting, and at his invitation the United States observer conveyed to the meeting a personal message of good wishes to the new Organization from President John F. Kennedy. The President's message concluded: "You of the Caribbean Organization now face a great opportunity for planning and promoting even more effective self-reliance and mutual cooperation. Your success will not only strengthen the welfare and dignity of man in the Caribbean area, but also it will strengthen the cause of freedom throughout the world. I and your friends, the people of the United States, extend to you every good wish in the work which lies ahead of you."[6]

Representatives and delegates of the members of the new organization then addressed the meeting in turn. Following the speeches, the chairman of the Council and the secretary general accompanied the governor out of the meeting room, and on their return, the chairman closed the formal inaugural session of the Caribbean Organization.[7]

At 9:30 A.M. on the following day there was a short ceremony at which the flags of the members of the Caribbean Organization were raised at the headquarters of the Central Secretariat in Hato Rey, and the national anthems were played. Following a brief speech by the chairman of the Council, the secretary of state of the Commonwealth of Puerto Rico addressed the gathering and on behalf of his government welcomed the Organization's Secretariat to Puerto Rico.[8]

At three o'clock that afternoon—the ceremonies having been concluded—the Caribbean Council began its first working session at the Secretariat headquarters.[9]

Structure of the Caribbean Organization

The full text of the Statute of the Caribbean Organization is included in the Appendix. Suffice it to note here that Article V provided that the governing body of the Organization was the Caribbean Council. In Article VI, dealing with the composition of the Council, it was declared that each member should be entitled to send to each session of the Council one delegate and such advisers as it considered necessary, but that the Republic of France should be entitled to send one *delegation* plus such advisers as it considered necessary.

Voting in the Council was on the basis of one vote for each member except that the Republic of France was entitled to have three votes, in recognition of its three territories in the Caribbean. Procedural matters were to be decided by a simple majority, substantive matters by a two-thirds majority (Article IX). However, the Organization's *budgets*, either annual or supplementary, had to be approved by a *unanimous* vote; that is, the total amounts involved had to be approved by all members. In the event that any proposed budget failed to receive a unanimous adoption the budget for the preceding year remained in effect (Article IX, Section 3). Hence any member of the Organization could at any session of the Council prevent the Organization from embarking on some new project simply by defeating the budget which provided for the new activity.

The parties to the agreement establishing the Caribbean Organization, the four metropolitan governments, were entitled to send observers to all meetings. These observers had the right to speak but not to vote. Likewise any prospective member of the Organization could send observers with the right to speak but not to vote (Article XII).

Meetings of the Council and Membership in the Organization

The Caribbean Council held five meetings altogether, as follows:

First meeting, September 6–15, 1961, at San Juan, Puerto Rico
Second meeting, March 13–16, 1962, at Georgetown, British Guiana
Third meeting, October 3–8, 1962, at Paramaribo, Surinam
Fourth meeting, September 23–27, 1963, at San Juan, Puerto Rico
Fifth and last meeting, November 30–December 4, 1964, at Curacao, Netherlands Antilles

The Statute of the Organization, Article III, specified the following territories as eligible for membership in the Organization:

Republic of France for the Departments of French Guiana, Guadeloupe and Martinique
Netherlands Antilles
Surinam
Bahamas
British Guiana
British Honduras
British Virgin Islands
West Indies
Commonwealth of Puerto Rico
Virgin Islands of the United States

At the first meeting of the Council in September 1961, the following areas were formally represented with a delegate (or delegation) present:

Republic of France
Netherlands Antilles
Surinam

British Guiana
West Indies
Commonwealth of Puerto Rico
Virgin Islands of the United States

The British Virgin Islands, as a prospective member, was represented by an observer. British Honduras was not present in any capacity, and it never participated in any way in the work of the Organization.

At the second meeting of the Council, in March of 1962, the same territories were again represented as members. The administrator of the British Virgin Islands had informed the secretary general that his government was eager to become a full member of the Organization as soon as the necessary arrangements could be made.

However, at that same second meeting in 1962 there was an ominous note about the future membership of the Organization. By March of 1962 when the Council met it was already known that the West Indies Federation was in the process of dissolution. The Caribbean Council had before it in fact a formal notice of withdrawal of membership from the West Indies, to take effect on December 31, 1962. Noting this change, the Council adopted a resolution urging the governments signatory to the agreement (the four metropolitan powers) establishing the Caribbean Organization to make the necessary arrangements for the units embraced within the Federation to join the Organization as separate members. Those units for the time being would be designated as "countries served by the Organization." A fatal flaw in the Organization structure had been discovered, namely, that the Organization itself was not in full control of its own membership arrangements. In retrospect it can be said that this marked the beginning of the end for the Caribbean Organization.

By the fifth and final meeting of the Council in 1964 the participants as full members included:

Republic of France
Netherlands Antilles
Surinam
British Virgin Islands
Commonwealth of Puerto Rico
Virgin Islands of the United States

Present as special observers for "countries served by the Organization" were representatives from the following British West Indies islands:

Antigua
Dominica
Grenada
Montserrat

Barbados
St. Vincent

Conspicuously absent were any delegates or observers from the two largest islands of the former Federation, Jamaica and Trinidad.

Also, the fifth meeting had before it notices of withdrawal which it had received from British Guiana, Surinam, and Puerto Rico. British Guiana, in fact, did not even attend the fifth meeting. Clearly the Organization had reached the end of its useful existence. These matters will be explored at greater length in chapter 13.

ACCOMPLISHMENTS OF THE CARIBBEAN ORGANIZATION

This case study of international organization in the Caribbean is of course more concerned with what the Caribbean Organization *was* than with what it *did*. That is, the main purpose of this book is to examine the successive agencies in the Caribbean as cooperative instrumentalities of the peculiar state system of the West Indies. However, these and all other international organizations are formed for the purpose of carrying out certain common purposes, and so some attention must be given to the actual substantive work of the Caribbean Organization.

The new Caribbean Organization had broadly the same terms of reference as the old Commission, with the addition of cultural activities (Article II of the Statute). The Organization thus began by continuing the work started by the Commission. The secretary general and the headquarters staff in Puerto Rico carried on after September 6, 1961, with no break in continuity from its service to the Caribbean Commission.

The projects undertaken by the Caribbean Organization and some of its accomplishments will be summarized here under the same headings used by the Organization in its publications. For a better appreciation of why the Caribbean Organization failed, however, note should be made that in these summaries which follow there is a great deal more of study, meet, coordinate, and publish than there is of direct purposeful activity.

Agriculture

In the field of agriculture,[10] during the more than three years of its existence the Caribbean Organization conducted two more successful demonstration tours, one relating to vegetables and food crops, held in Puerto Rico in February 1963, the other concentrating once again on the banana industry, held in Guadeloupe in February of 1964. The registered participants in the banana tour numbered 294, but at times there were more than 350 in attendance. Twenty-three countries were represented altogether, including, in addition to the banana-growing countries in the Caribbean, also Ecuador in South America and Ivory Coast and Guinea in Africa.

At the request of the Caribbean Organization, Dr. A. J. Oakes of the United States Department of Agriculture undertook in 1964 a grass expedition to the Republic of South Africa, as a result of which more than three hundred new grasses were introduced into the Caribbean region.

The Organization's Division of Natural Resources undertook the publication of a quarterly agricultural journal, *Caribbean Agriculture,* devoted to disseminating the results of Caribbean studies, research, and experience. This Division also maintained a clearinghouse for monthly collection and dissemination of information on the diseases of plants and animals. It conducted an exchange service of publications in the field of agriculture among scientists, technologists, and farmers in the area. In 1962 a report was published on *The Status of Research into the Problems of Animal Health and Production in Countries Served by the Caribbean Organization,* which drew together and summarized all of the research work in the area.

The standing advisory committees on Animal Health and Production, and on Fishery Development, were set up in collaboration with governments served by the Organization for the purpose of advising the Caribbean Council on all matters affecting the development of livestock and fisheries in the area. In May of 1963 the Caribbean Food Crops Society was established under the sponsorship of the Caribbean Organization.

Valuable documents relating to the Banana Demonstration Tour were prepared for publication in book form, and steps were being taken when the Organization ceased its work to establish a Caribbean-wide Banana Research Association.

Trade and Tourism

To promote the development of trade and tourism in the Caribbean area, the Caribbean Organization established and operated a highly successful service under the title Clearing House on Trade and Tourism Information.

The purpose of this service was to publish information and answer inquiries on markets in Caribbean products and on industrial and tourism development possibilities. This was accomplished through the publication of a monthly journal and a weekly trade bulletin. Both publications circulated among more than a thousand businessmen and government officials in the Caribbean and abroad. Results of a questionnaire circulated among users of this service indicated that the additional commerce generated through information made available by the Clearing House had a dollar value many times the total amount spent for the maintenance of the entire Caribbean Organization.

The Clearing House was also responsible for arranging survey visits and missions on trade, industry, tourism, and investment within the region. Plans had been made, prior to the termination of the Organization, for setting up a permanent trade exhibition of Caribbean products at the Secretariat.

The Organization's interest in stepping up regional trade in fruits, vegetables, and other food crops resulted in a survey conducted by a market analyst from Holland. The report on this survey was published by the government of the Netherlands under the title *Promotion of Intra-Caribbean Trade in Fruits and Vegetables.*

The Clearing House in 1964 published *Intra-Caribbean Trade,* a 359-page statistical report giving the value of intra-Caribbean imports and exports, intra-Caribbean trade as a percentage of the total trade of Caribbean countries, and the value of intra-Caribbean imports and exports by commodity and country of destination.

Economic Development Planning

As the work of the Caribbean Organization proceeded more and more of its activities came to be centered around a concept called the Caribbean Plan, patterned frankly after the Colombo Plan in southeast Asia.

At the special West Indian Conference in 1959 and at the thirtieth meeting of the Caribbean Commission in 1960 the secretary general was commissioned to prepare a Plan for the Caribbean area comparable to the Colombo Plan. Early in 1961 the secretary general visited most of the countries in the region, discussing proposals for a Caribbean Plan with heads of government and with private interests. From these consultations and from the deliberations of the Caribbean Council and other bodies associated with the Organization the Caribbean Plan took shape.

In brief the aims of the Caribbean Plan were to foster mutual assistance among the countries of the area; to help the countries to obtain assistance from external sources; and to harmonize development on a regional basis. Like the Colombo Plan the Caribbean Plan contemplated an annual review of the countries' development plans and the publication of an annual report. The Caribbean Organization did in fact publish a document called "The Caribbean Plan" in 1961 and then Caribbean Plan Annual Reports in 1962 and 1963. These were digests of economic development planning in the countries served by the Caribbean Organization, including agricultural, tourism, and industrial development investment possibilities.

A Standing Advisory Committee of the Caribbean Plan met frequently during the life of the Caribbean Organization and prepared numerous recommendations for consideration by the Caribbean Council.

Of all the meetings and seminars convoked by the Caribbean Organization, probably the most noteworthy was the Seminar on Planning Techniques and Methods, held in Puerto Rico in 1963 with the assistance of the Ford Foundation. Thirty-five participants, lecturers, and observers attended, representing twenty countries, international organizations, and universities in the area. British Honduras and the Dominican Republic— nonmembers of the Caribbean Organization—sent participants. Organizations represented included the Food and Agriculture Organization, World Health Organization, Organization of American States, Ford Foundation, University of the West Indies, University of Puerto Rico, Inter-American University of Puerto Rico, and the Inter-American Planning Society. From the lectures and discussions at this Seminar the consensus emerged that there was not only an urgent need to improve the planning procedures used in many of the countries of the area and to obtain the necessary trained staff for these purposes, but also that practical measures had to be taken urgently to start executing the development plans of the countries of the area. Following this Seminar the Organization published in 1964 a report on Planning for Economic Development in the Caribbean, a series of authoritative articles by many well-known economists and sociologists.

The Economic Division of the Secretariat also engaged in studying the possibilities of establishing a Caribbean Development Bank and a Caribbean Private Investment Company.

Transportation and Telecommunications

In the field of transportation a *Preliminary Report on Air and Ocean Transportation in Selected Countries* was prepared in 1962. Two meetings of representatives of the various airlines serving the Caribbean were held in August and November of 1964, during which discussions took place on the important matter of special fares for the stimulation of regional travel.

A survey of telecommunications needs in the eastern Caribbean was organized with the assistance of the United States Agency for International Development (AID). The report of this survey was published in 1962. Following upon this, a meeting on telecommunications was held at the Secretariat in April of 1964. This meeting was attended by representatives of government and state agencies, private telecommunications agencies operating in the area, and other interested agencies concerned. The decision of this gathering was that there should be established in the eastern Caribbean a telecommunications trunk route system reaching from Trinidad up the archipelago to the U.S. Virgin Islands and Puerto Rico, and from there to the outside world. It was contemplated that in all of the islands the internal telephone services would be improved and that eventually they would all be connected through feeders into the main trunk route, thereby enabling the establishment of adequate and uninterrupted telecommunication services throughout the area.

Nutrition and Health

The Caribbean Organization established a Standing Advisory Committee on Food and Nutrition (SACFAN) to advise the Caribbean Council on all questions pertaining to food and the improvement of nutrition in the area. The Food and Agriculture Organization, the World Health Organization, the Pan American Health Organization, and the governments served by the Organization collaborated with the committee. Surveys were made of the problems in food and nutrition and possible methods of improvement were studied. A Seminar on Food and Nutrition was held in 1961; the report of the meeting was published in 1962.

On the recommendation of SACFAN the Caribbean Council invited F.A.O., W.H.O. and the United Nations International Children's Fund (UNICEF) to establish a Caribbean Nutrition Center.

Cooperatives

A Standing Advisory Committee on Cooperative Development was set up by the Caribbean Organization in collaboration with the governments served by the Organization to advise the Caribbean Council on all matters affecting the development of cooperatives in the area.

In 1964, in collaboration with the International Labor Organization and with the Commonwealth of Puerto Rico, a regional Workshop on the Methods and Techniques of Cooperative Organization was held in Puerto Rico. The report of this Workshop was published by the Organization.

The Organization also published from its inception a *Cooperative Newsletter*. This was a quarterly publication designed to stimulate and record the activities of the cooperative movement in the Caribbean.

Education

The Caribbean Organization, in collaboration with the Inter-American University of Puerto Rico and the Political Science Association of Puerto Rico, organized a Seminar on Civil Service, which was held in Puerto Rico in January of 1963.

With financial assistance from AID, the Caribbean Organization in 1962 established one of its most important activities, the Caribbean Organization Fellowship Program. The purpose was to assist in the development of the countries served by the Organization by providing opportunities for higher education in the fields of agriculture, engineering, economics, public administration, and teacher education. More than eighty fellowships to universities in the West Indies and in the United States were awarded in 1963 and 1964.

The Library

The Caribbean Organization retained and developed the uniquely valuable library begun by the Caribbean Commission. During the tenure of the Caribbean Organization the library maintained exchange relationships with nearly fourteen hundred institutions and agencies whose publications the library received regularly. It was a depository for the United Nations and its affiliated agencies, for the European Community agencies, for the Organization for Economic Cooperation and Development (O.E.C.D.), for the Organization of American States, for the South Pacific Commission, and the Inter-American Statistical Institute. The library also organized a law collection of the most recently published laws of all the countries served by the Organization.

A monthly Selected List of Recent Additions was published. Other publications included *Bibliography of Development Plans* in 1963, *Bibliography of Caribbean Folklore* in 1963, and *Periodicals Lists* in 1963. The library also published regularly a Current Caribbean Bibliography.

Information and Cultural Affairs

The Information and Cultural Affairs Division of the Secretariat maintained liaison with news and public affairs agencies throughout the Caribbean. It disseminated information concerning the Organization, held press conferences and interviews, issued press releases, briefed groups visiting the Secretariat, and so on. This Division also prepared and distributed *The Caribbean,* the official monthly newsletter of the Organization. In cooperation with universities and other institutions of learning it began preparation of a Directory of Cultural Institutions and of a Dictionary of Caribbean Biography.

TAKING STOCK AFTER THREE YEARS OF SERVICE

All of the good works and useful projects of the Caribbean Organization ceased with the expiration of the Organization in 1965. In chapter 15 we shall see the extent to which some of these activities were revived, remodeled, and carried on at least for a time by Puerto Rico's new CODECA.

Dealing as it did with the age-old human problems of a poor and depressed area, the Caribbean Organization's own press releases and other publicity material often had a homey and down-to-earth quality which is not apparent in the summary given above of its meetings, publications, and other formal activities. To capture and preserve the flavor of the Organization's outreach to the people of the region and to recapitulate what its work meant to those people, there is in the Appendix material quoted from a series of radio scripts prepared by the Organization for broadcast in the Caribbean countries in connection with the celebration of Caribbean Day in 1964. In the light of the booster spirit expressed in these scripts it is a bit pathetic to note that these broadcasts were made only two months before the fifth meeting of the Caribbean Council at which the decision was made to terminate the Organization.

12 □ CONSTITUTIONAL DEVELOPMENTS DURING THE CARIBBEAN ORGANIZATION YEARS AND AFTER

In chapter 8 it was asserted that of all the factors which can be identified as having prompted the successive changes in the structures and activities of the agencies for regional cooperation in the Caribbean, one stands out as fundamental—namely, the constitutional growth in the direction of increasing self-government and independence in the region.

As we have already seen, and as will be explored at greater length in the next chapter, what mainly caused the Caribbean Organization to founder was the breakup of the West Indies Federation and the resulting inability of the Organization to include the units of the former Federation in its membership roster. There was also the negative attitude of France, speaking in the name of its Caribbean departments. And, in addition, there was the impatience of a progressive Puerto Rico with the shortcomings of the Caribbean Organization.

In this chapter, then, let us pause to bring up to date the constitutional developments in the Caribbean which have occurred since the Caribbean Organization began its career late in 1961.

Primary attention will of course have to be given to the British territories, including the dissolution of the Federation and the resulting independence for some of the islands and the evolution of the new status of Associated State of the United Kingdom for some of the others.

In view of Puerto Rico's increasing role in the Caribbean and the introduction of its CODECA to replace the defunct Caribbean Organization, a discussion of Puerto Rico's dialogue with itself over its future political status and its plebescite of July 23, 1967, will be included in this chapter as a principal item in the constitutional evolution of the Caribbean.

NETHERLANDS AND FRENCH AREAS

Little need be said about the Netherlands and French areas during the time span covered by this chapter, for there were no constitutional—as distinguished from political—developments indicative of any change of official status.

Dutch Areas

According to most observers it can be stated that the reformed kingdom of the Netherlands, after more than ten years of operation, has been favorably received by the vast majority of the citizens of the former Dutch colonies in the Caribbean.[1] For all practical purposes the degree of internal self-government is complete. The participation through the complicated but adequate formula for the preparation of kingdom legislation has been found to be effective and generally satisfactory to all parties concerned. Moreover, the attitude of the Dutch government, marked by self-restraint on the one hand and receptivity to change on the other, is said to have created a healthy political environment.[2]

Some of the younger elements from the population of the Netherlands Antilles, mostly students who have studied in Holland, would like to see more emphasis on the development of a local Antillean culture, perhaps with Dutch being eventually replaced by the native dialect called *papiamento* as the language of expression. However, both the constant threat of Venezuela, almost in sight from the shores of the "ABC" islands, as well as the lack of any potential resource which might offer a basis for greater economic or commercial activity, has made most of the Netherlands Antilleans take a realistic position concerning any political change in the relationship with Holland.[3]

In Aruba and Curacao both employment levels and per capita income have declined moderately in recent years due to the increasing automation of the two large oil refineries: Shell Curacao, N.V., and Lago Oil and Transport Company in Aruba. The economic decline has been only partially offset by the development of new tourist facilities. The result has been the closer association of the Netherlands Antilles government with that of Holland in the working out of long-range development plans and in the granting of financial assistance to the islands by the Netherlands government.

Surinam has displayed some concern over two possible areas of limitation in its status which some leaders in that country feel might be modified. According to the Charter of the Kingdom, foreign loans from other nations and from any international organization must be undertaken and negotiated only with the full approval of the kingdom government. So far Holland has always been willing to meet any reasonable request for financial assistance from Surinam, thus making it unnecessary to apply to foreign sources. Nevertheless, there are some Surinamese who feel that if their country had a more independent status it might become eligible for support from such operations as the Alliance for Progress. Furthermore, it is argued that as a part of the Kingdom of the Netherlands Surinam is not eligible for beneficial treatment as an underdeveloped nation, which she clearly is, under certain United Nations programs.[4]

On May 30, 1969, rioting, said to be the worst in the history of the Netherlands Antilles, broke out on the island of Curacao as a result of a wage dispute between Shell Oil Company, its contractors, and their employees. Union leaders alleged that the government of the Antilles was maintaining a low-wage policy in order to attract foreign investment. More than 150 persons were injured in the rioting, and approximately sixty million dollars worth of damage was done to business establishments in Willemstad, the capital, through fire and looting. At the request of the local government, the Netherlands government sent 300 royal marines by air to Curacao to help restore order.[5]

French Areas

The impact of French culture on Guadeloupe and Martinique has been greater than the English impact on any of its islands, even Barbados, the so-called "Little England" of the Caribbean. Therefore the action taken by the French in 1946 to incorporate the French Caribbean dependencies into the Republic as integral *départements* of France was in many ways the logical and natural outcome of historical forces. This assimilation of the French Caribbean communities did not provoke any protest at the time except by one or two isolated and independent persons. Even the numerous communists, including the great poet and man of letters of the Caribbean, Aimé Césaire, went along with integration in the hopes that perhaps with the aid of the then-strong French Communist Party the vestiges of colonialism would be wiped out once and for all.

Yet, as might have been anticipated, the incorporation of the Caribbean dependencies on a plane of equality with metropolitan France proved artificial and unsatisfactory in many ways. Political integration into the highly centralized government of France served not to satisfy aspirations for local political freedom but rather to accent the need and desire for self-government.[6] With virtually every governmental and administrative matter pertaining to the islands having to be referred to the appropriate ministries in Paris, examples of the same kind of annoying administrative frustration previously cited multiplied endlessly.

The result has been that some elements in the French Caribbean assert that the time has come to change the political status of Martinique and Guadeloupe in the direction of a greater autonomy. Authorities who study the situation closely can distinguish among the autonomist forces representatives of both communists and noncommunists, as well as some youth organizations.[7]

The communists demand an autonomy which would return to the people the administration of their own affairs, including agrarian reform, diversification of agriculture, industrialization, and reduction of the powers of the private monopolies in trade and transportation.

Aimé Césaire broke with the Communist Party in 1956 and formed his own Progressive Party of Martinique. He favors an administrative autonomy by which the islands could conduct their own local affairs within the French constitutional structure.[8] Césaire is presently serving as one of Martinique's three deputies to the National Assembly in Paris and also as mayor of Fort-de-France. It is, however, taken as indicative of the lack of political sophistication on the part of the people of Martinique that they elect Césaire to high office and also give a heavy vote to communists, while at virtually the same time giving a referendum vote in favor of de Gaulle as high as 85 percent, as occurred in October of 1962. Thus, it is virtually impossible to read into election statistics any true will of the French Caribbean peoples with regard to their future political status. Nearly all observers of the French Caribbean scene point to the indifference of the great majority of the population toward opening up the status issue. They seem to want to remain French and avoid taking any risks which would involve endangering the standard of living they have achieved under departmentalization.

Riots growing out of a strike by construction workers occurred in Guadeloupe late in May of 1967, resulting in five dead and sixty persons injured. It was generally conceded, however, that these disturbances reflected local economic and racial grievances and did not express dissatisfaction with the constitutional and political status of Guadeloupe.

In April of 1969, while the people of France as a whole rejected by 52.4 percent the constitutional reforms proposed by President de Gaulle, the result of which was de Gaulle's resignation, the people of Martinique and Guadeloupe voted heavily in favor of the proposals. In Guadeloupe the vote was: Yes, 33,945; No, 11,703. In Martinique the Yes vote (pro de Gaulle) was 71,592; No, 9,230.[9]

British Commonwealth Areas

A far greater number of changes occurred in the British areas of the Caribbean in the years after 1961 than in all of the rest of the region combined. The Federation dissolved; Jamaica, Trinidad, Barbados, and British Guiana became fully independent nations; and the remaining islands, as well as British Honduras, sought for some sort of compromise formula between the independence which they could not quite sustain and the colonial status which they were so eager to throw off.

End of the Federation

The West Indies Federation, which came into existence in 1958, was destined to have a short life. The commitment to the Federation principle on the part of the large islands, Jamaica and Trinidad, was largely the vision of leaders like Norman Manley in Jamaica and Eric Williams in Trinidad, who were able to understand and appreciate the common heritage of the West Indian society. But lesser politicians and an indifferent public caused the new nation's future to be clouded from the start.

In Jamaica, during 1961, political maneuvering between the premier, Manley, and the Jamaica Labour Party of his rival, Alexander Bustamente, resulted in the calling by the House of Representatives of a referendum on the question of continued membership in the Federation for September 19, 1961. Bustamente had originally favored federation, but in 1961 his party led the campaign against the Federation and in favor of separate independence for Jamaica.

The result of the referendum was as follows: in favor of continued membership of Jamaica in the Federation, 216,400 (46.2 percent); against the Federation, 251,953 (53.8 percent). The majority for secession was thus 35,553.[10]

Mr. Manley told a press conference that he accepted the people's decision "fully and absolutely." He attributed the result to three causes: (1) Jamaica's intense national spirit; (2) its geographical remoteness from the other units of the Federation; and (3) fears of federal taxation and of an "invasion" of people from the smaller islands in search of work.

In Trinidad, Eric Williams pointedly remarked that when you remove the numeral "1" from the numeral "10" the result is zero. Jamaica's defection meant the end of the Federation. It was an ominous note for the future of international cooperation in the Caribbean that Jamaica's referendum on secession from the Federation came just two weeks after the formal inauguration of the Caribbean Organization.

On April 18, 1962, in London, the West Indies Bill on dissolving the Federation became law. It empowered the United Kingdom government to provide by Order-in-Council for: (1) the secession of an individual colony from the Federation; (2) the dissolution of the Federation itself; (3) an interim authority (under a commissioner) to carry on the common services; and (4) the establishment of a new federation or any other form of government, for any of the colonies concerned.

The West Indies Federation was officially and formally dissolved by an Order-in-Council on May 31, 1962. The people of the British West Indies continued the process of liberating themselves from colonialism, but the first experiment in integrated nationhood had failed.[11]

Independence for Jamaica, Trinidad, Barbados, and British Guiana

The years 1962 through 1965 were marked by complex and largely fruitless conferences in London over the political future of the smaller units of the former Federation. Meanwhile, however, the three largest island territories of the Federation achieved full independence within the Commonwealth, as did British Guiana on the mainland of South America.

1. Jamaica. Jamaica, whose defection had caused the dissolution of the Federation, became independent at midnight on August 5-6, 1962, ending 307 years of British rule. The Queen was represented at the independence ceremony by Princess Margaret, and the United States was officially represented by Vice President Lyndon B. Johnson. Accepting independence for Jamaica was the new prime minister, Sir Alexander Bustamente, whose Jamaica Labour Party had defeated Norman Manley's People's National Party in April. On September 12, 1962, the seventeenth session of the United Nations General Assembly accepted Jamaica as a member of the United Nations.

2. *Trinidad.* On August 31, 1962, less than a month after Jamaica's independence, the other major unit of the former Federation, the territory of Trinidad and Tobago, likewise became an independent nation within the Commonwealth. The Queen was represented this time at the ceremonies by the princess royal. Accepting independence for his island nation was the prime minister, Dr. Eric Williams. As with Jamaica, Trinidad and Tobago was also accepted as a member of the United Nations in September of 1962.

An additional note of interest with regard to international organization affairs in the West Indies is the fact that on February 23, 1967, Trinidad was admitted to the Organization of American States as the twenty-second member. This marked the first admission of a new member since the O.A.S. was formed in 1948. Trinidad thus became the first British Commonwealth member of the hemisphere organization, since Canada has never joined.

3. *British Guiana.* British Guiana achieved full independence under its new name, Guyana, on May 26, 1966. Independence for this colony on the north coast of South America had long been delayed because of continuous internal strife between the two major racial and ethnic groups. The largest, and a predominantly rural group—some 268,000 people of East Indian descent—is represented by the People's Progressive Party, led by the pro-Marxist Dr. Cheddi Jagan. The approximately 184,000 Negroes are represented by the People's National Congress, under the leadership of Forbes Burnham.

Rioting between the two groups as early as 1953 had caused the British government to suspend the existing constitutional arrangements for British Guiana, occupy the territory with troops, and reimpose strict colonial rule. Further serious rioting in Georgetown, the capital, occurred in February 1962.

Meanwhile, however, slow progress was being made toward constitutional revision for British Guiana. By 1961 the territory was fully self-governing and Dr. Jagan became the first prime minister in September, following an election victory by his party in August 1961.

The British continued their efforts to find a basis for agreement among the parties on major constitutional questions. When these efforts failed and no prospect of a coalition was in sight, the party leaders agreed to ask the British government to settle the outstanding issues on its own authority. The British thereupon decided that a system of proportional representation should be instituted as a prelude to new elections. This was bitterly opposed by Jagan, who foresaw that he would lose his working majority. The elections were held, however, on December 7, 1964. Jagan's party obtained 45.8 percent of the votes and twenty-four seats in the House of Assembly. Burnham's party got 40.5 percent and twenty-two seats. But since Burnham was able to form a coalition with Peter D'Aguiar's minor third party, the United Force, which had won seven seats, Burnham became the prime minister. Jagan's party boycotted the Assembly for five months.[12]

With the radical Jagan out as head of government, the British were prepared to go ahead with independence, which came on May 26, 1966, leaving Guyana's racial and economic problems unsolved, however. Jagan and Burnham publicly embraced at the independence ceremonies but future prospects for the new nation were none too bright.

Guyana joined the United Nations as the 118th member on September 22, 1966, by unanimous action of the twenty-first General Assembly.

National elections in December 1968, resulted in a substantial increase in the representation of prime minister Burnham's People's National Congress party, enabling him to remain in power without coalition support. At a rally in Georgetown on February 23, 1969, Prime Minister Burnham announced that Guyana would become a republic on February 23, 1970.

4. Barbados. After 339 years of British rule, Barbados became an independent nation on November 30, 1966. The most easterly of the West Indian islands, Barbados has an area of only 166 square miles and a population of only 245,000. Accepting independence for his island nation from the Queen, represented by the Duke of Kent, was the prime minister, Mr. Errol Barrow. On December 9, 1966, Barbados was welcomed into United Nations membership, and in October of 1967 Barbados joined the Organization of American States.

Abortive Design for an East Caribbean Federation

After the West Indies Federation had been dissolved and Jamaica and Trinidad had become independent countries, it was for a time hoped that the eastern British Caribbean islands (the "Little Eight" of the former Federation) would establish a smaller federation and that this East Caribbean Federation could then emerge as a new independent nation in the Commonwealth. But this rather logical solution to the future status of the islands never proved possible. There was simply no feeling of unity on the part of the peoples of the islands or their political leaders. The title of a West Indian novel by S. Selvon is *An Island Is a World*; for most West Indians the island is indeed the most important symbol of his world.

Negotiations and conferences seeking to give birth to the new federation were complicated and protracted, as well as fruitless.

In May 1962, a conference held in London recommended the establishment of the federation and considered the steps necessary to achieve this goal. The matter was next brought before the first of a series of meetings of a Regional Council of Ministers of the territories.

Grenada decided not to participate in these discussions. The Regional Council of Ministers in April of 1965 considered a plan for a seven-member federation (minus Grenada). But Antigua refused to participate in these discussions; and in August of 1965, Barbados, having noted Antigua's withdrawal from the planning, decided to move toward separate independence.

The British government officially abandoned the plan for an eastern federation in December 1965, simultaneously with its announcement of a new concept under which the six islands should each become an "Associated State of the United Kingdom."

Associated States of the United Kingdom

The British Colonial Office published on December 30, 1965, a White Paper (Cmnd. 2865) in which it was proposed that six British island territories in the eastern Caribbean should each become an "Associated State of the United Kingdom"—a new status under which each island would be wholly responsible for its own internal affairs, with Britain remaining responsible for defense and foreign relations. The islands considered for the new status were: Antigua; St. Kitts-Nevis-Anguilla; Dominica; St. Lucia; St. Vincent; and Grenada. Separate consideration was proposed for Montserrat, which has a population of only 13,000.

The White Paper proposals included the following items:

1. The Queen would remain the head of state of each associated state, and there would be a Queen's representative in each island. There would also be a British commissioner for the region to represent British interests.

2. Each associated state would be able to amend its own constitution (by a two-thirds majority in the legislature and in a referendum) and, in the same manner, to terminate unilaterally its association with Britain, either by proceeding to full independence or joining some other state.

3. The British government would have legislative powers to discharge its responsibilities for the defense and foreign relations of the associated states. The British Parliament would not, however, have any powers to legislate for the associated states without their consent.

4. Safeguards for the maintenance of human rights, etc. would be entrenched in the constitutions of the associated states. A Superior Court for the region would be established to uphold these safeguards.

5. There would be the customary provisions for ensuring the neutrality of the civil service, police, and judiciary in the associated states.

6. Citizenship would continue to be established by the British Nationality Act unless an associated state established separate citizenship.

At a conference held in London from April 18 to May 4, 1966, it was agreed that Dominica, Grenada, St. Lucia, and St. Vincent would each have the status of an associated state. Antigua had already agreed to accept the status. It was further agreed that Britain would retain general responsibility for their defense and foreign relations; that the islands would in all other respects be self-governing; and that their special relationship with Britain could be terminated either by the island territory concerned or by the British government. A common judicial service was agreed upon for the four Windward Islands; other than the judiciary, however, each unit would be separately administered and would have parallel ties with Britain.

A third conference, which ended on May 26, 1966, set up a similar arrangement for the three-island federation of St. Kitts-Nevis-Anguilla.

Antigua, Dominica, Grenada, St. Kitts-Nevis-Anguilla, and St. Lucia officially became associated states during February and March of 1967. Change of status for St. Vincent was held in abeyance during most of 1967 owing to a constitutional dispute arising out of contested elections held in 1966, but by the end of the year St. Vincent had joined the others as an associated state.

A minor flurry over status, with almost comic overtones, began in 1967 when thirty-five-square-mile Anguilla declared its secession from the St. Kitts-Nevis-Anguilla federation. Voters of Anguilla—1,839 of them—went to the polls on July 11 and cast their ballots on the issue of independence. When the ballots were counted on a ping-pong table in the police station, the vote stood at 1,813 for independence, 5 opposed, and 21 ballots ruled void. Actually the island's council of government had already withdrawn Anguilla from the three-island group headed by St. Kitts in May 1967; the vote of the people in July merely ratified this secession decision. Anguilla applied for association with Britain, the United States, and Canada. When none of these nations agreed to adopt the orphan, its newly elected president, Peter Adams, flew to New York to begin a fund-raising drive and to confer with the United Nations. The reason for the secession centered around the charge of "neglect" of the island's needs by the leader of the group, St. Kitts, whose premier, George Bradshaw, threatened to use force to end Anguilla's "state of rebellion." Efforts proceeded during 1967 to patch up this quarrel and reinstate Anguilla as a member of the St. Kitts-Nevis-Anguilla grouping.

On January 8, 1968, Mr. Anthony Lee, a British Commonwealth Office official, arrived on Anguilla to act as administrator for one year, during which it was hoped that some resolution of the dispute could be worked out. In October of 1968 talks were held in London among Prime

Minister Bradshaw of St. Kitts-Nevis-Anguilla, Mr. Ronald Webster, self-styled chief executive of Anguilla's secession government, and British officials. No settlement was reached. On December 11, 1968, Mr. Webster announced that Anguilla would become a republic on January 8, 1969.

This development touched off a dispute and a series of confrontations between the Anguilla people and the British government which kept the issue of Anguilla's eventual status in doubt throughout much of 1969.

On February 6, 1969, the voters of Anguilla, by 1,739 to 4, indicated their wish to establish a republic and to sever all links with the British crown. In Basseterre, capital of St. Kitts, a statement was issued on February 8 saying that "the Government of the State of St. Christopher-Nevis-Anguilla rejects and condemns [Anguilla's proclamation of a republic] as being illegal and of no force and effect, and declares . . . that Anguilla is and continues to be an integral part of this unitary state by virtue of the Constitution of St. Christopher-Nevis-Anguilla."*

In March Anguilla was visited by Mr. William Whitlock, parliamentary under-secretary, Foreign and Commonwealth Office. His arrival caused rioting and shooting, as a result of which Mr. Whitlock announced that Anguilla was in the hands of gangsters and armed hoodlums.

Shortly before dawn on March 19, 1969, Anguilla was occupied by a force of three hundred British paratroops, airlifted to the Caribbean from the United Kingdom. Mr. Anthony Lee was reappointed British commissioner for the island.

On March 20, Mr. Webster sent a letter to Lee demanding the immediate withdrawal of British troops and proposing that a referendum be held presenting the islanders with three alternatives: (1) independence; (2) direct association with Britain; or (3) a return to the three-island federation.

Webster then went to New York to confer with Lord Caradon, British representative to the United Nations, and on March 28 Lord Caradon arrived in Anguilla for negotiations with regard to the situation. On March 31 Webster and Lord Caradon signed an agreement which provided, among other things, that the administration of Anguilla should continue to be conducted by Her Majesty's representative in full consultation and cooperation with representatives of the people of Anguilla. The association with St. Kitts and Nevis was at an end.

British troops were largely withdrawn by the end of March, but continued unrest on the island forced Lee to vacate his post as British commissioner. He was succeeded by Mr. John Cumber, former administrator of the Cayman Islands.

---

*St. Christopher is the formal name for the island which is universally referred to by the more familiar St. Kitts.

PUERTO RICO

Like the French and Netherlands areas in the Caribbean, Puerto Rico underwent no formal change in status in the years after 1961. But totally unlike its French and Dutch neighbors, Puerto Rico indulged in a great deal of debate and introspection with regard to its status. Exhaustive hearings on the subject of Puerto Rico's status were held throughout much of 1965 by a special United States-Puerto Rico Status Commission, and on July 23, 1967, the issue of Puerto Rico's status was for the first time in the island's history put to the voters in a special referendum. And in November of 1968 the voters dismissed from office the Popular Democratic Party, architect of the commonwealth, and ushered into power the administration of Governor Luis Ferré, leader of the statehood faction in island politics.

Status Commission

In 1962, the tenth anniversary of Puerto Rico's commonwealth status, the idea was conceived of examining anew the status of Puerto Rico in relation to the United States and to explore the possibilities for the future evolution of that status. The result was the eventual creation of the United States-Puerto Rico Commission on the Status of Puerto Rico.

This Commission held extensive hearings in Puerto Rico in 1965, the transcripts of which fill three thick volumes: one on the legal-constitutional factors, another on social and cultural factors, and the third on economic factors in relation to the status of Puerto Rico.[13] The Commission's report to the President of the United States, to the governor of Puerto Rico, to the Congress of the United States, and to the Legislative Assembly of Puerto Rico was released on August 5, 1966.[14] It is worth quoting at this point the conclusions of the Commission's introduction to its report, inasmuch as this marked the beginning of a long period of political struggle over the status question.

Conclusions

Before presenting its conclusions and recommendations, the Commission wishes to record its satisfaction that the bonds which unite Puerto Rico and the United States have been reaffirmed in the course of the Commission's work.

Both Puerto Rico and the United States share a common commitment to individual freedom, to fundamental human rights, and to the traditions of democratic, representative government. Both are vitally interested in the economic growth and in the political development of the Caribbean area, within which Puerto Rico has provided a worthy example of progress and stability. Finally, both Puerto Rico and the United States have pledged their resources and their efforts to the success of the Alliance for Progress in its historic mission for hemispheric development.

These mutual interests of Puerto Rico and the United States are the product of a history of increased understanding out of which has grown a creative association. The foundation for both the mutual interests as well as the creative association has been the common U.S. citizenship. In 1952, 77 percent of the people of Puerto Rico voted for their two principal political parties that advocated, although in different forms, a permanent union between Puerto Rico and the United States based upon common U.S. citizenship; and this percentage has since increased steadily with each election, reaching 94 percent in 1964.

Throughout its deliberations the Commission has been particularly aware of the intimacy of the relationship between the United States and Puerto Rico and of the obligation which the association imposes for the consideration of the wishes of the people of Puerto Rico. In full appreciation of the importance of the maintenance of a mutually satisfactory relationship between Puerto Rico and the mainland, the Commission presents the following conclusions from its study of the factors bearing on the present and future relationship between the United States and Puerto Rico.

The Commission's major conclusion is that all three forms of political status—the Commonwealth, Statehood, and Independence—are valid and confer upon the people of Puerto Rico equal dignity with equality of status and of national citizenship. Any choice among them is to be made by the people of Puerto Rico, and the economic, social, cultural, and security arrangements which would need to be made under each of the three status alternatives will require the mutual agreement and full cooperation of the Government of the United States. A first step toward any change in political status must be taken by the Puerto Rican people acting through the constitutional processes.

From the examination of the legal and constitutional factors affecting the status question, the Commission concludes:

1. The policy governing the relationship between the United States and Puerto Rico is and should continue to be based on the principles of mutual consent and self-determination.

2. In accordance with this policy and these principles, it is essential to any change in political status that Congress fully understand the wishes of the people of Puerto Rico in order that it can be properly guided in working with the people of Puerto Rico to carry out their wishes.

3. The right of the U.S. citizens of Puerto Rico to participate effectively in decisions affecting their present and future welfare is protected by the Constitution of the United States and the Constitution of Puerto Rico.

4. All three status alternatives—the Commonwealth, Statehood, and Independence—are within the power of the people of Puerto Rico and the Congress to establish under the Constitution.

5. As a form of political status, each alternative confers equal dignity and equality of status.

From the examination of the sociocultural factors affecting the status question, the Commission concludes:

6. Each of the three status positions contains an ideological dimension: Each involves a concept of the identity of the people of Puerto Rico, an interpretation of history, a way of life, and an aspiration of the future.

7. Each of the status alternatives is committed to the growth of Puerto Rico's culture and the preservation of the Spanish language. Each alternative would require a different form of adjustment to fulfill its commitment.

8. Insofar as the questions of ideology and of culture and language are involved in arriving at a consensus regarding their future political status, it is the people of Puerto Rico themselves who must resolve these questions.

From the examination of the economic factors affecting the status question, the Commission concludes:

9. An examination of the economy of Puerto Rico with reference to political status involves the problem of comparing a pattern of growth under an existing set of institutional relationships which has resulted in impressive economic development, with patterns of economic growth under alternative institutional arrangements proposed by the advocates of statehood and independence.

10. Despite the substantial rates of economic growth of the past two decades, the continued economic growth and development of Puerto Rico is imperative. Puerto Rico's average per capita income is still 40 percent below that of the lowest income State of the Union. Furthermore, only through continued, rapid growth will it be possible to resolve such problems as the persistent high rate of unemployment, the uneven development of the island, inadequate transportation and communications, and the continuing need for further development of education and other basic public services.

11. An immediate or abrupt change in political status would involve serious economic risks and dislocations. These could be offset by special economic and financial arrangements which, in the case of Statehood, would clearly involve financial assistance well beyond the levels Puerto Rico is today receiving. In the case of Independence the costs of an abrupt change could be much greater. To allow for the adjustments required by a change to either Statehood or Independence, a carefully designed plan of transition would be necessary.

12. As far as economic standards alone are concerned, estimates regarding the time intervals required for transitions depend upon projections utilizing such criteria as growth rates of per capita income, comparative wage rates with the mainland, rate of unemployment, levels of investment in the public and private sectors, and growth rates under each of the status alternatives. For Independence there are such additional criteria as alternative sources for financing capital investment and the development of new export markets.

Professional economists differ as to when these projected criteria may be fulfilled. Professional estimates begin at a minimum of 15 years to a much longer period for Statehood; and even longer for Independence* unless there is more rapid

---

*The economist representing the Independence Party estimated at an economic presentation on Feb. 8-9, 1966, that the necessary economic adjustments might be effected within a period of 10 years after the granting of independence, but also estimated that a period of as long as 20 years might be required to insure an adequate margin of safety.

economic development and integration of this hemisphere than can now be reasonably expected. However, the speed of Puerto Rico's economic growth is such that any current estimates might be better by actual experience.

13. As Puerto Rico continues to develop, a time will come when the economic structure can more readily absorb the impact of a change to Statehood or Independence. It is therefore in the interest of proponents of such change to maximize Puerto Rico's economic growth, for as further growth is achieved the people of Puerto Rico will be able to weigh more realistically the economic costs and advantages of each of the status alternatives.

From the examination of all the foregoing factors affecting the status question, the Commission further concludes:

14. An expression of the will of the citizens of Puerto Rico by popular vote on the question of whether they wish to continue Commonwealth status capable of growth and development, or to change to either statehood or independence would be helpful to all concerned. The Commission recognizes, however, that it is for the people of Puerto Rico to decide whether, when, and in what manner they wish to express their preference. Such an expression should precede any change in status.

In this regard, the Commission wishes to note Puerto Rico Law No. 95, passed June 21, 1960, which permits the people of Puerto Rico to express a status preference. This law provides that 10 percent of the qualified electorate can bring about a plebiscite on the status issues without further legislation or executive action. Under this or any other law of similar intent that the Legislature of Puerto Rico is empowered to enact, the wishes of the people of Puerto Rico may be expressed.

Plebiscite

Late in December of 1966 the Legislature of Puerto Rico, on the petition of 10 percent of the registered voters, called for a plebiscite on the status question to be held on Sunday, July 23, 1967.

The ballot presented to the people of Puerto Rico offered three choices, represented by three symbols familiar to all Puerto Ricans: the Mountain for commonwealth (Estado Libre Associado); the Palm Tree for statehood; and the Wheel for independence.

The following is an English translation of the ballot as given to its readers by the *San Juan Star* on July 21, 1967:

The Ballot and What It Means

At the top of the ballot are written the words: Plebiscite on the political status of Puerto Rico. Held the 23rd of July of 1967.

Above the mountain symbol are the words: I vote in favor of commonwealth.

Above the palm tree symbol: I vote in favor of statehood.

Above the wheel symbol: I vote in favor of independence.

Underneath the three symbols there is a text explaining what the three votes mean. That text says:

A vote in favor of commonwealth will mean:

1—Reaffirmation of the Commonwealth established through mutual agreement under the terms of Law 600 of 1950 and of Joint Resolution 447 of 1952 of the United States Congress as an autonomous community permanently associated with the United States of America.

2—The inviolability of common citizenship as primary and indispensable basis of the permanent union between Puerto Rico and the United States;

3—The authorization to develop commonwealth in accordance with its fundamental principles up to the maximum of self-government compatible with common defense, common market, common currency and the indisoluble bond of United States citizenship;

4—That no change in the relations between the United States and Puerto Rico will have effect unless it has previously received the acceptance of the majority of votes cast in a referendum specifically called for that purpose.

A vote in favor of statehood will mean:

Authorization to request from the United States Congress the admission of Puerto Rico into the American union as a federated state.

A vote in favor of independence will mean:

Authorization to demand from Congress Puerto Rico's independence from the United States of America.

Another statement at the bottom of the ballot explains what is needed to win. It says:

A majority vote in favor of any of the status formulas constitutes a mandate of the people of Puerto Rico to the Resident Commissioner, as its representative in the federal sphere, to act within the scope of his official functions in accordance with the will of the people expressed through said vote.

There was general understanding that, whichever way the balloting went, nothing would really be altered with regard to Puerto Rico's status unless or until the U.S. Congress should act. It was noted, for example, that Hawaii had petitioned Congress no fewer than twenty-three times for statehood before it was admitted to the Union, and that the vote in favor of statehood in Hawaii often exceeded 80 percent. Nevertheless a lively campaign was waged throughout the commonwealth, complete with posters, banners, speeches, sound trucks, rallies, and all the usual paraphernalia of a political contest.

Although there were only three choices on the ballot, four major positions developed with regard to the plebiscite.

Pro-commonwealth forces were led by the venerable Don Luis Muñoz Marín, a senator following his retirement as governor.*

---

*The Commonwealth's governor, Roberto Sanchez Villella, member of the ruling Popular Democratic Party, had to stay out of sight during the campaign. His reputation with the people had suffered because of a divorce scandal earlier in the year.

The pro-statehood faction, for this plebiscite, was led by the well-known Ponce industrialist, Luis A. Ferré, who in 1968 was to be elected governor. The Statehood Republican Party officially boycotted the plebiscite; Ferré's action in campaigning therefore represented a split in the ranks.

The independence campaign for this contest, the smallest and poorest of the three factions, was headed by University of Puerto Rico professor Hector Alvarez Silva.

In addition there was an antiplebiscite movement made up of defecting factions from all three of the major positions, each of which for its own reasons wished to persuade the voters to boycott the election. There was, first of all, the traditional statehood Republican Party, led by Miguel A. Garcia Mendez. This group maintained that for American citizens the only conceivable political goal is statehood; therefore a ballot which purports to offer alternative choices is a fraud. Only to a plebiscite on which the issue was "Statehood, yes or no" would they go. Then there were the various independence factions, ranging from moderate to radical, who maintained that political freedom is the natural right of all peoples and is not subject to manipulation by a vote. Finally in the antiplebiscite camp were the so-called "Sovereigntist" who debated the question whether the electorate was sovereign and hence able to choose a political status for Puerto Rico.

All of the parties and factions were guilty of making emotion-charged statements, and none was above quoting material out of context from the Status Commission report. Boiled down to their basic essentials these were the main arguments:[15]

In favor of continuing the commonwealth: the close association with the United States has allowed Puerto Rico to make rapid economic and social progress while maintaining her personality as an autonomous, essentially Latin society. While it gets grants of federal aid the commonwealth is exempt from federal taxes. This, plus relatively low wage scales and the lack of tariffs on exports to the mainland, has encouraged the intense and rapid industrialization of the island. Thus, since Puerto Rico elects its own governor and its own legislature, makes its own laws and runs its own affairs, save for the bother of foreign relations and defense, it really has the best of two worlds. The federal taxation which would come with statehood would be a crushing burden to the island in its present stage of development.

In favor of statehood: Puerto Rico is in an inferior position with relation to the fifty states. Puerto Ricans may be American citizens but they are second class ones. They cannot vote for the President and they have no voting representation in Congress, whose legislation nonetheless applies to Puerto Rico. As a state Puerto Rico would qualify for even greater federal aid. Its representatives in Congress could vote and express the will of the Puerto Rican people with regard to such matters as the Vietnam war, of which most Puerto Ricans disapprove but for which its young men are drafted. Taxation would not be a great burden. Special arrangements could be made for Puerto Rico until it reached the level of the other states. Besides, eight out of ten Puerto Ricans would pay no federal taxes anyway under current schedules.

In favor of independence: Puerto Rico as it exists now is merely an outpost of American colonialism. It is embarrassing that Puerto Rico is one of the last of the dependent areas of the world. Like other small countries Puerto Rico has a right to complete freedom. This is the only dignified goal for a proud people. An independent Puerto Rico could still remain closely associated with the United States, and the United States could be expected to continue favoring Puerto Rico with generous aid, as it has done with the Philippine Republic, which received its independence in 1946. There may have to be economic sacrifices in gaining independence, but this would be a small price to pay for freedom. In any case the economic ties with the United States should be cut now, before the island's economy becomes any more closely integrated with the mainland's. Finally, independence is the only hope if we wish to retain our language and culture intact.

As was widely anticipated the vote was rather heavily in favor of continuance of the commonwealth. The result of the plebiscite was as follows:

Commonwealth:	425,081 votes (60.5 percent)
Statehood:	273,315 votes (38.9)
Independence:	4,205 votes (0.6)

However, 34.2 percent of the island's registered voters failed to turn out, thus allowing all of the antiplebiscite factions to claim victory.*

*By the exercise of what some Puerto Ricans call "Peronista arithmetic," this is how the boycotters claimed victory. The following is an article from the *San Juan Star* of July 26, 1967:

'Don't Vote' Group Claims It Succeeded

The Sovereigntist Antiplebiscite Concentration yesterday said that 59 per cent of the island's voting population rejected both commonwealth and statehood by not voting in Sunday's plebiscite.

Claiming a "resounding victory," the sovereigntists pointed out that only 66 per cent of 1,067,000 registered went to the polls.

"If it is taken into account that over 50,000 foreigners were allowed to vote and that the machinery of the colonialist government, with its economic resources, exerted all pressures which colonialism usually exerts to perpetuate itself, it is evident that the forces of patriotism and Puerto Ricanship obtained a resounding victory," the organization said in a written statement.

"The victory, however, is bigger than those figures," it added.

The total of Puerto Ricans of voting age, the statement said, are not the 1,067,000 registered but 1.7 million, "according to the latest official census from the U.S."

Postplebiscite Politics

Following the plebiscite, former Governor Muñoz Marín is reported to have said, "This settles the status question." He was very wrong; the plebiscite settled nothing. Puerto Ricans have delighted in arguing over their status since Spanish days. It is the theme that has overshadowed all other issues in Puerto Rican political life since the turn of the century.

Considering the percentage of nonvoters, as well as the number of those who cast their ballots, there was something in the plebiscite results for everybody. The statehood advocates looked upon the nearly 39 percent in favor of that option as virtually the start of a bandwagon.

Puerto Rico's general election coincided with that of the United States, in November of 1968. Denied renomination by the Popular Democratic Party, Governor Roberto Sanchez Villella ran as an independent. The official nominee of the majority party was Luis Negron Lopez; Muñoz Marín campaigned for him vigorously.

Heartened by the size of the statehood group in the plebiscite, Luis Ferré decided to run for governor in 1968. He made a campaign pledge, however, that he would not consider his election a mandate to seek statehood. To divorce himself once and for all from the old statehood party, Ferré formed his New Progressive Party (Partido Nuevo Progresista) as a vehicle for the campaign.

Ferré's election victory, with less than 45 percent of the vote over a badly divided opposition, was indeed hardly a mandate to seek rapid change of the island's political status.* However, Governor Ferré remains convinced that statehood should be the ultimate objective for Puerto Rico, and he quietly passed the word in his new administration that the groundwork was to be laid for nudging Puerto Rico in the direction of eventually joining the Union. As will be seen in chapter 15, this change of policy had rather ominous consequences for Puerto Rico's leadership role in Caribbean integration.

IN RETROSPECT

What we now call the West Indies was actually the very first non-European region of the world to be colonized by Western Europe, begin-

---

This means, according to the group, that 75 per cent of the "genuine" electoral forces rejected commonwealth and that "annexationism" only obtained 16 per cent of that force.

"Therefore, there is a contingent of 59 per cent of persons of voting age who repudiate the colony and annexation," the statement said.

"This is the true Puerto Rico: that which rejects all forms of political inferiority and rejects assimilation because it does not want to cease existing. It is the sovereigntist Puerto Rico."

*New Progressive Party (Ferré), 390,964 votes: 44.3 percent; Popular Democratic Party (Negron Lopez), 367,355 votes; People's Party (Governor Sanchez), 87,800 votes.

ning as early as the voyages of Columbus in the fifteenth century. European colonization of Asia and Africa came much later, yet nearly all of those formerly dependent areas have long since emerged into independence. Only in the Caribbean do we find these scattered bits and pieces of once proud empires—a holdover, it seems, from a bygone era. The West Indies has been one of the last areas of the world to be transformed by the modern tides of nationalism and political emancipation. Yet those powerful forces are at work, even on these small and remote islands and territories, as this chapter and chapter 8 have demonstrated. They have contributed not only to the transformation of the West Indies but also to the changing patterns of international structures which it is the purpose of this book to describe.

13 □ THE END OF ANOTHER ERA: TERMINATION OF THE CARIBBEAN ORGANIZATION

"The Caribbean Organization broke down mainly because it was a formal structure paralyzed by protocol that sprang from a bewildering array of governmental forms." By contrast the new CODECA would be "a form of organization designed to find ways to slip around the problems of sovereignty, protocol, and diplomatic snags." In this succinct fashion did Andrew Viglucci, managing editor of the *San Juan Star*, explain to his readers in Puerto Rico the demise of the Caribbean Organization after a little more than three and a half years of service to the West Indies.[1]

At the fifth and last meeting of the Caribbean Council, held in Curacao from November 30 to December 4, 1964, the Caribbean Organization finally foundered on the twin rocks of the ever-growing formal autonomy of many of the territories in the region, side by side with the stubbornly persisting economic and even political dependency of most of them on the metropolitan powers.

The shift of pattern in 1961 from Caribbean Commission to Caribbean Organization was a logical and creative adaptation to the political evolution which had occurred in the region since 1946. It reflected the natural desire on the part of the Caribbean territories to take in hand their own regional organization. The Caribbean Commission, made up of the four metropolitan powers, was a nagging, even humiliating, reminder to the Caribbean territories of their long colonial status which they believed they were so eagerly shaking off.

But the metropolitan powers had *not* vanished from the West Indies scene in 1961, nor had they yet been removed by 1964. No exchange of one charter instrument for another altered the basic facts of life in the region. Puerto Rico, the Netherlands Antilles and Surinam, and especially the French territories, remained firmly and formally linked politically with the United States, Holland, and France, respectively. Jamaica and Trinidad had moved on to independence within the Commonwealth but still of necessity looked to Great Britain, to the United States, to Canada, and to the international organization community for aid, trade, and other assistance. The other islands of the former Federation were moving toward a quasi-independence, or administrative autonomy, but their small size and their poverty would necessitate their continued heavy dependence upon the mother country and the outside world generally.

Thus in 1964 there was still no *effective* control over their own destinies by the territories in the West Indies. An *international* organization in the Caribbean had proven to be a misnomer, despite the words of the Statute and the formal structure of the Caribbean Council, for there were in truth no real *nations* in the area. The Caribbean Council could still in the final analysis do little more than seek to bring to bear on the problems of the West Indies the decision-making power and the resources of the metropolitan governments and their agencies. The Caribbean Organization, like its predecessor, could recommend, propose, coordinate, study, publish, and administer. But it never did dispose of sufficient resources, generated from within its own membership, to attack with vigor the basic problems of the Caribbean. Nothing much had changed since 1961.

Errol Barrow, the prime minister of Barbados, attending the first session of CODECA in Puerto Rico in July of 1965, was quoted in the press as having said of CODECA that "at least it was started by a Caribbean country and not by one of the metropolitan countries," as was the case with the old Caribbean Organization. Barrow also said that with CODECA "you don't break up the organization if you can't agree on something." This is another advantage the new outfit would have over the old Caribbean Organization, he said.[2]

Thus from November of 1964 to July of 1965, the Caribbean was witness to still another stage in the evolution of regional structures, another shift of level in the remarkable and persistent desire of the region to find a formula for truly effective cooperation in meeting the needs of the Caribbean.

First, however, the breakup and dissolution of the Caribbean Organization must be examined, so that the lessons for the future contained in that story may be recorded.

Background Causes

The Caribbean Organization was beset almost from the beginning with constitutional, procedural, budgetary, and even political problems with which it was powerless to cope.

In the first place, the breakup of the West Indies Federation in 1962 deprived the Organization of its largest charter member. By normal logic, of course, the way for the Organization to respond to the dissolution of the Federation would have been simply to admit as separate members the ten individual units which had made up the Federation. This solution, however, never proved possible, and the British islands which had made up the Federation were never again fully a part of the activities of the Caribbean Organization.

Jamaica and Trinidad joined the United Nations and looked forward also to the possibility of joining the Organization of American States. For these two new nations, then, having to pay to the U.N. and receiving benefits from its complex of activities, it no longer seemed necessary or important to participate in the Caribbean regional organization. Jamaica addressed to the third meeting of the Council a request for information about membership, but no further steps toward membership were ever taken. As for Trinidad, its negative attitude toward the Organization might be anticipated so long as Eric Williams remained its head of government.

As for the "Little Eight" of the former Federation, the British Windward and Leeward Islands plus Barbados, they would indeed have benefited from full membership in the Caribbean Organization, and they were in fact eager to rejoin the Organization. This simple question of membership, however, clearly revealed to the Organization what its Caribbean sponsors, in their euphoria at taking over their regional organization, had forgotten or overlooked. This was simply that the agreement authorizing the Caribbean territories to set up the Caribbean Organization was itself a four-power document entered into by Great Britain, France, the United States, and the Netherlands in 1960. Thus it could be altered only by those same metropolitan powers. In this agreement the signatory powers had unfortunately specified "The West Indies" as one of the countries eligible to become a member of the Organization. With the disappearance of "The West Indies" from the political map, what was clearly needed was a simple revision of the four-power agreement to permit an altered roster of membership in the Caribbean Organization. This was never accomplished, however, and all that the Caribbean Council could do in its second, third, and fourth sessions was adopt resolutions pleading with the metropolitan powers to amend the basic agreement.

At the third meeting, for example, the Council noted that at its second meeting it had adopted a resolution: (i) requesting the governments signatory to the agreement to take the necessary steps to enable territories formerly embraced within the Federation of the West Indies to join the Organization; (ii) expressing the hope that those territories would join the Organization as soon as possible; (iii) authorizing the secretary general to regard these territories as countries *served* by the Organization until December 31, 1962.[3]

Records of the third meeting indicate that the secretary general advised the Council that this resolution of the second meeting had been forwarded to the governments concerned on April 6, 1962, and that he had subsequently invited each of these governments to send a representative to the third meeting of the Council.[4]

The realization dawned in Puerto Rico and elsewhere in the area that the Caribbean countries had not come as far as they had hoped in the direction of regional autonomy.

Contributing greatly to the dissatisfaction with the Caribbean Organization structure was the fact that France, a metropolitan power, retained full membership in the Organization and on the Council because of the unusual constitutional status of its territories as departments of France. It is true that in practice the French delegation to the Council meetings consisted of leaders from Martinique, Guadeloupe, and French Guiana, but close behind them at the table sat officials from the ministries in Paris, in adviser status. It became quite apparent to the other delegations that the men from Paris were controlling the French position in the Caribbean Organization.

It was at best an awkward situation to have one of the metropolitan powers present at Council meetings made up otherwise of local delegations. At the very least it tended to inhibit free discussion of local Caribbean affairs because any such discussion often tended to be critical of the metropolitan powers and their administration of the affairs of the West Indies. But to the Republic of France was attributed more than just an awkward and embarrassing presence in the Organization.

It will be recalled that in the original arrangements for membership and voting in the Caribbean Organization, it was provided that each member should have one delegate and one vote at Council meetings, except for France, which should have one "delegation" and three votes, in recognition of the participation in the Organization by Guadeloupe, Martinique, and French Guiana. Thus, prior to the disappearance of the West Indies Federation, France had held three out of ten votes in the Council, and after the loss of the Federation France held three votes out of nine. Since substantive matters had to be decided in the Council by a two-thirds majority, France, with three votes, held very close to a veto over decisions by the Council. If, however, as many as eight of the ten units which made up the Federation had been admitted to the Organization, each as a separate member with a vote, this would have increased the voting strength of the Council to seventeen, of which France would have continued to hold only three. The French stated flatly that this would have created an unbalanced situation, and in the final analysis France never agreed to revision of the four-power agreement. In all fairness to France, however, it should be noted that there was perhaps some logical reason for delay in accommodating the British islands in the Organization, since among the possibilities being discussed for their political future was that of an Eastern Caribbean Federation. Such a unit would in fact have been a much more logical candidate for membership in the Caribbean Organization than the separate tiny islands.

The French also tended to sound a negative note at Council meetings and at budgetary conferences, urging always a limited and restricted role for the Caribbean Organization with corresponding reductions in expenditures.[5] Since in budgetary proceedings a unanimous vote was required for any changes in the budget, France's view with regard to the scope of the Organization was a controlling voice.

It was widely alleged in the Caribbean that France never really accepted the idea that her Caribbean dependencies might wish to participate actively in a purely regional association, or that they might benefit from so doing. In fact the situation that developed with France in the Caribbean Council seemed to parallel, though on a much smaller scale, the similar difficulties being encountered with France in the European Common Market over matters having to do with the nature of the association and the voting strength of its members. Thus even in the remote and relatively minor affairs of the West Indies, General de Gaulle's concept of French primacy had to be upheld.

Difficulties with France also served to remind participants in the Caribbean Organization that they were not entirely free of the other metropolitan powers either. In the Statute of the Organization it was provided that the signatory parties to the agreement were entitled to send to all meetings held under the auspices of the Organization observers with the right to speak but not to vote. Thus every session of the Council was attended by "observers" from the United States, Great Britain, and the Netherlands, in addition of course to the "delegation" from France. All of the nagging criticisms which had plagued the Caribbean Commission throughout its lifetime, asserting that it was really nothing but the compliant tool of the colonial powers, were hurled once again at the Caribbean Organization. Newspapers of the region blossomed with "I told you so!" editorials.

By its third anniversary in September of 1964, the Caribbean Organization could list as its members the following:

France, for the Departments of Guadeloupe, Martinique, and French Guiana
Surinam
Netherlands Antilles
British Guiana
British Virgin Islands
Puerto Rico
Virgin Islands of the United States

The following other territories enjoyed special observer status which entitled them to receive the same services as members except that they did not have a vote on the Caribbean Council (and paid no dues to the Organization):

Antigua
Barbados
Dominica
Grenada
Montserrat
St. Kitts-Nevis-Anguilla
St. Lucia
St. Vincent

British Honduras and the Bahamas were noted as "prospective members" who might join the Organization whenever they wished.

Clearly the whole structure was disjointed and truncated. The Organization was attempting to serve an area far broader than its membership and financial support warranted. Consequently it was never able to realize its full potential for benefiting the area. Worthy as its accomplishments were, there was always the feeling of what might have been—with a larger membership and more adequate resources.

The budget of the Organization for 1964[6] is quite revealing:

France	18.558139%	$ 70,806.54
Netherlands Antilles	8.989099	34,396.92
Surinam	7.249274	27,658.81
British Guiana	4.316529	16,469.24
British Virgin Islands	0.250000	953.85
Puerto Rico	51.387252	196,062.40
Virgin Islands of the U.S.	9.249707	35,191.24
		$381,539.00

Nearly all of these funds had to be spent in paying the salaries of the Secretariat staff and covering the rental of the office in San Juan. Whatever good works and worthwhile projects were to be sponsored by the Organization thus had to be undertaken with funds provided by one of the large international organizations, by the U.S. government, or by private foundations. Clearly some more adequate organizational arrangements were needed.

Professor Thomas G. Mathews, director of the Institute of Caribbean Studies of the University of Puerto Rico, added an interesting final comment on the failure of the Caribbean Organization.[7] Perhaps, he said, the Caribbean Organization never really got off the ground because it tried so hard *not* to be political—this is an era when the politics of nationalism and anticolonialism were in the air, not only in the West Indies but throughout the underdeveloped world. In concentrating on social and economic good works the Caribbean Organization appeared to be just an extension of colonial policies. Not, he added, that what the Organization was doing did not need doing, not that its activities were not highly worthwhile. But the sentiment in the area during those years was quite a bit reminiscent of Kwame Nkrumah's often quoted: "Seek ye first the *political* kingdom."

The United Nations and its associated agencies do many good works in the social and economic and cultural realms, Professor Mathews pointed out, but still the U.N. is chiefly noted and publicized for being a political sounding board and a center for diplomacy. If only the Caribbean Organization had had some sort of general assembly where delegates could gather periodically and sound off, passing resolutions denouncing the shortcomings of the metropolitan powers, for example, then probably all of the territories in the region would have stood in line to join the Organization, including Trinidad. At the same time, however, the Secretariat of the Organization could quietly have gone on with its social and economic good works.

The Formal End of the Caribbean Organization

On December 23, 1963, the Secretariat of the Caribbean Organization received official notification from the governor of British Guiana that as of December 31, 1964, British Guiana would cease to be a member of the Organization. By letter received in the Secretariat on April 17, 1964, the minister-president of Surinam notified the secretary general that Surinam would withdraw from the Caribbean Organization effective April 17, 1965.[8]

The fifth meeting of the Caribbean Council was scheduled to meet in Curacao from November 30 to December 4, 1964. Just a week before the meeting was to convene the Secretariat received one additional message, from the government of Puerto Rico, which meant the death of the Caribbean Organization.

By letter dated November 18, 1964, and delivered by special messenger on November 23, 1964, the governor of the Commonwealth of Puerto Rico notified the secretary general that Puerto Rico elected to cease to be a member of the Caribbean Organization with effect on December 31, 1965.[9] Since Puerto Rico was by then contributing 51 percent of the Organization's budget, the withdrawal of Puerto Rico clearly signalled the termination of the Organization.

The fifth meeting of the Council took place as scheduled, in Curacao, Netherlands Antilles, from November 30 to December 4, 1964, but it necessarily confined itself to final reports and to the making of administrative and procedural arrangements for the disbanding of the Organization. Ironically, the fifth meeting had before it a cablegram from the under-secretary for foreign affairs of the Dominican Republic inquiring about membership in the Caribbean Organization for his country.[10]

The fifth meeting was opened by Dr. N. Debrot, governor of the Netherlands Antilles and host for the meeting. Dr. Debrot outlined the course of international cooperation in the Caribbean and concluded:

One cannot easily give a categorical answer to the question whether in the Caribbean Organization that succeeded the Anglo-American Commission and the Caribbean Commission a definite means for cooperation has been found. It is after all, not difficult to meet the demands for constitutional and cultural desiderata with statutory provisions. The statutory provisions contain nothing more than a fiat for what had already been changed and approved, while the cultural provisions mean nothing more than a card of admittance to a new field of activities without any concrete commitment beforehand. The difficulty arises however in the case where a realistic approach is wanted. Reality changes from one day to another and therefore it also demands an approach by people with the necessary tact and experience to follow these changes. Whether an approach is realistic or not can only be determined by the practice of daily life.[11]

Addressing the Council next, C. W. J. Jonckheer, chairman for the fifth meeting, observed that it was incredible that more than two years after the dissolution of the Federation of the West Indies, steps had not been taken to permit the units of that Federation to join the Organization, even though eight of them had applied for membership. After pointing out that three of the member governments had decided to withdraw from the Organization, Mr. Jonckheer emphasized the point made by Dr. Debrot that it was open to debate whether the Caribbean Organization constituted the definitive form for regional cooperation. However, he called for good will, patience, and foresight in order to demonstrate that the peoples of the Caribbean had the necessary maturity to follow the compelling trend of the time—regional cooperation. It was urgent, even imperative, that a new path be found for cooperation among all those who shared such ideals. To fail to do so, he stated, would be a disservice to the Caribbean area. Mr. Jonckheer referred especially to the work being done by the Clearing House on Trade and Tourism Information, the survey of the fruit and vegetable trade of the area, the efforts made to arrange for a better communications system for the area, the steps taken to encourage and improve the standard of economic planning, the successful agricultural tours which had been arranged, and the valuable fellowship program which had been in operation for two years with the financial assistance of the United States Agency for International Development.

The Council then reluctantly decided that since three members (British Guiana, Surinam, and Puerto Rico) had given notice of withdrawal from the Organization, the continuation of the work of the Caribbean Organization was no longer possible.

The reason given by the government of British Guiana for its decision to withdraw was that benefits of membership were insufficient to warrant continued participation. This was due in part to the restricted membership of the Organization which inhibited the wide regional planning and economic assistance required for the country's urgent needs.

In his speech the delegate of Surinam stated that the reasons which led his government to give notice of withdrawal in no way reflected upon the good and important work done by the Organization in the past. Surinam could, however, no longer participate in an organization which had become too small, and it considered that a broader regional cooperation should be attained.

Stating that within the limited scope of its functions the Caribbean

Organization had been a success, the delegate for the Commonwealth of Puerto Rico recalled that all endeavors to expand membership so that a wider span of Caribbean peoples could be included in the Organization had not met with the necessary measure of success. Membership in the Organization had needlessly hampered the cultural and technical exchange programs of the commonwealth, which felt it could do more if it undertook these programs outside the limited scope of the Organization.

Taking into consideration the implications of the decision of the three members of the Organization to withdraw and the financial consequences thereof, the Council unanimously adopted a resolution under which it: (1) decided that the operations of the central secretariat would be terminated not later than December 31, 1965; (2) requested that the parties signatory to the agreement establishing the Caribbean Organization take such steps as would be necessary to terminate the agreement on December 31, 1965, or as soon thereafter as possible; (3) recommended that a working group comprised of all members, including the withdrawing members, the special observers, and all other interested democratic countries in the area, convene at the earliest possible date to develop a formula or a series of formulas to provide for regional cooperation in the social, educational, and cultural fields; and (4) recommended that before April 15, 1965, a meeting of these governments be convened at the highest possible level to decide the form and nature of future regional cooperation.

The representative of Puerto Rico then declared that his government would be prepared to convene the working group and the meeting of high-level government representatives in Puerto Rico at dates to be announced later. The Council recorded its intention that the secretary general should terminate the appointments of staff, cease the operations of the secretariat, and dispose of the Organization's assets at such date as he should decide. Consistent with the orderly termination of the operations of the Organization, the date for final closing should be around the middle of 1965.

The Council had before it a number of matters relating to regional cooperation, but discussion of these matters took place under the shadow of the decision to dissolve the Organization. The Council considered the annual report of the Caribbean Plan. The purpose of the review was to afford governments an opportunity to harmonize their development planning and to identify opportunities for cooperation among governments through regional projects. With regard to private financing of development projects, the Council noted that investment capital was available and could be used to finance development projects in the Caribbean if adequate means were taken to channel it. However, adequate facilities did not yet exist in many of the Caribbean countries to identify investment opportunities and to establish complete and detailed projects. The Council agreed that a private investment company would be of great value in this respect.

The Council received the report of C. N. de Boer on the promotion of intra-Caribbean trade in fruits and vegetables. Dr. de Boer had conducted a market survey and analyzed the fruit and vegetable situation in the Caribbean countries. He concluded that most of the countries of the Caribbean were deficit areas with regard to supplies of fruits and vegetables. This, he stated, was due largely to the traditional concentration of agricultural activities on one or a few export crops and the reluctance of farmers to engage in an enterprise for which marketing might prove difficult and risky. Accordingly, expansion of trade in fruits and vegetables was primarily dependent on increasing production. Some coordinated planning was essential, Dr. de Boer felt, in order to avoid too many countries having exportable surpluses at the same time. He warned that self-sufficiency was not necessarily the wisest policy. Specialization by each country in the type of production for which it was best suited would be the best course, he stated.

Discussing factors hampering intra-Caribbean trade, Dr. de Boer emphasized the need for all countries to seek as wide a spread of trade outlets as possible rather than to depend on one or a few traditional markets. In addition, he stated, lack of trader initiative was one of the basic deficiencies affecting the expansion of intra-Caribbean exchange. Traders and businessmen tended to be satisfied with existing and well-known channels of trade and were too easily convinced that difficulties of communications and transport were insuperable. Finally, Dr. de Boer emphasized that a strong focal point was indispensable to any efforts to develop economic cooperation. In this connection he stressed the important role which the Caribbean Organization could play and should be suitably equipped to play in the development of intra-Caribbean trade.

With regard to expansion and harmonization of the tourist industry, the secretary general reported on the discussions initiated concerning the introduction of a "limited time, unlimited use" ticket for visitors to the area. He also noted that he had intended to seek the Council's approval for authority to proceed with a detailed study of package tours and expansion of hotel and tourist investment facilities. The Council approved the recommendation for the establishment of a Caribbean nutrition center and instructed the secretary general to forward it to the Food and Agriculture Organization, the World Health Organization, and the United Nations Children's Fund with the request that they give favorable consideration to the establishment of the center.

Regarding the activities of the central Secretariat, the Council decided that all work on long-term projects should cease immediately. Where projects were in an advanced stage and could be completed in a relatively short time, the Council agreed that every effort should be made by the secretary general to complete them or to arrange for them to be taken over by member governments or by other organizations or agencies in the area.

The Council agreed, however, that further action should be taken on the Clearing House on Trade and Tourism Information and that arrangements should be made to leave the files and documentation in a state which would enable the service to be continued by any association which might be formed in the future.

Noting the advanced stage of the discussions and negotiations on a private investment company, the Council was of the opinion that the group in Puerto Rico formed to advise the secretary general on the study of this project would be in a position to take all further action leading to the establishment of the company. Since the distribution of the new grasses selected in South Africa by the United States Department of Agriculture was an extremely important project for the livestock industry in the Caribbean, the Council agreed that the secretary general should make every effort to arrange for the distribution to be carried on by some other agency.

Realizing that in the process of liquidating the Organization the secretary general might need instructions and decisions, the Council appointed a Liquidation Committee composed of representatives of the member states. The Committee was empowered to act in all respects on the Councils's behalf in accordance with the decisions made at the fifth Council meeting and the principles agreed upon for the closing of the Secretariat.

Final Report

The secretary general's final report to the member governments adds the final details to the story of twenty-three years of formal international organization in the West Indies.[12]

By March 19, 1965, the secretary general had received from the United States Department of State confirmation that the four parties to the agreement for the establishment of the Caribbean Organization (the four metropolitan powers) had withdrawn from the agreement effective December 31, 1965.

As agreed by the Council at its fifth meeting, all activities of the Secretariat in 1965 were directed toward the orderly winding up of the Organization, and work on projects of a long-term nature was ceased immediately after that meeting. As regards those projects which were in an advanced stage and which could be completed in a relatively short time, every effort was made to complete them or to arrange for them to be taken over either by member governments or by other organizations or agencies in the area. The technical divisions functioned until the end of February, and the other services of the Secretariat were closed down progressively so that by June only a small administrative staff remained to attend to the final details of the liquidation process.

The final issues of *The Caribbean* (newsletter) and the quarterly

Caribbean Agriculture were dated in December 1964 and distributed early in 1965. Donations from private banana interests, supplemented by funds from the Organization's own limited 1965 budget, permitted the publication of five hundred copies in English of the papers of the Banana Demonstration Tour of 1964.

Perhaps the two most important issues to be resolved in the termination of the Organization were what was to become of the Caribbean Organization Fellowship Program and what was to be the fate of the Organization's library.

It will be recalled that the Caribbean Organization Fellowship Program began in 1963 with a grant of $100,000 from the United States Agency for International Development. In the second year of operation a further grant of $200,000 was received from AID. At the end of 1964 some eighty students were enrolled under the program at universities in the Caribbean and in the United States. Following discussions with AID in April of 1965 an agreement was reached under which AID would make a final grant of $250,000 to complete the program by assuring that the students then studying could complete their university work. It was agreed that no new fellowships would be awarded under this final grant and that the Caribbean Organization would work out the necessary arrangements with the universities concerned for administering the fellowships.

With regard to the library, the Council had decided at its fifth meeting that:

1. The Library should be maintained as a unit.
2. It should be retained in the area for the benefit of the whole area, this service to include the loan of books by mail as well as research on request.
3. The collection should continue to be developed and expanded along the present lines of specialization in Caribbean affairs, so that it might continue to be a source of reference for students and research workers studying conditions in the Caribbean area.

In addition, it would be the responsibility of whoever was awarded custody of the library to arrange for its removal by the middle of June and to bear whatever packing and transportation costs might be involved.

Requests for the library were received from two member governments of the Organization, an international agency, and four universities:

Commonwealth of Puerto Rico
Virgin Islands of the United States
International Labour Office
University of Puerto Rico
   Institute of Caribbean Studies, Rio Piedras campus
   College of Agriculture and Mechanical Arts, Mayaguez campus

Inter-American University of Puerto Rico
University of the West Indies
  Vice-Chancellor
  Pro-Vice-Chancellor, Trinidad campus
World University, Puerto Rico

After discussing the merits of each request, the Liquidation Committee unanimously agreed that the library should be handed over in trust to the government of the Commonwealth of Puerto Rico when the Secretariat closed on June 30, 1965. In arriving at this decision the Committee took into account Puerto Rico's undertaking to maintain and develop the library in accordance with the wishes of the Caribbean Council. By the time this decision was made it was known that Puerto Rico was in the process of setting up CODECA. As it turned out CODECA moved into the same quarters that the Secretariat had occupied, so the library did not have to be disturbed and it never ceased operations.

On June 17, 1965, at 3:30 P.M., Dr. Carlos J. Lastra, secretary of state of the Commonwealth of Puerto Rico, visited the Secretariat and, on behalf of his government, officially accepted the library of the Caribbean Organization to be held in trust in accordance with the decisions and wishes of the Caribbean Council.

And on June 30, 1965, at 4 P M , the Central Secretariat of the Caribbean Organization terminated its operations.

14 □ FROM FORMAL TO INFORMAL INTERNATIONAL COOPERATION AND THE ROLE OF PUERTO RICO

By the time of the fifth—and what proved to be the final—meeting of the Caribbean Council late in 1964 it was widely known that Puerto Rico was well along in planning for the agency which would be offered as successor to the dying Caribbean Organization.

As it was noted in the last chapter, the Council, in its final meeting, adopted a resolution which, among other items, recommended that a working group comprised of all members including the withdrawing members, the special observers, and all other interested democratic countries in the area convene at the earliest possible date to develop a formula to provide for regional cooperation in the social, educational, and cultural fields.

Following the adoption of this resolution the delegate from Puerto Rico informed the Council that he had been authorized by his government to state that it would be prepared to convene the working group and a meeting of government representatives at a high level in Puerto Rico, at dates which would be announced shortly.

The San Germán Conference

Early in 1965, therefore, Puerto Rico invited the governments of each of the Caribbean islands and of the Guianas to send representatives to a conference which would seek a new approach to the problem of regional cooperation in the Caribbean. The result of this invitation was the Conference on Economic Coordination in the Caribbean, held at San Germán, Puerto Rico, from May 17 to May 19, 1965.

This Conference served to bridge the gap between the expiring Caribbean Organization and what was to replace it. Twenty-five delegates attended, representing Antigua, Barbados, British Guiana, British Virgin Islands, Grenada, Jamaica, Montserrat, Netherlands Antilles, Puerto Rico, St. Lucia, St. Vincent, Trinidad and Tobago, and the U.S. Virgin Islands. In order that the evolution of the new structure would not be flawed by the presence of outsiders, as in the past, representatives from the metropolitan governments were not invited to the Conference. The absence of France and of the French Caribbean territories was conspicuous.

It immediately became apparent to the delegates at this Conference in San Germán that Puerto Rico's purpose in calling it was to lay before the meeting its proposal for a new approach to regional cooperation—an approach which, because of its informal nature, was thought to have a greater possibility for success than the Caribbean Organization. This proposal was for the establishment by Puerto Rico of a public corporation to be an instrumentality which, with the joint efforts of all the Caribbean islands, would be able hopefully to turn effective regional cooperation and exchange into a reality. The main agenda of the San Germán Conference consisted of Puerto Rico's exposition of its proposals and the evaluation of them by the other delegates. The final act of the Conference was to give endorsement in principle to the Puerto Rican proposal.

On June 15, 1965, therefore, Governor Roberto Sanchez Villella of Puerto Rico signed into law an act of the Puerto Rican Legislative Assembly creating, as an agency of the Puerto Rican government, the Caribbean Economic Development Corporation, which from its title in Spanish (Corporación de Desarrollo Económico del Caribe) is derived the acronym CODECA by which the new agency became known. The full text of the law creating CODECA is recorded in the Appendix. Following the creation of CODECA, a meeting of heads of governments was called on July 26, 1965, at Dorado, Puerto Rico. At that time the leaders attending were advised of CODECA's creation and of its plan of action. This new informal system was agreed to in principle.

Concept and Purpose of CODECA

The passage of the act creating CODECA was hailed in the press as launching Puerto Rico's "Little Marshall Plan" for the Caribbean. In the official release CODECA was described as a public corporation created by the government of Puerto Rico as an expression of its interest in the continuation and intensification of Caribbean economic development on a regional basis.[1] What was not known in 1965, of course, was that the mandate of the new CODECA to work toward Caribbean development would all but expire within four years. The election in 1968 of Governor Ferré to replace the administration whose aim had been to use CODECA's activities to enhance the lustre of the commonwealth status of Puerto Rico spelled the effective end of the CODECA dream.

These matters will be explored in the next chapter but here we need to go back and set forth what the potentialities were for CODECA in 1965, under the law passed that year.

CODECA became under the law an agency of the government of Puerto Rico with its own juridic personality and not subordinate to any other agency or department of the government. Its Board of Directors was required to be entirely of Puerto Rican composition. The secretaries of state and commerce of Puerto Rico and the administrator of the Economic Development Administration became members of the Board ex officio, and two additional members were to be selected by the governor, at least one of whom had to be from the private sector of the economy.

CODECA's mission was to promote exchange of goods, experience, and cooperation among the countries of the Caribbean region. Under the law which created it, the Corporation had broad powers to carry out surveys and research in the field of economic, social, cultural, or other kinds of possible regional cooperation; to administer and initiate programs and activities designed to increase commercial, agricultural, and industrial production throughout the Caribbean region; and to initiate programs that might lead to a greater exchange of persons and ideas. CODECA was empowered to grant services or enter into contracts and execute whatever other instruments might be necessary or convenient for its purposes. It could grant economic or other incentives in order to promote the rendering of services or the creation of enterprises that might be necessary to increase the economic development of the Caribbean region. CODECA was also given the power to grant loans that might promote the development of the Caribbean. It could provide technical and specialized services to governments and to persons or to private enterprises either in Puerto Rico or elsewhere, and it could request the services of specialists from other governments or from private agencies.

Among the powers granted to CODECA for the purpose of increasing trade in the Caribbean was the authority to organize, purchase, or in any other way acquire, subsidiary companies, associations, or corporations. It could exercise partial or total control over such subsidiary organizations, and it could participate in the management, administration, or functioning of Puerto Rican firms or firms of foreign origin.

Another power held in reserve by CODECA was the authority to issue its own bonds as a means of raising capital. In addition, the Corporation was authorized to administer scholarship programs for higher education and for vocational education.

CODECA could enter into contract with any government in the area or with several governments, whereby CODECA would carry out research or implement any economic program of regional benefit. CODECA was also to be the spokesman for Puerto Rico in the field of regional economic cooperation and the channel of communication with the government of Puerto Rico in these matters.

CODECA thus had actual and potential powers far in excess of those possessed by the Caribbean Organization or its predecessors.

In presenting their plans for CODECA to the San Germán Conference, spokesmen for Puerto Rico pointed out that in a situation such as is found in the Caribbean today, with its kaleidoscope of rapidly changing political, economic, and social conditions and relationships, no classical solution to regional economic development can be applied successfully. Whatever system is evolved would have to be sufficiently flexible to adapt almost automatically to the changes that will occur in the area.

CODECA thus was thought to embody this new approach of informal economic cooperation. Its establishment did not require ratification by other countries, nor did there have to be any provisions for formal accession or withdrawal of members. No change in the political constitution of any participating country either internally or in its relationship with a metropolitan power or with neighboring territories would affect its relationship to the CODECA system.

Another factor of importance that was stressed to the delegates at San Germán was that of voluntarism. No country would have to contribute to or participate in any project except those which would benefit it. On the other hand, lack of interest by some countries in a project of regional scope would not prevent others from carrying it out.

The financial burden in the new system would be reduced to a minimum by the elimination of a permanent international secretariat and of fixed annual assessments. Under this new concept the countries participating in a project would be assessed for that specific project according to a weighted system based on a sliding scale. CODECA began its existence in 1965 with an annual appropriation from the Legislative Assembly of Puerto Rico of $200,000. This was used to maintain the office staff and to begin planning for future projects.

The fundamental concept which was said to make the CODECA system workable was that while certain territories in the Caribbean were not yet fully sovereign, still each country in the area had certain inherent powers as a corporate body which were not affected by its continuing relationship with a metropolitan power. Among these inherent powers was the right to create public corporate bodies and the right to contract for services. Thus it was within the power of each country in the Caribbean, whether independent or otherwise, to enter freely into contract with CODECA and with CODECA's counterpart agencies in other territories. Each participating country would thus be responsible for reaching agreement with CODECA and with its partner or partners that might be involved in the execution of each regional project to be undertaken by the system.

The basic recommendation made by CODECA to the other countries in the area was that each one designate a specific office within a given ministry or department, preferably one dealing with commerce; or, in the fashion of CODECA, create a special agency to deal with all matters pertaining to Caribbean coordination. This office would serve as the single liaison in regional cooperation and would perform for its government the same services that CODECA would perform for the government of Puerto Rico. These offices would maintain constant communication with CODECA, which agreed to serve as a central clearinghouse and depository for information that might be of value in the growth and development of the region.

It was the plan that at given intervals, but at least once a year, representatives of CODECA and of its counterpart agencies would meet as a working group in what could be called a socio-economic council, to discuss the needs of the region and to determine the program of action for the coming year. This Council would prepare each year a set of recommendations to be undertaken by the governments, and the Council would also serve as a board of advisers for CODECA. In this capacity it would guide and assist in the implementation by CODECA of the various programs for regional development.

Finally, it was planned that there be established a body at the highest possible level, but not below ministerial rank, which could meet when necessary to discuss and resolve problems of regional cooperation that may come to light. A function of such a council would be the establishment of overall long-term plans, goals, and timetables for regional development and coordination. These would be passed down to the Socio-Economic Council for elaboration and implementation through technical committees, CODECA, or the subsidiary agencies, as may be appropriate. Each government's participation would be the responsibility of its regional coordinating office, or of CODECA in the case of Puerto Rico.

Thus Puerto Rico's grand design for informal international cooperation in the Caribbean took shape as a replacement for the defunct Caribbean Organization. The accompanying diagram was among the materials presented to the San Germán Conference in 1965.

It will be noted that there was no provision on this chart for any participation by the metropolitan governments.

INFORMAL SYSTEM OF CARIBBEAN COORDINATION

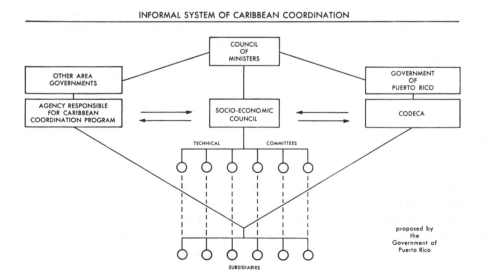

Dr. Luis A. Passalacqua Christian, formerly an officer of the Department of State of Puerto Rico, was named the first executive director of CODECA.

A Mid-Career Assessment of the CODECA Concept

As has already been indicated, the cycle of an independent CODECA lasted about four years, from 1965 to 1969. The institutional history and development of the agency will be explored in the next chapter, but by way of a further study of what Puerto Rican officials envisioned for CODECA we can at this point look ahead briefly to mid-career, 1967, when CODECA, still struggling to get its substantive work started, took stock of its position relative to the needs of Caribbean development. Officials of the corporation on that second anniversary in the summer of 1967 attempted to evaluate CODECA's progress and to look critically at the tasks lying ahead.

By mid-1967, comparing its visible and tangible achievements with what had been accomplished by the Caribbean Organization, CODECA had relatively few achievements to boast of. In fact, to somewhat cynical observers in Puerto Rico outside of the organization it appeared as though the Puerto Rican government had killed the Caribbean Organization and its worthwhile activities and had offered to the Caribbean region very little in the way of any substitute good works.

While acknowledging the validity of this judgement as of July 1967, Dr. Passalacqua and other officials of the corporation insisted that CODECA had not really had time yet to make its mark on the Caribbean region.[2] Dr. Passalacqua explained that there were actually three levels to CODECA's present and future operations: research, promotion, and action.

Emphasis throughout the first two years had been largely on research, with promotion and action yet to come. During this first period, then, CODECA was ostensibly doing no more than the Caribbean Organization had done. But in looking ahead to the promotion and action phases, the differences between its mode of operation and that of the old Caribbean Organization would hopefully begin to become apparent.

As a multilateral agency the Caribbean Organization's decisions and recommendations had to represent in effect the minimum consensus acceptable to the delegates to the Council. Its output (according to CODECA officials) consisted of very little more, usually, than: it would be a good idea to increase the tourist trade; it would be a good idea to industrialize; it would be a good idea to diversify agriculture, or to improve public health, or to train better teachers. Meetings on subjects such as these were held; seminars and workshops were conducted; and perhaps a newsletter or an exchange service was started.

But (again according to CODECA officials) the Caribbean Organization by its nature never could *promote* its plans, defend them against criticism, or offer to contract for their detailed implementation. The Organization itself consisted of the multinational Council, while the Secretariat had to operate in such a way as to please its many masters. The Organization remained, in other words, what it was planned to be: a consultative and advisory body.

CODECA would supposedly suffer from none of these shortcomings, and therefore its progress could conceivably exceed by far the achievements of the Caribbean Organization. CODECA could, for example, make a complete feasibility study on a given project, produce detailed plans and justifications, set up pilot projects, suggest funding sources, and finally even contract both to get the funds and to see the job through.

Even the research phase of CODECA's work would be much more thorough than the efforts of the Caribbean Organization ever were, according to Dr. Passalacqua. He noted, for example, that the Caribbean Organization once decided that it might be beneficial to a certain island if a modern seaport were constructed there. The Organization proceeded to hire consulting engineers who quite understandably concluded that indeed a modern seaport could be constructed on that island and that the cost of the undertaking would be approximately so many millions of dollars. While a study of this sort, duly prepared and presented to the island government, was said to satisfy the Caribbean Organization, CODECA would want to ask: *should* a seaport be built on that island? Would the future progress of that island be better assured by devoting its scarce resources to some *other* use, and why?

Everyone would agree that the islands of the West Indies need more teachers and better trained teachers. But CODECA was asking searching questions about the whole direction of education. Is the British-style, classically oriented school system best suited to the former British islands, or would their future development be better assured by more technical and vocational training? In asking this question CODECA was, of course, only raising once again the matter that was referred to as early as the 1942 ten-point long-range program for the Caribbean.

Everyone would likewise agree that the tourist traffic should be increased; also that industrialization should occur, and crops should be diversified. But how can changes in all of these sectors be dovetailed with each other on relatively small islands? If sugar production is partially mechanized, canefield workers are freed for vegetable farming and the island is better off for not having to import as much food as formerly. But *will* the canefield workers switch over to truck farming? How can they be trained to the new work and induced to attempt it?

The Caribbean Commission and the Caribbean Organization never ceased publicizing their conclusion that there was a great shortage of shipping in the Caribbean and that the governments concerned ought to do something to relieve the situation. This conclusion was thought to be self-evident from the known facts that shipping charges were among the highest in the world and that service was erratic and unsatisfactory. CODECA, however, apparently for the first time, made an actual count of the ships available to the area. It found that there are some 120 shipping lines operating and that in both numbers and tonnage capacities the West Indies is quite adequately endowed with shipping. It was therefore necessary to probe deeper to discover the true reasons for the unsatisfactory service. CODECA officials surmised that the poor service might be due in large part to the lack of adequate warehousing facilities on most of the islands. CODECA therefore planned to undertake a pilot project of erecting modern warehouses on several of the islands, with the expectation that improved shipping service to those islands would result and that the other islands would then want modern warehousing facilities also.

Thus although the *subjects* for research undertaken by CODECA were the time-worn ones, such as tourism, airline scheduling, tariff reduction, vocational school training, maternal health care, and others that had been studied time and time again, by the Caribbean Commission, by the Caribbean Organization, and by other interested agencies, CODECA felt that a fresh look at these subjects was nevertheless justified. New questions would be asked, new approaches attempted. Old conclusions would be considered suspect, new premises would be sought. And, even more important, the research, when completed, would include in each case specific and detailed plans for carrying out the recommended project—complete with an offer by CODECA to enter into contracts to get the job done.

Would not the other islands consider this a high-handed approach on the part of CODECA and Puerto Rico? Perhaps, but since CODECA was not a membership agency no country was obligated to participate in or help to pay for any project which did not suit it. CODECA would be perfectly willing to hear and discuss suggestions from the other islands. CODECA planned in fact to call meetings and seminars. But rather than get delegates together who would, for example, solemnly resolve that better maternal care is needed in the Windward Islands, CODECA would lay before the meeting—and be prepared to defend—a detailed and complete *plan* for better maternal health care, including the offer to start with pilot projects and eventually contract on a larger scale to get the job done once and for all. Suggestions would be listened to and objections entertained, but CODECA would insist that the work get under way and would offer itself as the agency to do the job—or to arrange to have it done. CODECA felt that if substantial progress were ever to be made in the Caribbean some agency such as itself would have to undertake the responsibility. With the metropolitan powers fast fading out of the picture, Puerto Rico and its agency, CODECA, were willing, even eager, to assume the burden.

PUERTO RICO'S ROLE IN CARIBBEAN AFFAIRS

Why was Puerto Rico so willing to assume the burden of Caribbean development in 1965? Although by 1969, with the installation of the Ferré administration committed to progress toward statehood, Puerto Rico's interest in shouldering the burden of Caribbean affairs was sharply diminished, no record of the CODECA years would be complete without an attempt to understand and document the remarkable phenomenon of the island's devotion to regional affairs during the years when the commonwealth status was being shaped and refined.

In the inaugural address following his election in 1948, President Harry Truman enunciated the now famous Point IV statement:

We must embark on a bold new program for making the benefits of our scientific advances and industrial progress available for the improvement and growth of underdeveloped areas. More than half the people of the world are living in conditions approaching misery. Their food is inadequate. They are victims of disease. Their economic life is primitive and stagnant. Their poverty is a handicap and a threat both to them and to more prosperous areas.

Shortly afterwards President Truman was visited by Governor Muñoz Marín of Puerto Rico, who called the President's attention to the sensation which his statement had already created in the world. At this point the President may have begun to wonder whether the governor of Puerto Rico was leading up to a request that Puerto Rico be included among the poor, underdeveloped countries which could apply for benefits under this Point IV policy.

If so the President was treated to a pleasant surprise, for what the governor proposed was no less than that Puerto Rico should *help* the United States government implement the Point IV program. Muñoz went home and persuaded the legislature of Puerto Rico to appropriate funds to begin the island's participation in Point IV. These funds were appropriated even before the U.S. Congress approved of Point IV; additional funds were appropriated by Puerto Rico in following years, at a steadily increasing rate. Thus Puerto Rico, struggling to solve its own problems and poorer by far than the poorest state, became the only part of the American union other than the federal government to contribute actively toward American economic aid programs.

Thirteen years later, another President, the late John F. Kennedy, shortly before his inauguration in January 1961, declared:

The hemisphere needs a fundamental effort, a revolutionary effort in the best sense, to satisfy the desire of the Latin American peoples for a civilization that shall be great materially, as it already is spiritually. Puerto Rico has been a laboratory that has enabled thousands of Latin American public officials, intellectuals, and students to observe the remarkable development of democracy and economic growth by a people who have really chosen to work out their destiny in close association with the United States.

Throughout this story of international cooperation in the Caribbean, Puerto Rico came to play an increasingly significant role in the shaping of events. In 1946 a Puerto Rican was named as one of the U.S. commissioners to the Anglo-American Caribbean Commission. In 1957 the Puerto Rican delegation to the seventh session of the West Indian Conference threatened to boycott future sessions until the Commission structure should be reorganized in accordance with the wishes of the Caribbean territories. In 1959 the Puerto Rican delegation to the special session of the West Indian Conference placed on record such a generous bid for the Commonwealth to become the headquarters site for the new Caribbean Organization that in 1960 the Secretariat moved from Trinidad to San Juan. Puerto Rico became the most liberal contributor of all of the members to the budget of the Caribbean Organization. And, finally, in 1964 the Puerto Rican government killed the Caribbean Organization and the next year launched as its own creature the successor agency for international cooperation in the Caribbean.

The answer to the question why Puerto Rico came to play such a major role in the affairs of the Caribbean has essentially two parts: (1) effective Caribbean cooperation was thought to be good for Puerto Rican business; and (2) Puerto Rico's predominant role in Caribbean affairs added lustre to the island's unique commonwealth status. Of these two answers to the question I sincerely believe, after talking with many Puerto Rican officials, that the second reason was the stronger of the two. Puerto Rican officials believed that their commonwealth status must not be allowed to settle into a static relationship of dependence upon the United States. Only as the status was continually redefined in the light of Puerto Rico's economic progress, only as the status was allowed to evolve and mature, would the commonwealth relationship prosper.

Over the years Puerto Rico sought to serve as a "bridge" between the United States and Latin America, interpreting and explaining to each party the culture of the other. Puerto Rico participated actively in U.S. aid programs, offering itself as the host island for technical training and for demonstration visits from countless thousands of delegations from all around the world. Within the Caribbean Puerto Rico sought to become more and more the principal rather than the agent of American policy in the region—in so doing to show the world the benefits of a peaceful and creative relationship with the United States. And, finally, Puerto Rico sought in every way possible to enhance its own remarkable economic progress; this included efforts to increase the island's trade with the outside world, thus widening the market for goods produced in the dollar area.

We turn, then, to the direct question: why did Puerto Rico take so seriously the alleged shortcomings of the Caribbean Organization that it deliberately destroyed that Organization in order to set up another in its place as its own creature? Are the affairs of the Caribbean really that important to an island which is increasingly integrated into the American economic sphere? In other words, what difference did it truly make to Puerto Rico that the Caribbean Organization was not performing up to the full potential of a regional agency in the West Indies? The answer is a mixture of history, world ideological conflicts, and plain dollars and cents business considerations.

If it had been possible in the years 1965 to 1967 to put the question to a panel of Puerto Ricans, from the governor and the secretary of state down to officials of the Commerce Department and of CODECA, I believe that what would have emerged would be somewhat as set forth below. What follows, then, is a composite of what was said on this subject —some of it addressed to me in many interviews and much of it as it appeared in speeches, publications, and testimony before the United States-Puerto Rico Status Commission.

The late President Kennedy and many others have paid tribute to Puerto Rico's participation in the U.S. foreign aid program toward Latin America. Beyond that we have made a positive contribution toward an understanding between the underdeveloped countries of the entire world and the United States. The first contribution of Puerto Rico to these foreign aid programs came with their birth when in 1949 President Truman announced the famous Point IV doctrine. Don Luis Muñoz Marín, at that time our governor, proposed that in view of the success and the experience we gained in our fight against underdevelopment through our Operation Bootstrap, Puerto Rico could become a center to show what a people can do to rise out of the ashes of misery, armed with courage and faith.

Breathing life into this proposal, even before the Congress of the United States had taken action, our Legislature appropriated funds for these new undertakings.

The first program that we organized was technical cooperation. From its beginning in May 1950 to the end of June 1954, this program operated under the Planning Board of Puerto Rico. On July 1, 1954, it was transferred by law to the Department of State of the Commonwealth. From May 1950 to June 1953 this program attracted 766 persons. In the following year 968 visitors came to the island, some 200 more than during the preceding thirty-seven months.

The importance of this program is revealed by the fact that more than 15 percent of all visitors going to the United States under training programs sponsored by the Agency for International Development, and more than 62 percent of the participants from Latin America, are sent to Puerto Rico. This makes our island the single largest training center for economic development. The importance of this program is further revealed by the accelerated growth of our courses for training in public administration, which is of course of vital importance to the underdeveloped countries. This single item accounts for almost 25 percent of the total number of participants.

This program also includes labor relations, education, home economics, criminology, rural electrification, and many other areas of economic development. This technical cooperation program, by June 30, 1964, had brought to Puerto Rico a total of 13,824 people from all over the world. But, it is not only under these programs of the federal government that people come to Puerto Rico. They are sent for training by the United Nations and specialized agencies, by the Organization of American States, as well as the United Nations Technical Assistance Board, the International Labor Organization, and UNESCO; and other international agencies, including the Alliance for Progress, have also requested and received the services of Puerto Rican technical experts to carry out their programs throughout the world.

There is a second program, the educational and cultural exchange program, which was inaugurated in 1955. This program, during its first year, brought 189 people to Puerto Rico. In 1964–65, 671 arrived for a total of 6,277 in nine years.

There is still a third program, and this is the one in which we include CODECA. It is called the conference and special visits program. It has brought more than 8,000 people to Puerto Rico since 1952. Under this program Puerto Rico has hosted a number of international conferences, such as the Federation of Coffee Growers of America, the Conference on Human Resources at the Middle Level, the Inter-American Red Cross Conference, the World Congress on Planning and Housing, and many others.

Now, this program has included some of the more than two hundred conferences arising out of Puerto Rico's participation in the efforts to develop the Caribbean region which have arisen on this island. The government of Puerto Rico has taken an active part in the Caribbean regional programs, especially through the former Caribbean Organization.

The Caribbean Organization faced a number of difficulties which it was unable to overcome. It was devoted to advisory and consultative views and positions. It was also hampered by a lack of interest in many of the

Caribbean countries because they accused it, rightly or wrongly, of being a colonially sponsored organization since it was based on a treaty between the United States, Great Britain, the Netherlands, and France.

In December 1964, in the face of the rapidly decreasing membership of the Caribbean Organization it was decided to disband this organization. At this time we in Puerto Rico realized that this would create a tremendous gap in the potential for developing a stable region in the Caribbean.

In order to prevent what we felt would be a very unhealthy lapse between the demise of the Caribbean Organization and any attempt to re-create a new international organization, and also in order to forestall as much as we could the growing feeling of unrest in the Caribbean, Puerto Rico decided to continue to work at Caribbean economic coordination. The result of this decision was the creation of our Caribbean Economic Development Corporation, or CODECA.

The corporation is designed to foster coordinated regional development in the economic field. In order to do this we felt that it would be more to the advantage of the Caribbean regions, considering the variety of political relationships that exist, if this were done on an informal basis rather than through the medium of a formal treaty or a formal international organization. The difficulty of getting agreements sometimes, as for instance between the various particles of the British Empire in the Caribbean and the mother country as to exactly what was going to be said at a conference table, was a big one, and we had the same problem because of the French relationship to its islands, which are departments of France.

The general reception to our idea of an informal arrangement was quite favorable, and when we presented the idea of CODECA we found that the various islands, both independent and dependent, were quite interested in the idea—to the extent that many of them inquired into the establishment of similar organizations.

CODECA is interested in developing regional programs. There are many areas in which joint action among the islands of the Caribbean and the countries of Central America and North and South America could be of great value. For example let us take the matter of trade. The degree of intra-Caribbean trade is only about 4 percent of the total trade of the Caribbean islands. It is our observation that this trade could be increased considerably, that there are many products which are produced in Puerto Rico or in other islands which could profitably be traded but which are not at the moment being traded for lack of knowledge or difficult access to markets—a question of productivity in some cases perhaps, a question of transportation or of tariffs in others.

Take, for example, the clothing industry. When the Arrow Shirt Company—to name one firm—first put up a plant in Puerto Rico it had two aims: (1) to sell shirts to Puerto Ricans and (2) to produce Arrow shirts cheaply for shipment to, and sale in, the United States. But by now

Arrow has such a capacity for production, both in the United States and in Puerto Rico, that the Puerto Rican plant can easily supply all of the island's market for Arrow shirts and it can also help the stateside operation by running the production of certain styles or models for general sale in the U.S. Yet there is capacity for still more. Why not, then, develop a market for Arrow shirts in the other Caribbean islands? But first we must help those islands develop economically so that their people can afford to buy shirts. It is a simple fact of economic life that the more developed a place is the more it trades with other developed places. So it can be reduced to the simple proposition that if Puerto Rico wants to step up intra-Caribbean trade it must help the other islands to prosper economically.

If Puerto Rico can work up a market for Arrow shirts in Barbados, for example, the sales of which would be for U.S. dollars, the Arrow company is bound to be happy, and the U.S. government will be delighted because this would help improve the dollar balance of trade, help curb the gold outflow. But the problem is that the U.S. offices of the Arrow company—or of any other company that has branch plants in Puerto Rico— might overlook the possibilities of the West Indies. They might be trying too hard to get into the European Common Market, for example. We in Puerto Rico feel that we are in the best position to work up and sponsor trade in the Caribbean.

The Arrow shirt example is only one of many, of course. Another example is the avocado, which we Puerto Ricans consume in great quantities. The avocado which we grow in Puerto Rico is a seasonal fruit. Other islands of the Caribbean grow the same fruit during our off season. In those islands the avocados simply rot for lack of a market. Trade with Puerto Rico is the obvious solution.

Another example: our hotel industry uses a great quantity of garden vegetables. Garden vegetables are grown in most of the Caribbean, but as of now this culture is often not profitable because of a lack of transportation to other markets in other islands and because of low productivity.

Now, it is in fields like this that CODECA has taken a particular interest. These had to come first because these were the more difficult to develop and would take the longest time. CODECA got started on them right at first.

We are therefore now engaged in a study to determine the best modes of transportation and the best shipping itineraries that can be arranged in the Caribbean, with a view to facilitating the import and export of goods.

There are other fields in which we can profitably assist, and one of them is tourism. A coordinated development of tourism in the Caribbean would be of great value to all of the islands. We have the problem again of communications and of facilities, so that one of the things we are interested in particularly is the development of hotel training facilities. The other islands have made many requests for this type of training.

In concrete dollar terms what does all of this Caribbean trade amount to? Well, Puerto Rico's exports to *all* foreign countries are now running at about 50 million dollars a year. But still Puerto Rico is showing an enormous trade deficit with the external world. Thus anything we can do to step up exports will help balance the accounts, will help improve the U.S. balance of trade, and so on. To cite one non-Caribbean example, Puerto Rico *buys* from Spain 10 million dollars worth of goods every year, mostly olive oil and allied products. But Puerto Rico *sells* to Spain only about $100,000 worth of goods every year. Therefore anything Puerto Rico could do to step up sales to Spain would be helpful.

Detailed analysis of trade statistics will reveal that mainland United States exports something around 2.5 billion dollars worth of goods to the Caribbean every year (this includes Haiti and the Dominican Republic). If Puerto Rico could only assume one *tenth* of that trade it would mean 250 million in additional exports for us. This, in the face of our current $50 million per year in foreign trade, would be a tremendous boost for Puerto Rico. In our present stage of development every $20,000 of exports from Puerto Rico creates one job directly and two indirectly. So it would be quite an item for us if we could step up interisland trade.

We know of course that what is supposed to be a great obstacle to this intra-Caribbean trade is the existence of a patchwork of conflicting tariff and preference patterns, overlaid by habitual and historical trade routes with the metropolitan countries. Yet our studies have shown that these obstacles might be overcome more easily than would be suspected. Take, for example, linen products, which Puerto Ricans produce. The island of Jamaica has a Commonwealth preference tariff of 20 percent on linens and a general tariff of 30 percent. To sell linens to Jamaica Puerto Rico would have to pay the general tariff of 30 percent. Yet our studies have shown that Puerto Rico could land linen products in Jamaica, pay the 30 percent duty, and still offer them for sale in the stores of Jamaica at prices cheaper than exporters from the United Kingdom or Canada could offer, paying only the preferential duty of 20 percent.

With many other products the same is true. In the Netherlands Antilles the tariff schedule is practically zero, and it is the same for everybody, including Holland. So there is no problem whatever of stepping up trade with those islands.

Obviously so long as Puerto Rico's stage of development is about mid-course, our trade with highly developed areas like Western Europe will be mostly in agricultural products, while our trade with underdeveloped areas like most of the Caribbean islands will be in manufactured items and consumer goods. But in the long run as development progresses, both in Puerto Rico and in the other islands, trade patterns will shift more toward manufactured goods in both directions—which would be fine with us because there is more profit for everybody in that kind of trade.

Looking ahead many years, if Jamaica, for example, likes trading with Puerto Rico and would seek to buy Puerto Rican goods cheaper, we could drop the gentle hint: one way would be for you to lower your tariffs on American (and Puerto Rican) products. If they answer they could not do that because it would interfere with their Commonwealth ties, we will whisper, "So what? Will you in the long run get more benefit from maintaining your Commonwealth preferences, or from moving toward freer trade with the vast dollar area? Of course you will want to continue being friends with Britain, keep up your cultural exchanges, be proud of your British heritage and all that. But business is business. Why not sign up for *trade* with the dollar market and with Puerto Rico. Let the Commonwealth preferences go, if need be."

Yes, this is where we infuse politics into trade relations. But you really cannot disassociate economics and politics. We Puerto Ricans know that the politics of the region and of the world vitally affect our own progress. In the 1950s and early 1960s when the pro-Marxist Cheddi Jagan was the political leader in British Guiana it made would-be Caribbean investors jittery. Fidel Castro in Cuba has of course been a tremendous burden for Puerto Rico to bear, because most people do not know the geography of the Caribbean and they tend to think that when one island or colony is in turmoil the whole region is shaky. In 1965 when President Johnson sent U.S. marines into the Dominican Republic the Puerto Rican government had to dispatch a delegation to New York to reassure the holders of Puerto Rican bonds that Puerto Rico was not at all involved in the disturbances and that life in Puerto Rico remained peaceful, orderly, prosperous, and democratic.

Thus we Puerto Ricans believe that we simply must have effective Caribbean economic cooperation, for both the commercial and the political benefits that will flow from it. We fear that with the British presence about to be virtually withdrawn from the eastern Caribbean a dangerous instability may develop in those islands, given their extreme poverty and backwardness. In view of how recent events elsewhere in the region have affected us we want at all costs to preserve stability in the *eastern* Caribbean.

Moreover, we believe that the model of a peaceful, progressing, and cooperating eastern Caribbean will be an instructive example to the rest of the world, in contrast with the strife-torn, dictator-ridden, communist-infested western Caribbean. The world taunts the United States for being an imperialist in Latin America. Castro-type guerrilla movements are offered as the only hope for Latin America to throw off the yoke of Yankee colonialism. So we Puerto Ricans feel that if our commonwealth can lead the way to orderly and progressive cooperation in the Caribbean this will tend to refute the charge that Uncle Sam is an imperialist bully and that Puerto Rico is his servile colony.

Those of us in the government of Puerto Rico who commute almost monthly to Washington believe that the U.S. State Department has no policy for the eastern Caribbean worthy of the name. There is little or no technical assistance, Peace Corps, or development loans for those islands so long as they remain the responsibility of Great Britain. We therefore wish to have our new regional system in operation when the British finally pull out, so that channels will exist and projects will be in operation for immediate outside assistance to those islands. If at that time AID and other U.S. and international agencies wish to give assistance Puerto Rico will propose using the facilities of CODECA for the orderly distribution and management of such resources. If, however, little or no outside help materializes, Puerto Rico feels it must be prepared to go it alone. In either case CODECA is our chosen instrument. To arguments that the British will continue to be interested in the welfare of the islands through the Associated States concept we must reply that the metropolitan powers have had four hundred years to make something of those islands and still they are sunk in poverty and despair.

This, then, is our case. This is our reason for setting aside the Caribbean Organization and for going ahead with plans for Caribbean development—centering on Puerto Rico alone if need be. The job simply has to be done.

Thus little Puerto Rico, so recently wallowing in its own poverty and backwardness, strode to the center of the stage in the eastern Caribbean, attempting to be the leader rather than the follower of U.S. policy in the region, attempting to set the pace for regional international cooperation. It was said that in ten years or so legends might be painted on walls in the Caribbean islands saying "Puerto Ricans, go home." If so this would have been the ultimate mark of the Commonwealth's maturity in international affairs.

One Puerto Rican official expressed the rationale for CODECA this way: anybody from the outside who visits the Windward and Leeward islands and really sees their incredible poverty comes away either a missionary or a revolutionary. With CODECA Puerto Rico planned to play the missionary role, thereby hopefully thwarting the revolutionaries, communist or otherwise.

The next chapter must deal with the failure of CODECA to live up to this high promise.

15 □ THE CODECA CYCLE

TAKING UP THE BURDEN

CODECA began operations on July 1, 1965, the day after the Caribbean Organization Secretariat ceased functioning. CODECA accepted in trust the library, archives, and files of the Caribbean Organization, and it moved into the offices vacated by the Secretariat in the Teachers Association Building in Hato Rey.

Several of the Puerto Rican staff members of the Caribbean Organization were carried over as employees of CODECA. The new corporation also acquired by purchase the tangible assets of the Caribbean Organization, and it served as the informal custodian of the affairs of the Organization, handling correspondence and answering inquiries which for some months after were addressed to the Caribbean Organization.

With this latest shift of pattern, therefore, the primary responsibility for international cooperation in the Caribbean had come to rest in 1965 in its new public corporation of the Puerto Rican government.

INSTITUTIONAL DEVELOPMENT OF CODECA

CODECA began its existence in 1965 with an annual appropriation from the legislature of Puerto Rico of $200,000 for fiscal year 1966. This was increased for 1967 to $255,000, and for 1968 the appropriation reached $369,000. By July of 1967 the permanent staff reached a maximum of forty-eight. The budget for 1969 shrank to $273,000, and the final liquidation budget for fiscal 1970 was just over $250,000.

As noted in the last chapter, the basic recommendation made by CODECA to the other countries in the area was that each one designate a specific office within a given ministry or department, preferably one dealing with commerce; or, as in the fashion of CODECA, create a special agency to deal with all matters pertaining to Caribbean coordination. By the second anniversary of CODECA in 1967 the governments of Barbados, Guyana, Dominica, Jamaica, Montserrat, St. Vincent, Grenada, and the Netherlands Antilles had officially designated agencies to serve as liaison with CODECA. For example, Montserrat designated for this purpose the permanent secretary of the Ministry of Trade and Production. No territory created a separate public corporation comparable to CODECA, however.

The first meeting of the Socio-Economic Council, which would have served as a board of advisers for CODECA (see chart on page 168), was scheduled for late in 1966, but no meeting of this projected body ever occurred. Likewise the plan to establish another high-level body, which could meet when necessary to resolve problems of regional cooperation, remained only in the planning stage.

For reasons of internal politics, centering on the public debate over the status question preceding the plebiscite of July 23, 1967, the Puerto Rican government sought to play down any emphasis on CODECA during the first half of 1967. The administration felt that publicity for CODECA would be used by both the statehood and independence factions to reflect unfavorably on the commonwealth status. Statehood forces would presumably have argued that Puerto Rico was violating its relationship with the United States by engaging in foreign relations, while the independence people could argue that since Puerto Rico was acting like an independent republic it might as well be one. CODECA never got into stride after this politically inspired deemphasis of 1967.

CODECA Projects

CODECA's first work program, for 1966 and 1967, included the following ten items:

1. A program of aided self-help housing, with plans for a pilot project on the island of St. Vincent.
2. Research on, and the drafting of legal documents for the establishment of a Caribbean Investment Corporation, or CARINCO, which will be a major subsidiary agency of the CODECA system.
3. Study of the problems of maritime transport in the Caribbean.
4. Study for the development of an agency for the coordination of the tourist industry in the Caribbean.
5. Study looking toward the establishment of a uniform system of statistics for the countries of the Caribbean, as a basic aid to regional planning.
6. Establishment by January, 1967, of a Caribbean Hurricane Insurance Company (CHIC).
7. Study of commercial fisheries in the Caribbean.
8. Establishment of a "little Peace Corps," or Educational Service Corps (CESCO) among the Caribbean territories.
9. A scholarship program, continuing and developing the Fellowship Program of the Caribbean Organization, hopefully with the continuing financial assistance of AID.
10. Maintenance and further development of the library received in trust from the Caribbean Organization.

Unfortunately there was considerable erosion of this original work program as the initial two-year period wore on.

The projected self-help housing project on St. Vincent (no. 1, above) was held in abeyance because of alleged political instability on that island. Even before this point was reached, however, the discovery was made that additional research would be needed on mortgage financing before the project would be feasible.

The study looking toward the development of an agency for the co-ordination of the tourist industry in the Caribbean (no. 4) was held up for lack of funds.

Establishment of a Caribbean Hurricane Insurance Company (no. 6) was stalled for lack of interest in a season remarkably free of devastating storms.

The study of commercial fisheries in the Caribbean (no. 7) was under-taken, not by CODECA but by the Food and Agriculture Organization of the United Nations, with headquarters for the project in Barbados. CODECA, however, served as a coordinating agency for the Caribbean region, offering technical help, and serving as the liaison agency with the participating specialists.

The hoped-for scholarship program (no. 9) died, owing to a denial of funds by AID. CODECA went ahead however with plans for a Vocational Training Center and a Productivity Center.

With regard to the proposed Caribbean Investment Corporation (CARINCO) (no. 2), a detailed and comprehensive report on the legal and financial factors affecting the establishment of the company was sub-mitted in December 1966 by the law firm of Baker & McKenzie, working under the supervision of the Government Development Bank of Puerto Rico. The report was generally favorable to the project. It recommended that CARINCO be incorporated in the Netherlands Antilles. Additional reports and studies were published toward the end of 1967 with regard to this project.

Caribbean Regional Library

The library taken over from the Caribbean Organization and held in trust for the region was systematically expanded and made more useful to the West Indies, under the capable direction of the new director, Mrs. Paulita Maldonado de la Torre. It was officially designated the Caribbean Regional Library.

Conscious of the need for a bibliographic center for the region, the Caribbean Regional Library and CODECA called a conference in Hato Rey, March 28 and 29, 1967, to deal with this need. The major libraries of the Caribbean islands and the Guianas, as well as interested institutions and organizations from outside the region, were invited to send representa-tives to the conference to discuss the design for the planned center. This conference for the establishment of a bibliographic center for the Caribbean was attended by twenty-two delegates from the Caribbean and by eight delegates from outside the area.

True to its concept of moving beyond the study and discussion stage into purposeful action, the Caribbean Regional Library and CODECA announced at this conference that they had already contracted for the services of the System Development Corporation of Falls Church, Virginia, to design a bibliographic center. The conference gave its unanimous endorsement to the project, and the Library and CODECA announced they would seek the financial support needed to implement the project as a whole.[1] With the assistance of the University of Puerto Rico Library, the first of a new series of monthly bibliographic reports was issued in June 1967. The format of this first report was that of a computer printout, photographically reproduced by CODECA. Studies and experimentation are continuing with regard to designing the best method for the storage and retrieval of bibliographic data.

The number of visitors to the library and the number of requests for interlibrary loans increased steadily during 1966 and 1967.

Publications

Other major projects completed by CODECA during 1967 included the publication of the first volume of what was planned to be a new annual series: *Caribbean Statistical Annual*. These volumes would bring together more up-to-date and comprehensive information than had ever before been available in a single publication.

Another major publication in 1967 was the *Study on Tariff Barriers in the Caribbean*. This volume not only contained information on the subject but, in keeping with CODECA's desire to get ahead with the job, it also recommended solutions to the tariff problem.

Still another major publication was *Study on Cooperatives*, expanding on the interest in this subject demonstrated over many years by the Caribbean Commission and Caribbean Organization.

Finally, CODECA by 1967 was preparing for publication reports on the problems of maritime transport in the Caribbean—materials which will eventually require two or more volumes for distribution.

CESCO Pilot Project

Undoubtedly the most notable achievement recorded by CODECA in its first two years was the successful operation of a pilot project of the Caribbean Educational Services Corps (or CESCO).

The site selected for the pilot project was the island of Tortola, in the British Virgin Islands. Working with the government of Tortola and with the other governments of the Caribbean region, CODECA was able to begin the CESCO experiment in the school year 1966–67. Three volunteers from the Caribbean converged on Tortola in time to begin the fall term: Miss Nerida Cruz from Puerto Rico; Miss Dinah Evans from Guyana; and a Mr. Watson from Jamaica.

True to the tradition for innovation established for the Caribbean by the Caribbean Organization and its predecessors, CODECA scored another first with this CESCO pilot project. It constituted the first *multinational* volunteer service program in the world.

Another innovation in voluntary educational services was the CESCO concept that its volunteers had a duty not only to teach the children in the classrooms but also, through seminars and demonstrations, to help upgrade the performance of the local teaching staffs.

On the basis of the Tortola experience CODECA went ahead with plans for establishing CESCO as a permanent regional program of providing volunteer educational services to the Caribbean area. In addition to the governments of the region CODECA also communicated with the International Secretariat for Voluntary Services, the U.S. Peace Corps, the Canadian University Service Overseas, the British Voluntary Service Overseas, the U.N. Technical Assistance Board, the Canadian External Aid Office, and other such services relative to soliciting volunteers for CESCO. All of these agencies expressed interest in the project and offered help in varying degrees in the years to come.

To remind ourselves once again of the very basic, down-to-earth nature of the work which has to be done by CODECA to meet the needs of the region, and to provide a documentary record of this significant innovation, there is entered in the Appendix the full text of the evaluation of the CESCO pilot project made at the close of the first school term in December 1966.

A LOST OPPORTUNITY

CODECA's life cycle, like that of the Caribbean Organization before it, spanned a period of approximately four years. When the voters of Puerto Rico elected Governor Luis Ferré in November 1968, they signed the death warrant of CODECA as an independent agency. With its aim of grooming Puerto Rico for statehood, the new administration had no place in its plans for an agency which sought to create for Puerto Rico a role as leader in Caribbean international cooperation.

As a political appointee of the previous Popular Democratic Party administration, Dr. Luis A. Passalacqua Christian felt compelled to resign as executive director in January of 1969. The stated aim of the new administration with regard to CODECA was that it should be transferred to the Department of Commerce of Puerto Rico, where it would continue to perform certain residual research and administrative functions. This transfer to the Commerce Department, however, would require new legislation to amend the law of 1965 creating CODECA, and the legislature of Puerto Rico met and completed its work for 1969 without enacting any such new legislation. Thus CODECA continued through 1969 a shadowy existence, its work all but at a standstill, its personnel depleted, and its morale low. Mr. Manuel Velázquez Borges served as acting executive director in 1969 pending the possible appointment of a new director or the eventual transfer of the agency to the Commerce Department.

In retrospect, CODECA never really recovered from the period of politically dictated quiescence surrounding Puerto Rico's status plebiscite of 1967. The plebiscite was almost immediately followed by increasing political disorientation and uncertainty, in the midst of which CODECA projects never had a real chance to get started. Appropriations by the legislature for CODECA for the fiscal years 1968, 1969, and 1970 ($369,000; $273,000; and $254,000, respectively) were never large enough to do much more than maintain the staff and the library. In fact the library accounted for more than half of the expenditures by CODECA during these three years, as it continued to increase both its holdings and its services to the region. It could truthfully be said that the Caribbean Regional Library, as it is now called, stands as the one permanent structure of Caribbean cooperation which has survived all of the changes of pattern at the official level.

The critical turning point in the institutional history of CODECA came late in 1968. At that time Governor Sanchez had on his desk a letter to the President of the United States, drafted in CODECA, asking the President's approval for Puerto Rico to join the newly announced Caribbean Development Bank. Attempting to skirt the constitutional technicalities growing out of the fact that Puerto Rico was neither a state nor a territory, the Puerto Ricans expected that the President could delegate to a Puerto Rican plenipotentiary the right to sign a treaty on behalf of the United States in which it would be provided that Puerto Rico would join the Development Bank as a full member, apart from any question of membership by the United States itself. Had this arrangement been agreed to, CODECA would have been strategically placed to be the liaison and backstopping agency for Puerto Rico in its dealings with the bank. Through membership in the bank, Puerto Rican delegates would have had access to decision-making about basic development projects in the West Indies. They could have asserted the willingness of Puerto Rico to lend its industrial know-how and the output of its diversified economy to the projects undertaken by the Bank. The six million dollars which Puerto Rico would have had to contribute as its share of the bank's capitalization would be returned many times over in the added trade that Puerto Rico would have shared through its participation in the bank.

With the bank connection established, CODECA's request for funds to get on with its other projects would have been hard for the legislature to deny. But all of this never came about; in the political chaos immediately preceding the 1968 election the letter to the President of the United States from the governor of Puerto Rico was never sent. The result of the election of course was the new administration of Governor Ferré, the resignation of Dr. Passalacqua as director, and the rapid eclipse of CODECA. In Washington, too, the new administration of President Nixon sought to restudy its whole approach to the problems of the hemisphere. Governor Ferré announced that he would not object to Puerto Rican participation in the bank, but the initiative and the money would have to come from Washington. In any event CODECA's role in this approach to the problems of the Caribbean was at an end.

Final CODECA Diary

When the administration of Governor Ferré took office in January of 1969, CODECA found itself with a new Board of Directors. For the benefit of the new Board the CODECA staff drew up early in 1969 a document summarizing the projects for 1967 and 1968 and stating the agency's goals for the future if the decision were made to allow CODECA to continue its existence.

Since this chapter must conclude by recording the chronicle of CODECA's two final years, it would appear altogether fitting to let CODECA largely speak for itself. What follows here, then, is my translation from Spanish of selected portions of CODECA's report of 1969 to its new Board, interspered with additional observations that I gleaned from personal interviews and from other documents. Original subject headings of the CODECA document will be used for this commentary.

Summary Translation of CODECA's 1969 Report to New Board of Directors

Introduction

The work of CODECA has up to now been dedicated essentially to the preparation of studies and the evaluation of possible projects which would contribute to the well-being of the Caribbean region. CODECA has limited itself to these tasks not through inclination but because of the scarcity of the resources which it has had available for its work.

The plans, studies, and projects to which CODECA has given emphasis derive from three principal sources: useful projects, including those left over from the former Caribbean Organizations; projects which implement the recommendations of the Conference on Economic Coordination of the Caribbean, held at San Germán in 1965; and projects initiated by CODECA itself or entrusted to it by the government.

Joint Dominican Republic-Puerto Rican Economic Commission

On October 18, 1967, the United States, Puerto Rico, and the Dominican Republic announced simultaneously the creation of a Joint Dominican Republic-Puerto Rican Economic Commission, to engage in technical planning and to work toward increasing the commercial, economic, and social relationships between the two countries.

The governor of Puerto Rico designated CODECA to be the secretariat of the Puerto Rican section of the new Commission. CODECA was active in the organization of the first plenary conference of the Commission, held in the Dominican Republic in November of 1967. Likewise, CODECA assisted the Department of State of Puerto Rico in organizing the second plenary conference which was held in San Juan from August 14 to August 16, 1968.

[Thus, by way of comment, we have here in embryo the concept of a new departure in Caribbean integration—the creation of a formal structure uniting an independent republic with a nonsovereign commonwealth, across a boundary of diverse national linkage and in the absence of a tradition of prior association. The Dominican Republic was never a formal part of the Caribbean Commission or the Caribbean Organization, although the fifth and final meeting of the Caribbean Council in 1964 did have before it a request from the Dominican Republic regarding the possibility of membership.]

[Puerto Rican officials looked forward to the generation of a considerable trade between their island and the Dominican Republic. A third meeting of the new Commission was scheduled for October 1969.]

Work Accomplished during Fiscal Year 1967-68

A. CODECA:
1. Continued the Information Services on Animal Health in the Caribbean, and prepared the first annual report on animal health.
2. Continued preparing a comparative study on airline schedules and airport facilities.
3. Discontinued the analysis of the Puerto Rican experience in economic development and its possible application to other countries, for lack of the necessary funds.
4. Because the necessary constitutional processes were not completed in St. Vincent, CODECA could not implement the program of self-help housing and mortgage insurance on that island. Nevertheless the agency offered technical assistance on these problems to other areas which asked for it. To the extent that its resources permit, CODECA will extend the concept to other receptive areas.

5. Continued the Voluntary Educational Services Corps (CESCO).
6. For lack of resources, CODECA could not undertake the projected study of the economic strategy required for the industrialization of the Caribbean.
7. As part of its normal functions, CODECA participated in a series of activities and regional conferences on the possible creation of a Caribbean Development Bank, and completed a study of the possible participation of Puerto Rico in the bank.
8. Published the preliminary study of a Caribbean Plan.
9. In collaboration with the United Nations, CODECA completed a partial analysis of the techniques used by industries oriented toward export.
10. Discharged the duties of executive secretariat to the Joint Dominican Republic-Puerto Rican Economic Commission.
11. Prepared an evaluation of the plan for the economic development of the Dominican Republic for the Puerto Rican delegates to the Joint Commission.
12. Began a study of the possible effects on the economy of Puerto Rico of changes in the tariff structure of the United States which might grow out of discussions held in Geneva under the auspices of GATT and U.N. Conference on Trade and Development (UNCTAD). In the study emphasis will be given to the possible competitors of Puerto Rico in the context of the discussions referred to above.
13. Completed and sent to press a *Study of Maritime Transportation in the Caribbean.*
14. During the year CODECA participated as observer in the following conferences: Caribbean Mental Health Association, Barbados; Inter-American Statistical Institute, Venezuela; Fisheries, Barbados; Seminar on Acquisition of Latin American Library Materials, U.S.A.; Conference on National Accounts, sponsored by CODECA and the Planning Council; and Conference on Agriculture, St. Lucia.
B. Caribbean Regional Library:
15. Published and distributed volumes 9-11 (Part II), corresponding to the years 1959-61, and volume 15, corresponding to 1965, of the Current Caribbean Bibliography.
16. Carried through the processing of the publications received from January to December of 1967 and transferred the information to IBM punch cards. This information will constitute the volume corresponding to 1967 for the Current Caribbean Bibliography. The total number of publications

included is 1,916. The following agencies and governments participated in this project by submitting information: the University of Puerto Rico; the University of the West Indies (Jamaica and Trinidad); Jamaican Institute; Library of Congress; University of Florida (Gainesville); Department of Education, Virgin Islands of the United States; Haiti; Guadeloupe; Pedro Henriquez Urena National University (Dominican Republic). For the first time this volume will include the location of the publications in the libraries of the region.

17. Completed the first phase looking toward the creation of the Bibliographic Center for the Caribbean.

18. Provided briefing to three librarians from the U.S. Virgin Islands with a view to assuring uniformity of the data which is required for the Current Caribbean Bibliography. The Library will offer such briefings to librarians of other institutions.

19. Sent a Library employee to University Microfilms, Ann Arbor, Michigan, to receive training in the use of microfilm cameras.

20. In accordance with an agreement between University Microfilms and CODECA, the Library installed a microfilm camera and a Xerox machine in order to assess the demand for copied material. Among the institutions which solicited this fee service are the following:

   (1) National Agricultural Library, Washington, D.C.
   (2) University of Florida Library, Gainesville
   (3) University of Kentucky Library
   (4) Westhem Corporation, Ltd., Canada
   (5) Northwestern University Library
   (6) West India Reference Library, Jamaica
   (7) Public Library, Tortola, Virgin Islands
   (8) Goshen College, Indiana
   (9) Harvard University
   (10) Library of the State Agricultural University of the Netherlands
   (11) Institute of Caribbean Studies, University of Puerto Rico
   (12) Interamerican University, San Germán, Puerto Rico
   (13) Arnold & Porter, Washington, D.C.
   (14) Twentieth Century Fund, Washington, D.C.
   (15) Banco Popular, Puerto Rico
   (16) University of Puerto Rico
   (17) Hamburisches-Welt Wirtschafts Archiv, Germany

21. Processed sixty-six interlibrary loans to institutions in Puerto Rico and abroad.

22. Requested fifty-six interlibrary loans from other institutions.
23. Participated actively in the thirteenth seminar on acquisitions of Latin American library materials. Our library is actively affiliated with this project.

Goals for Fiscal Year 1968–69*

A. CODECA:
1. Will continue the Information Service on Animal Health in the Caribbean.
2. Will continue preparation of the comparative study on airline schedules and airport facilities.
3. Will continue the Voluntary Educational Services Corps (CESCO). [Actually CESCO came to an end in fiscal 1968–69. All of the islands need additional teachers; by the same token each island is reluctant to contribute personnel to the Corps.]
4. Will continue analyzing the effect on the economy of Puerto Rico of the establishment of the Caribbean Development Bank, and of the possible participation by Puerto Rico in the bank.
5. Will continue performing the duties of executive secretariat to the Joint Dominican Republic–Puerto Rican Economic Com mission. CODECA organized and participated actively in the second plenary conference which took place in San Juan from the 14th to the 16th of last August (1968).
6. Commenced a study of wages in the Caribbean.
7. Will commence a study of the financial institutions in the Caribbean.
8. Began a study of the tax structure in the Caribbean.
9. Will continue participating in regional activities to strengthen the economic and socio-educational relations between Puerto Rico and the other islands of the Caribbean.
10. Completed the first part of a study on maritime transportation in the Caribbean.
11. Published the first number of the *Statistical Annual of the Caribbean*, which covers up to the year 1966, with projections to 1975. There are plans to publish all the data for other years in supplementary or revised editions.
12. Continued negotiations with the government of St. Kitts for the establishment of a women's underwear factory on that

*This list was drawn up shortly after the mid-point in the fiscal year. For that reason some items are in past tense while others are future tense.

island. In the last year CODECA completed a study of the viability of such a factory at the request of the St. Kitts government.

13. Continues giving advice on housing and mortgage guarantees to various islands in the Caribbean.

14. Will continue observing the efforts of the developing nations to obtain preferential tariff treatment in the U.S. market.

15. Will publish this year the study, "A Strategy of Regional Economic Development for the Caribbean," prepared by the firm of Clapp & Mayne.

16. During the month of February we will hold the CESCO Conference, which will be attended by representatives of ministries of education and other officials in the area interested in volunteer services.

17. During the year we will participate in various conferences in the area, in accordance with our policy of having observers and participants on behalf of Puerto Rico. We will participate in the conference of the Tourist Association, San Juan; Fisheries, Barbados; Conservation of Natural Resources, Trinidad.

19. During the year we will reproduce copies of a "Survey of Industrial Incentives and Tax Laws of the Caribbean," material which will be of great utility for present and potential investors in the area.

B. Caribbean Regional Library:

20. Will continue improving and reforming the structure of the library as far as funds will permit.

21. Will publish volumes 12–14 (1962–64), volume 16 (1966), and 17 (1967)—which will bring the Current Caribbean Bibliography up to date.

22. CODECA and the library will be hosts to the 14th seminar on the acquistion of Latin American library materials, to be held in Puerto Rico in June 1969.

23. Will continue inventorying the books left by the Caribbean Organization, in accordance with the recommendation of the Comptroller of Puerto Rico.

24. Will continue preparing the Current Caribbean Bibliography for 1968.

25. Will continue offering reproduction and microfilm services.

26. Will continue efforts to obtain economic assistance for the establishment of the second phase of the Bibliographic Center for the Caribbean.

27. Will prepare new bibliographies on specific subjects, for example, economic development plans.

List of Projects for Fiscal Year 1969–70

The following studies and projects for which funds are solicited will be undertaken or continued in the coming fiscal period:

A. CODECA:
  1. Promotion of the image of Puerto Rico in the Caribbean.
  2. Study of the port and warehouse facilities in the Caribbean area.
  3. Study of the possibility of creating a Caribbean Institute of Public Administration.
  4. Publication of the second number of the *Statistical Annual of the Caribbean.*
  5. Study of the problems facing the tourist industry in the Caribbean area and of the potentials for increasing the traffic.
  6. Will continue exercising the appropriate duties of the executive secretariat of the Joint Dominican Republic–Puerto Rican Economic Commission.
  7. Will continue a study on the usefulness of establishing a regional vocational school.
  8. In coordination with the Planning Council and the University of Puerto Rico, CODECA will institute a seminar on statistical methods for civil servants of the Caribbean.
  9. During the fiscal year 1969–70 the following conferences will be held on the initiative of Puerto Rico:
     (a) on maritime transport (date not yet set)
     (b) Caribbean Investment Company (CARINCO)
B. Caribbean Regional Library:
  10. Will take inventory for correcting and completing the records maintained by the Caribbean Organization, and will catalog the international organization documents which compose the major part of the body of material still to be cataloged.
  11. Will prepare card indexes of the books already cataloged, to bring up to date all of the records and archives of the library —a job which has not been completed previously because of lack of secretarial assistance.
  12. Will continue offering reference services, requests for which increase daily.
  13. Will continue cataloging and processing publications received by the library.
  14. Will continue preparing and distributing the Current Caribbean Bibliography.
  15. Will continue offering Xerox and microfilm copying service.

16. Will put into operation the Bibliographic Center, preparations for which will have been completed by the library.

A FINAL LOOK AT PUERTO RICO AND CODECA

Thus with a much abridged and yet unlikely to be attained list of projects for fiscal 1969-70, CODECA faced its demise as an independent agency. With its death would perish also, at least temporarily, the hope of creating for Puerto Rico a role as leader and innovator in Caribbean integration.

Partisans on all sides of the status issue agree that Puerto Rico's position vis-à-vis both the United States and the outside world cannot remain static. It must be a role which is steadily evolving. Evolution may be toward the goal of union with the other fifty states, as the statehood faction insists; or it may be toward sovereign independence, as the forces favoring that option insist. Even the commonwealth enthusiasts of the Popular Democratic Party believe that the Estado Libre Associado status requires constant redefinition and the constant addition of new dimensions to the autonomous stature of a growing and prospering polity. At heart most P.D.P. members have a sentimental predilection toward independence, but this romantic vision is restrained by the practical advantages of continued association with the United States. Rafael Hernandez Colon, president of the Senate and probable heir to the mantle of Muñoz-Marín as leader of the P.D.P., is quoted as having said, "If we could, then I think we should be an independent nation. But we can't, and that's the reality." The fact that upwards of fifty of the members of the United Nations have fewer people, far less wealth, and a much lower degree of development than does Puerto Rico seems not to sway the thinking of the commonwealth partisans.

As the Status Commission reported in 1966 (see chapter 12), all three of the status alternatives proposed for Puerto Rico—statehood, independence, or an evolving commonwealth—are compatible with the dignity and well-being of the island. In the election of Governor Ferré the voters may, or they may not, have given the green light to progress toward statehood. As the duly chosen executive, however, Señor Ferré reserves the right to lay the groundwork for an eventual statehood bid. In the light of this new policy the kinds of projects that CODECA was involved in or was planning for the future were unwise and even bordered on disloyalty to the United States. In any event, this will be the island's conception of its external affairs at least until the election of 1972. As a loyal candidate for statehood Puerto Rico will defer to Washington in all matters of external relations in the Caribbean.

Partisans of the P.D.P. and those who helped create the CODECA pattern of informal international cooperation naturally enough remain unconvinced regarding this new official outlook. Without retracting any of the arguments cited in the justification of Puerto Rico's role in Caribbean affairs in the last chapter, friends of CODECA in 1969 returned with renewed emphasis to the argument of *scale*.

As a petitioner for statehood—or even as the fifty-first state—Puerto Rico has to compete in Washington for favors and attention with the claims of the other and larger areas of the United States and with the demands of virtually the entire outside world. When faced with the Vietnam war abroad, and with problems of inflation, poverty, racial imbalance, and environmental pollution at home—to cite only the more obvious examples—the requirements of little Puerto Rico are necessarily low on the list of priorities, so far as Washington is concerned. But as a commonwealth growing in its freedom to engage in regional foreign relations and in its skill in playing this role, Puerto Rico could draw up its own list of Caribbean priorities and view the affairs of the region in what to Puerto Rican eyes is the proper scale.

Let one important example suffice to show what these Puerto Ricans mean. The following is a portion of an address given by Dr. Passalacqua before a meeting of the local International Studies Association convention in San Juan early in April of 1969.

We are all aware of the United Nations Conference on Trade and Development, UNCTAD, and that one of its recent proposals, endorsed by the United States, calls for the developed countries to grant unilateral trade preferences to the manufacturers and semi-manufacturers of the underdeveloped countries. We are also aware of the fact that the United States Government is now conducting a study of some 200 items on which such preferences could be granted. We are further aware of the fact that a task force of some 100 businessmen, industrialists, academicians and government officials have rendered a report to the President recommending that such preferences be granted to Latin America. Finally, we are aware that a study carried out by the U.S. Department of State on U.S. policy in the Caribbean also recommends this. At least we should be aware of these facts. They have all been in the press since December. They are, taken together with repeated statements by the President, the Secretary of State and other high officials on a "trade not aid" approach to Latin America, a clear indication of a new foreign trade policy.

However, if you were to compare the list of products under consideration with the list of products exported by Puerto Rico to the United States, you would be astonished at their similarity. Included in the list are goods that represent a very high proportion of Puerto Rico's exports to the United States perhaps as much as 40 per cent.

Since it is generally recognized that production costs in Puerto Rico are much higher than elsewhere in Latin America and the Caribbean, it should follow that our free-market arrangement with the United States provides us with a competitive advantage over other countries. If, however, trade preferences were to be established, the competitive advantage would disappear and might even become a very serious disadvantage because competitive goods could invade the Puerto Rican market place also. This would adversely affect not only our export market but even our domestic market. It would also affect decisions as to the location of new industrial plant and the expansion . . . or contraction . . . of what we have.

It may well be in the national interest of the United States to grant such trade preferences, but no degree of self-delusion can hide the fact that it would certainly *not* be in the national interest of Puerto Rico. Our common market system situation would become meaningless and we would need to seek new markets to replace the old and a new line of production.

Here is an extreme case. But there are many where the difference is one of degree. Many events in the Caribbean that deserve only passing notice from the United States, if any at all, have an important effect in Puerto Rico. The existence and success of the Caribbean Free Trade Area and the Caribbean Development Bank are of considerably greater importance to Puerto Rico than they are to the United States. So is Anguilla. So is the future of the Dominican Republic. So is Jamaica's rejection by the O.A.S.

If we were to rely solely on U.S. foreign policy to foster Puerto Rico's interests in these matters, we would wait in vain. If they are to know what our interests are we must tell them. If we are to tell them we must formulate a foreign policy, a Puerto Rican foreign policy.

The End of the Line

The shifting patterns of regional international cooperation in the West Indies which for some twenty-seven years cut across the boundaries and the diverse national heritages of a kaleidoscopic region apparently will end with the demise of CODECA in 1969. The line of descent which this book has attempted to trace from Anglo-American Caribbean Commission, to Caribbean Commission, to Caribbean Organization, and finally to CODECA threatens to peter out, perhaps for good, in the termination of CODECA as an independent agency.

I must refrain from making any value judgment on this latest turn of events. As a student of international organization and related phenomena I have remained intensely interested in these changing structures and would naturally be delighted to see further experimentation and innovation. But of course the people of Puerto Rico and of every other island and territory in the Caribbean have a perfect right to view their relations with far-off metropoles and with other peoples in the West Indies in any way they choose.

It was to study the phenomenon of international organization in an area of the world which presented the poorest imaginable soil for the sprouting of such structures, that this research was undertaken in the first place. Such were the hurdles to be overcome in the setting up of international organizations in a region where there were essentially no nations that, as we have seen, the creative innovations that were inspired added to the world's storehouse of international political experience. If now, however, new nations in the region such as Jamaica, Trinidad, Barbados, and Guyana wish to look outward toward larger international systems than the Caribbean can offer, and if the remaining territories in the region have reached new milestones in their struggle to discover their political identities, then it may indeed be the opportune time to record an end to the patterns of international cooperation begun with the A.A.C.C. and to wait while the processes of political introspection work themselves out in the Caribbean. It could well be that by 1969 the mixture of status-seeking and self-study among the political units of the West Indies is such that for the time being no truly international cooperative organization such as those described in this book can now be sustained.

The hard facts of geography, small-scale territories, and political isolation and neglect which have for centuries been characteristic of the West Indies remain unchanged, however, whatever the colors on the political map of the region may seek to exhibit. Thus it is interesting that even while what this book has described as the mainstream thread of international organization in the Caribbean comes to an end with CODECA, other efforts at international cooperation were being attempted in limited and piecemeal fashion elsewhere in the West Indies. It will be the purpose of the next and final chapter to take a brief look at these other experiments.

16 □ ALTERNATIVE STRATEGIES FOR CARIBBEAN INTEGRATION

In 1968 the Institute of Caribbean Studies of the University of Puerto Rico published a basic and much needed study by Professor Aaron Segal, entitled *The Politics of Caribbean Economic Integration.*[1] In this pioneering work Professor Segal discusses at length the various strategies which have arisen in recent years to foster the *economic* integration of the West Indies.

Economic versus Political Integration

Economists and political scientists argue interminably over whether it is basically economics or politics which informs and determines the destiny of nations and international systems. All they can agree on is that it is impossible and largely fruitless to try to separate the two phenomena. The making of an economic decision by a government or by an international organization is an act of politics; economic conditions and possibilities often determine the boundaries within which political decisions can be made.

It has been the purpose of this book to examine the successive structures which have worked toward international cooperation in the Caribbean. Looking upon these agencies as *international organizations,* that is, as bodies whose members are separate and diverse political entities, the study has been primarily oriented toward the political. The West Indian Conferences of the Caribbean Commission and the Caribbean Council of the Caribbean Organization were *political* bodies in the truest sense. But of course the content of their work consisted to a large degree of *economics* —along with matters of social, cultural, and technical cooperation, health, education, and so on.

The theme of Professor Segal's study is that political integration has not succeeded and will not work in the West Indies. He notes:

The current discussion of regionalism is virtually unanimous that economic integration should not extend to political integration or unification. It is rejected on grounds of both desirability and practicality. The failures of the Caribbean Organization and the West Indian Federation have left widespread distrust of political regionalism. It has been identified with the undue influence of the metropolitan powers. Introduction of questions of political distribution of power is considered certain to reawake past memories, provoke hostility, and curtail the chances of economic cooperation. The diversity and incompatibility of political systems and experiences, the enormous differences in size, wealth and population between the islands, and the overwhelming predominance of national loyalties and identifications are all fundamental obstacles to political integration. What is desired is the minimum of political consensus required to permit economic integration to be initiated. There are few expectations that the learning experience of successful economic integration will somehow generate politicization.[2]

Professor Segal's last remark in the paragraph quoted above refers indirectly to the tremendous amount of work which has been done in the last fifteen years by theorists of international integration. Noteworthy among these theorists are Ernst Haas and Philippe Schmitter.

Does the economic integration of a group of nations automatically trigger political unity? Or are the two processes quite distinct, requiring deliberate political steps because purely economic arrangements are generally inadequate for ushering in political unity?[3] This is the basic question posed by Haas and Schmitter relative to the automaticity of the link between economic and political integration. Their thesis is that "under modern conditions the relationship between economic and political union had best be treated as a continuum."[4] Their reason for making this assertion is best summarized by the following passage from their work:

Linkages between economic objectives and policies, on the one hand, and political consequences of a disintegrative or integrative nature, on the other, are of a "functional" character: they rest very often on indirection, on unplanned and accidental convergence in outlook and aspiration among the actors, on dialectical relations between antagonistic purposes. They also frequently contain elements of creative personal action by administrators who seize upon crises, the solution of which upgrades common interests among the actors; hence they include an organizational component which may, depending on the organization, be of dominant significance. Integration can be conceived as involving the gradual politicization of the actors' purposes which were initially considered "technical" or "noncontroversial." Politicization implies that the actors, in response to the initial purposes, agree to widen the spectrum of means considered appropriate to attain them. This tends to increase the controversial component, i.e., those additional fields of action which require political choices concerning how much national autonomy to delegate to the union. Politicization implies that the actors seek to resolve their problems so as to upgrade common interests and, in the process, delegate more authority to the center. It constitutes one of the properties of integration—the intervening variable between economic and political union—along with the development of new expectations and loyalties on the part of organized interests in the member nations.[5]

Professor Segal doubts that in the West Indies successful efforts at economic integration will generate politicization, this process generally referred to in the literature by the shorthand expression, "spillover."* Therefore in studying current integration efforts in the West Indies Professor Segal thinks it would be more profitable to concentrate on those strategies which look toward closer economic cooperation. Yet hardly any student of these phenomena doubts that from successful organs of international economic cooperation a certain degree of spillover to the political is almost certain to occur, not only as the decision-makers of the organization respond to crises which arise in the process of economic union but also as the actors simply make the kinds of decisions which will safeguard their collective economic welfare.

We are back to a matter of definition again, but when decisions are jointly made to safeguard economic arrangements which have been made through collective international action, such an output can fairly be labeled "political" in the broadest sense.

Let us therefore examine the strategies identified for us by Segal and then look briefly at the emerging agencies of limited international cooperation in the Caribbean. We must suspend judgment for now whether these efforts will eventually spill over into political integration of some sort among the countries of the West Indies.

First Strategy: The CODECA Concept

Professor Segal cites as the first strategy of proposed economic integration in the Caribbean the approach selected by CODECA. Although when he wrote his analysis Professor Segal had no way of knowing that CODECA was soon to be phased out, his description of the CODECA approach is nevertheless worthy of examination for the permanent insights such a study offers. According to Segal:

CODECA eschews regional preferential trade arrangements and prefers to concentrate on limited, specialized and technical services not readily available at the national level. CODECA tacitly accepts the political and economic *status quo* in the Caribbean including the prevalence of external over regional economic integration . . . .

CODECA seeks to organize regional functional cooperation in such areas as improved statistical services and national accounting, a coordinated technical assistance program to provide volunteer teachers to the smaller islands, a proposed regional bibliographic center and service, a regional air and maritime transport. CODECA rigorously avoids the political presence of non-Caribbean powers

---

*Spillover has been defined as a convergence of goals and expectations to support any given step in integration in which assurance of original goals requires further actions which create further conditions and need for more action. The initial task and grant of power to central institutions creates situations dealt with only by expanding the task and grant of power. See Leon N. Lindberg, *The Political Dynamics of European Economic Integration* (Stanford University Press, 1963), p. 10.

which proved so fatal to the Caribbean Organization and initially requests nothing more than appointment by each government of a high-ranking civil servant as liaison officer for Caribbean projects . . . .

The CODECA strategy is to provide direct and useful experience of limited functional tasks which have a low political content. It is a learn-to-crawl-before-one-walks strategy based on a realistic appraisal of the prevailing insularity, suspicion and lack of contact among the islands. It is a strategy which minimizes risks and permits losses or failures to be isolated without jeopardizing other programs. It is a strategy comparable to that pursued by the U.N. Economic Commission for Latin America (ECLA) in Central America during the period 1950–1958, prior to the signing of the first Central American regional free trade treaty. CODECA envisions modest functional tasks as building a climate of mutually beneficial exchange and confidence to enable a development strategy for the Caribbean based on tourism and agricultural diversification to be presented.[6]

Second Strategy: Caribbean Free Trade Association (CARIFTA)

According to Professor Segal:

The second strategy is that embodied in the draft Caribbean Free Trade Association (CARIFTA), negotiated in 1965 between Antigua, Barbados and Guyana and due to come into operation in 1967. Copied almost verbatim from the EFTA agreement, CARIFTA calls for nothing more than a modest and gradual elimination of tariffs and other trade restrictions. It provides for a regional secretariat with little more than statistical and administrative functions and no supranational authority. CARIFTA requires the minimum sacrifice of political sovereignty and offers little room for task expansion. It is considered to be the most that governments can be induced politically to accept under present circumstances while offering the prompt short-term advantage of increased trade flows . . . .

The CARIFTA strategy has been endorsed by the Incorporated Chambers of Commerce and Industry of the Commonwealth Caribbean. This organization sent a delegation of local industrialists and businessmen throughout the Commonwealth Caribbean in September–October 1966 to promote the idea of a phased free trade area. The report of this delegation considers a free trade area to be the only immediately politically feasible form of economic integration. There is also business resistance to the more active public sector role, including planned location of new industry, which an economic union might imply.[7]

Third Strategy: Proposals by Economists of the University of the West Indies

The third strategy is that proposed in the series of studies concerning economic integration commissioned in 1965 by the governments of Jamaica and Trinidad and being published in 1967 by a group of young economists associated with the University of the West Indies (UWI). These studies depend on the concept of a subregional economic community of the Commonwealth Caribbean, intended to rationalize existing and future production regionally through the planned organization of economic complementarity. It is not only that the UWI economists are *dirigiste* whereas the businessmen favor removal of restrictions on trade. The UWI studies emphasize the planned pooling of economic resources at the regional level, both to create a larger internal market and to enhance external bargaining power for the Commonwealth Caribbean as a region. The flaw in these studies is that they fail to analyze the political arrangements and political process required to achieve this degree of economic integration. These proposals necessitate an implied or explicit degree of supranational authority.[8]

Summary Comparison of the Three Strategies

Professor Segal notes that:

The three strategies are not so much in conflict as at cross purposes. The CODECA strategy is intended to embrace as much of the Caribbean as is politically possible, through provision of specific tasks and services. It is a strategy which emphasizes flexibility without confronting sovereignty. The CARIFTA strategy concentrates on present trade flows and its primary economic objective is trade diversion rather than trade creation. It is intended to permit industrialists to make more efficient use of existing capacity through marginal preferential access to wider markets but does not commit governments or firms to future activity. The UWI strategy emphasizes stimulation of new economic activity based on regional rather than national resource allocation. It promises the largest economic benefits but asks short-run economic and political sacrifices.[9]

THE NEW AGENCIES OF ECONOMIC COOPERATION

Even as CODECA's mandate runs out, bringing to a close the pattern of cooperation first envisioned in the Anglo-American Caribbean Commission in 1942, new structures are arising in the Caribbean to attempt in other ways and in limited areas to advance some of the goals which CODECA and its predecessors sought to achieve.

In particular we shall take a brief look at the Caribbean Free Trade Association and its Commonwealth Regional Secretariat; the Caribbean Development Bank; and the Regional Development Agency in Antigua. At this writing none of these agencies has had time to make a significant mark on the affairs of the West Indies, so we must leave it to be assessed in later years how well these new organizations fared in their assigned tasks.

Caribbean Free Trade Association (CARIFTA)

Professor Segal identified as his second strategy for economic integration in the Caribbean the formation of the Caribbean Free Trade Association (or CARIFTA). As he indicated in the passage quoted from his work, the original CARIFTA agreement was negotiated in 1965 between Antigua, Barbados, and Guyana. The Association did not, however, come into operation in 1967, as anticipated by Segal.

The original CARIFTA agreement, signed on December 15, 1965, between Antigua, Barbados, and Guyana, was initially intended to come into force on September 1, 1966. By that date the agreement had been ratified by Antigua and Barbados, but Guyana's ratification was not completed until December 30, 1966.[10]

Since the original agreement was open to accession by all other Commonwealth countries in the Caribbean area, representatives of twelve of the Commonwealth islands and territories met at Georgetown, Guyana, on August 17, 1967, and decided to recommend to their governments that the agreement be modified to become the basis for freeing the trade of the entire region, not just that of the three original signatories.[11]

Proposals and recommendations for a revised CARIFTA agreement were discussed at a conference of heads of government of twelve Commonwealth Caribbean countries, held in Bridgetown, Barbados, from October 24 to October 28, 1967. At this conference it was agreed that free trade among the Caribbean countries should be introduced by May 1, 1968. This was subject to agreement on a list of reserved commodities which would not be affected immediately but would be freed within a five-year period for the developed members and within ten years for the less developed member countries.[12]

Another meeting, this time of the ministers of trade of the area, was held in Guyana in February 1968, for the purpose of making final adjustments and amendments so that it might apply to the expanded region. Jamaica did not attend this meeting, thus foreshadowing some difficulties which would lie ahead in starting operations under CARIFTA. From Kingston it was announced that the various agencies and departments of the Jamaica government and the pertinent interest groups in Jamaica had not had time to study the modified CARIFTA proposals.[13]

May 1, 1968, arrived to find only one other country—Trinidad—having formally adhered to the CARIFTA agreement in addition to the three original signatories. Jamaica continued to have misgivings about an economic union with the smaller, underdeveloped eastern Caribbean islands.

By July 1, 1968, however, all of the eastern islands and island groupings had completed arrangements to associate with CARIFTA, and on June 23 Jamaica had fallen into line. Jamaica's application was formally accepted on June 28, 1968. In the final analysis Jamaica could not afford to cut herself off from a potentially important regional market and thus lose some of its attractiveness to investors—particularly in comparison with Jamaica's great rival, Trinidad.[14]

With Jamaica in place only two territories of the Commonwealth Caribbean indicated as potential members of CARIFTA were absent: British Honduras and the Bahamas.

The CARIFTA agreement calls for free trade among the signatories, subject to certain qualifications as stated in the treaty. Two lists of area-origin goods are included, on which duties will be reduced gradually. Annex B lists fourteen products on which duties will be phased out over five years for the developed countries (20 percent per year); these include, for example, tobacco, radio and TV sets, and leather footwear. The less developed countries are allowed to maintain pre-CARIFTA duties on these products for five years and 50 percent of original duties for an additional five years.

Annex D calls for similar five-year elimination of the "effective protective element" in duties on beer, stout, and ale; gin; vodka and whisky; petroleum products; and rum. The less developed countries are given ten years to eliminate the protection of rum.

Article 38 of the agreement gives Guyana the right to impose quantitative restrictions on petroleum products from other members for fifteen years. This is to allow Guyana to protect its newly established refining industry. Article 39 serves as an escape clause for the less developed members, to enable them to foster industrial development.[15]

Along with the main agreement are two concurrent protocols on local agricultural production. Members are to reduce their extrazonal imports of twenty-two basic food commodities in three years to 30 percent of their 1966 level. The Secretariat will allocate markets among the CARIFTA producers and it alone will sanction imports from outside the area. An annual conference will set market prices. The second protocol allows the imposition of quantitative restrictions on sugar, to prevent movement of this commodity from one producing area to another because of different price-setting arrangements.[16]

As for the structure of CARIFTA, Article 28 of the agreement provides for a Council to supervise the application of the agreement and keep its operations under review. Each member is to be represented on the Council and have one vote. Article 28 further provides for the establishment of a Commonwealth Caribbean Regional Secretariat to be the principal administrative organ of the Association. The Council may entrust the Regional Secretariat with such functions as it considers necessary to assist it in accomplishing its tasks for the Association.

Headquarters for the Caribbean Regional Secretariat, and hence the administrative center for CARIFTA, have been established at Georgetown, Guyana.

Indications from the first year of operations under CARIFTA are encouraging. Both Jamaica and Guyana have sent trade missions to other

CARIFTA countries, and Trinidad and Barbados have begun vigorous promotional campaigns.

As a direct result of the new arrangements, Jamaica received an order for 500,000 yards of cotton fabric from Trinidad in October 1968; and Trinidad in turn received from Jamaica an order for 5,000,000 boxes of matches. These and other items of new business are generally taken as evidence of a genuine desire to expand regional trade.[17]

Caribbean Development Bank and Regional Development Agency

Both the Caribbean Development Bank and the Regional Development Agency owe their inception to recommendations made in the *Report of the Tripartite Economic Survey of the Eastern Caribbean (January–April 1966)*, drawn up by six distinguished scholars and financed jointly by the governments of Canada, the United Kingdom, and the United States. Excerpts from this report, dealing with a regional approach to development programming, are included in the Appendix.

The Tripartite Survey was followed in 1967 by a mission sent to the region by the United Nations Development Program. The result of this mission was a set of concrete proposals for a Caribbean Development Bank.[18]

The conference of heads of government of twelve Commonwealth Caribbean countries meeting in Bridgetown, Barbados, in October 1967, which agreed to the setting up of CARIFTA, also resolved to proceed with the creation of the Caribbean Development Bank. In brief, the plan conceives of a bank with a capital of U.S. $50 million, 30 million subscribed by the regional members and 20 million subscribed by the non-regional members: Canada, the United Kingdom, and the United States. The regional members are stated to be Barbados, Guyana, Trinidad, Jamaica, and the associated states, plus Montserrat and St. Vincent. The Bahamas and British Honduras are considering membership; and, as noted in the last chapter, CODECA in 1968 was in the throes of seeking for Puerto Rico an avenue for membership in the bank.

Half of the subscribed capital would be paid in annual installments over a period of four years, 50 percent of this in gold or convertible currencies. Later a fund of 20 million dollars would be raised to provide "soft loans" for non-self-liquidating infrastructure projects. This latter fund would perform a "soft loan" function similar to that of the International Development Association (IDA), in the structure of the International Bank for Reconstruction and Development, the World Bank. Had CODECA succeeded in launching its Caribbean Investment Corporation (CARINCO), that agency could eventually have performed for the Caribbean Development Bank members the same service that the International

Finance Corporation (IFC) does for the World Bank, that is, to encourage development through the actual purchase of shares in new enterprises.

Jamaica caused difficulties in the setting up of the bank, just as she did with the evolution of CARIFTA. On April 11, 1968, Jamaica announced withdrawal from the planning for the bank.[19] The question at issue was where the headquarters for the bank should be located. Jamaica insisted that the bank be located in Kingston, where adequately trained personnel experienced in fiscal management would be available. Jamaica also maintained that locating the bank in the eastern Caribbean would overplay that area's role in the development of the Commonwealth Caribbean. Jamaica suggested that headquarters be in Kingston with a branch office in the eastern islands.

An international conference was held on Antigua on April 27-28, 1968, at which it was decided that the bank should be located at Bridgetown, Barbados, despite the objections of Jamaica.

At this writing a draft charter for the bank has not been approved and therefore no loans have been processed or other business transacted.

Following the recommendations of the Tripartite Economic Survey of 1966, a Regional Development Agency has been set up on the island of Antigua. Members of the Agency are Barbados and the Associated States, plus St. Vincent and Montserrat. Canada, the United Kingdom, and the United States are "cooperating countries" but not members. The specter of the metropolitan powers sitting at the conference tables with the countries of the region, which so haunted the affairs of the Caribbean Commission and the Caribbean Organization, is raised again in the form of these outside "cooperating countries." The addition of Canada to the list of outside powers is interesting, inasmuch as Canada never possessed territories in the West Indies.* The Caribbean does indeed provide a fascinating study of political phenomena. One is led to wonder what effect these outside powers will have on the work of the Regional Development Agency, other than to be the source of financial aid. It is, of course, significant in this connection, however, that we are dealing here with an agency whose constituency is limited to the Commonwealth Caribbean and does not extend to countries sensitive of their autonomy like Puerto Rico and the Netherlands Antilles.

The organs of the Regional Development Agency are the Board of Directors, the Regional Development Committee, and the Executive Secretariat, located in St. John's, Antigua. The purposes of the Agency, on behalf of and for the benefit of the participating governments, are as follows:

---

*It is widely believed in the West Indies that when the Associated States concept was being developed Antigua pleaded with Canada to be allowed to become a Canadian province.

1. To promote activities in the fields of tourism, industrial development, agriculture, forestry, fisheries, and the use of industrial materials.

2. To promote the development of regional and external communications both by air and sea.

3. To obtain from abroad technical services in such fields as:
   a. Technical education
   b. Land use, town planning and cadastral survey
   c. Regional statistical services
   d. Specialized training programs
   e. Market research and intelligence services

4. To carry out development planning and feasibility studies.[20]

It is devoutly to be hoped that the executive secretary, Mr. George E. Williams, is aware of the research which has already been done in all of these subjects over a period of more than a quarter of a century by the Caribbean Commission, the Caribbean Organization, and CODECA. The West Indies deserves better than simply another round of starting from scratch.

In May of 1968 the United States Agency for International Development signed technical assistance agreements with the Regional Development Agency to help the latter to establish a Regional Statistical Service; to contract for a study on the future of tourism in the eastern Caribbean; and to contract for assistance in organization and planning. In May of 1969, as a result of contract assistance from A.I.D., the Regional Development Agency published a 288-page report entitled *The Future of Tourism in the Eastern Caribbean.* The report was written by H. Zinder and Associates, Washington, D.C., based on field work carried out in October of 1968.

Canada has provided assistance in elementary school construction, specialized technical training, and is undertaking a study of the air transport needs of the area. The United Kingdom has prepared a study on vocational training and has offered assistance in other fields.[21]

To anyone who has followed the work of the Caribbean Commission, Caribbean Organization, and CODECA, the foregoing has a decidedly familiar ring. From the point of view of the peoples and governments of the West Indies it is somewhat depressing that these projects are being carried out *for* them by Canada, the United Kingdom, and the United States.

By Way of Conclusion

Inasmuch as these new agencies of economic cooperation and integration are arising even while CODECA is dying, the story of international organization in the Caribbean cannot be declared at an end. Within just over twenty-five years this region of the world which had (and which has) virtually none of the makings of international organization nevertheless has produced not one but as many as six distinct patterns of institutional cooperation.

The Caribbean has often been referred to as a "political laboratory" because of the strikingly different political and constitutional orders found there, and because of the great diversity of cultures, languages, races, and levels of income and development. In view of the efforts at international cooperation described in this book the Caribbean might also be considered an "integration laboratory." Despite the great heterogeneity of historical, cultural, and national heritages, the West Indies islands and territories nevertheless have much in common as they confront the modern world.

The one consistent theme which revealed itself in every change of pattern, from Anglo-American Caribbean Commission to CODECA, was the region's urge to expel the metropolitan powers from decision-making with regard to regional cooperation. As most of the territories moved steadily in the direction of autonomy, self-government, and independence, the natural urge was to be rid of the nagging reminder of colonialism which was represented by the participation of the metropolitan governments in the regional institutions. Thus there was the intense pressure first to sustain the West Indian Conference, then to scrap the Caribbean Commission altogether in favor of the Caribbean Organization. The Caribbean Organization in its turn foundered largely because the region discovered to its chagrin that it had not completely frozen out the metropolitan powers after all. In this light, then, CODECA was the ultimate swing of the pendulum in the direction of Caribbean regional affairs strictly in the hands of Caribbean people. Yet Puerto Ricans are also American citizens. The metropolitan powers are hard to eliminate from the affairs of the West Indies. The new Regional Development Agency does not even try.

In retrospect it can be said that the Caribbean Organization came too soon, though it certainly was not too soon for the people who created it. It was, nevertheless, an immature attempt on the part of the West Indies to run their own international show, and because it came too soon it failed. The Caribbean Organization therefore had to give way until a new pattern of international cooperation could emerge. Puerto Rico took up the burden of keeping the spirit of cooperation alive and carrying on the good work.

It is therefore ironic that, after all of the effort to which Puerto Rico went in forcing the changes of pattern from Caribbean Commission to Caribbean Organization and then from Caribbean Organization to CODECA, she should be the one to drop out of the integration movement almost altogether while seeking to move toward statehood.

Puerto Rico's current indecision about its role in Caribbean affairs had an earlier parallel in Jamaica's efforts to find its niche in the larger world. At the time that Barbados was applying to join the Organization of American States in 1967, Jamaica was under some pressure to join the O.A.S. too. But at a press conference in London in September of 1967 Prime Minister Hugh Shearer said that Jamaica had decided "after long and careful consideration" to opt for Europe rather than America. Referring to his country's interest in association with the European Economic Community, or Common Market, the prime minister stated that membership in the O.A.S. and the E.E.C. are *de facto* if not *de jure* mutually exclusive. He said, "we choose Europe because the hard facts of our economic life are that Britain and Europe are more important to us than America."[22] And, as we have already seen, Jamaica dragged its heels with both CARIFTA and the Caribbean Development Bank.

Trinidad and Barbados have joined the O.A.S. Guyana would too except that it has a border dispute with Venezuela, and O.A.S. rules do not permit application from a country while a member has a territorial claim against it. With these extra-Caribbean associations made or pending, with Puerto Rico looking toward statehood, with Jamaica choosing Europe over America, and with the French territories apparently very little interested in Caribbean ties, this may indeed be a bleak season for large-scale integration movements and true international organization experiments in the West Indies.

It is perhaps significant of the current state of West Indies affairs that the two newest structures—CARIFTA and the bank, with their associated bodies—are, so far, limited in their constituency to the British (or Commonwealth) Caribbean, and that the role of the metropolitan powers is again recognized. The forces of nationalism are indeed producing strange effects in this area, and the Caribbean remains a political laboratory.

I will not venture to predict whether CARIFTA, the bank, and the Regional Development Agency will eventually enlarge to take in a scope wider than the Commonwealth Caribbean. What can be surely asserted, however, is that the potential benefits from cooperation and coordination in the entire Caribbean area are just as apparent today as they were in 1942, or in 1946 when the four-power Caribbean Commission was formed. In the 1970s, no less than in the 1940s, 1950s, or 1960s, the Caribbean would profit from cooperative efforts in such areas as tropical agriculture, marine biology, economic planning statistics, low-cost housing design and construction, health, and education. The question is, will some agency or agencies now in existence or yet to be born take up the burden of coordination, research, and action in these areas?

The answer is almost surely yes. The West Indies region remains crisscrossed with international organization ties. It is an area of concern for the United Nations and its Economic Commission for Latin America (which has a regional office in Trinidad), for the O.A.S., and even for the E.E.C. and the O.E.C.D. Nearby are the Central American Common

Market, the Latin American Free Trade Area, and the Inter-American Development Bank. It was noted in the very beginning of this book that by the action of a sort of Parkinson's law, the secretariat structures of international organizations always seem to generate the willingness and the facilities for doing worthwhile jobs in their region beyond the stated purposes in their charters. The Caribbean Commission may have helped formulate the modern concept of international cooperative technical assistance, which then spread to the South Pacific and to the Colombo Plan and all around the world. Every major international organization in the world engages to some degree in international cooperative technical assistance. If SEATO, a military alliance, can devote a great part of its resources and energy to international cholera research and treatment, then surely some international agency situated in or near the Caribbean will step in to fill the void left with the demise of CODECA. Whether in the Caribbean there will be spillover from the economic to the political, there will almost certainly be spillover to research and technical assistance. Such spillover might well come from the activities of the Commonwealth Caribbean Regional Secretariat at Georgetown or from the Regional Development Agency on Antigua. For the benefit of the long-suffering and neglected peoples of the West Indies we can only hope that some new pattern of area-wide international cooperation will manifest itself promptly and that it will soon produce solid achievements.

APPENDIXES

A. □ AN AGREEMENT FOR THE ESTABLISHMENT OF THE CARIBBEAN COMMISSION (1946)

The Governments of the United States of America, the French Republic, the Kingdom of the Netherlands, and the United Kingdom of Great Britain and Northern Ireland, whose duly authorized representatives have subscribed hereto,

Being desirous of encouraging and strengthening cooperation among themselves and their territories with a view toward improving the economic and social well-being of the peoples of those territories, and

Being desirous of promoting scientific, technological, and economic development in the Caribbean area and facilitating the use of resources and concerted treatment of mutual problems, avoiding duplication in the work of existing research agencies, surveying needs, ascertaining what research has been done, facilitating research on a cooperative basis, and recommending further research, and

Having decided to associate themselves in the work heretofore undertaken by the Anglo-American Caribbean Commission, and

Having agreed that the objectives herein set forth are in accord with the principles of the Charter of the United Nations

Hereby agree as follows:

ARTICLE I
Establishment of the Caribbean Commission and Auxiliary Bodies

There are hereby established the Caribbean Commission (herein-after referred to as "the Commission") and, as auxiliary bodies of the Commission, the Caribbean Research Council and the West Indian Conference (hereinafter referred to as "the Research Council" and "the Conference" respectively).

ARTICLE II
Composition of the Commission

1. The Commission shall consist of not more than sixteen Commissioners appointed by the Governments signatory hereto (hereinafter referred to as the "Member Governments"). Each Member Government may appoint four Commissioners and such alternates as it may deem necessary. Each such group of Commissioners shall form a national section of the Commission.

2. Each Member Government shall designate one of its Commissioners to be the Chairman of its national section. Each such Chairman, or in his absence, the Commissioner designated by him from his national section as his alternate, shall be a Co-Chairman of the Commission and shall preside over meetings of the Commission in rotation according to English alphabetical order of the Member Governments, irrespective of where a meeting of the Commission may be held.

ARTICLE III
Powers of the Commission

The Commission shall be a consultative and advisory body and shall have such legal capacity as may be necessary for the exercise of its functions and the fulfilment of its purposes.

ARTICLE IV
Functions of the Commission

The functions of the Commission shall be as follows:

(1) To concern itself with economic and social matters of common interest to the Caribbean area particularly agriculture, communications, education, fisheries, health, housing, industry, labor, social welfare and trade.

(2) To study, formulate and recommend on its own initiative, or as may be proposed by any of the Member or territorial Governments, by the Research Council or the Conference, measures, programs and policies with respect to social and economic problems designed to contribute to the well-being of the Caribbean area. It shall advise the Member and territorial Governments on all such matters, and make recommendations for the carrying into effect of all action necessary or desirable in this connection.

(3) To assist in co-ordinating local projects which have regional significance and to provide technical guidance from a wide field not otherwise available.

(4) To direct and review the activities of the Research Council and to formulate its rules of procedure.

(5) To provide for the convening of the sessions of the Conference, to formulate its rules of procedure, and to report to the Member Governments on Conference resolutions and recommendations.

ARTICLE V
Meetings of the Commission

1. The Commission shall hold not less than two Commission meetings each year. It is empowered to convene and hold meetings at any time and at any place it may decide.

2. At all such meetings the four Co-Chairmen, or their designated alternates, shall constitute a quorum.

ARTICLE VI
Method of Arriving at Decisions

The Commission shall be empowered to determine the method of arriving at its decisions, providing that decisions other than those relating to procedure shall not be taken without the concurrence of the respective Co-Chairmen or their designated alternates.

ARTICLE VII
The Research Council

The Research Council, together with such Research Committees as the Commission may establish, shall serve as an auxiliary body of the Commission with respect to scientific, technological, social and economic research for the benefit of the peoples of the Caribbean area.

ARTICLE VIII
Composition of the Research Council

1. The Research Council shall consist of not less than seven and not more than fifteen members who shall be appointed by the Commission having special regard to their scientific competence. At least one member of each Research Committee shall be a member of the Research Council.

2. The Research Council shall elect a Chairman from among its members. A Deputy Chairman of the Research Council shall be appointed by the Commission and shall serve on the Central Secretariat.

3. The present composition of the Research Council and of its Research Committees shall be deemed to be effective from the 1st day of January, 1946.

ARTICLE IX
Functions of the Research Council

The functions of the Research Council shall be:

(a) To recommend to the Commission the number and functions of the technical Research Committees necessary to provide specialized scientific consideration of Caribbean research problems.

(b) In the interest of the Caribbean area to ascertain what research has been done, to survey needs, to advise concerning desirable research projects, to arrange and facilitate cooperative research, to undertake research assignments of a special nature which no other agency is able and willing to carry out, and to collect and disseminate information concerning research.

(c) To recommend to the Commission the holding of Research Council and Committee meetings and also of meetings of scientific, specialist and extension workers, and to facilitate an interchange of experience among the research workers of the Caribbean.

ARTICLE X
The Conference

The Conference shall be an auxiliary body of the Commission. The continuity of its existence shall be ensured by means of regular sessions.

ARTICLE XI
Composition of the Conference

1. Each territorial government shall be entitled to send to each session of the

Conference not more than two delegates and as many advisers as it may consider necessary.

2. Delegates to the Conference shall be appointed for each territory in accordance with its constitutional procedure. The duration of their appointments shall be determined by the appointing governments.

ARTICLE XII
Functions of the Conference

The sessions of the Conference shall provide a regular means of consultation with and between the delegates from the territories on matters of common interest within the terms of reference of the Commission as described in Article IV hereof, and shall afford the opportunity to present to the Commission recommendations on such matters.

ARTICLE XIII
Meetings of the Conference

1. The Commission shall convene the Conference at least biennially, on such date as the Commission shall decide. The location of each session of the Conference, which shall be in one of the territories, shall be selected in rotation according to English alphabetical order of the Member Governments.

2. The Chairman of each session of the Conference shall be the Chairman of the national section of the Commission in whose territory the session is held.

ARTICLE XIV
Central Secretariat

1. The Commission shall establish, at a place within the Caribbean area to be agreed upon by the Member Governments, a Central Secretariat to serve the Commission and its auxiliary bodies.

2. A Secretary-General and a Deputy Secretary-General shall be appointed by the Commission under such terms and conditions as it shall prescribe. On the occurrence of a vacancy in the office of Secretary-General the position shall not be filled, except for special reasons approved by the Commission, by a candidate of the same nationality as the outgoing Secretary-General, regard being had to the desirability of continuity in the administration of the Commission's business. It shall, however, be open to the Commission at its discretion to reappoint any Secretary-General for a further term. The Secretary-General shall be the chief administrative officer of the Commission and shall carry out all directives of the Commission.

3. The Secretary-General shall be responsible for the proper functioning of the Central Secretariat and shall be empowered, subject to such directions as he may receive from the Commission, to appoint and dismiss such staff as may be deemed necessary to ensure efficient conduct of Commission business, provided that the appointment and dismissal of the Assistants to the Secretary-General shall be subject to approval by the Commission.

4. In the appointment of the Secretary-General, officers and staff of the Central Secretariat, primary consideration shall be given to the technical qualifications and personal integrity of candidates and, to the extent possible consistent with this consideration, such officers and staff shall be recruited within the Caribbean area and with a view to obtaining a balanced national representation.

5. In the performance of their duties, the Secretary-General and the staff shall not seek, receive or observe instructions from any government or from any other authority external to the Commission. They shall refrain from any action which might reflect on their position as international officials responsible only to the Commission.

6. Each Member Government undertakes to respect the exclusively international character of the responsibilities of the Secretary-General and the staff and not to seek to influence them in the discharge of their responsibilities.

7. Each Member Government undertakes so far as possible under its constitutional procedure to accord to the Secretary-General and appropriate personnel of the Central Secretariat such privileges and immunities as are necessary for the independent exercise of their functions, including inviolability of premises and archives of the Central Secretariat. The Commission shall make recommendations with a view to determining the details of the application of this paragraph, or may propose conventions to the Member Governments for this purpose.

ARTICLE XV
Finances

1. The salaries, allowances and miscellaneous expenditures of the Commissioners and their staffs, and of delegates and advisers to conferences, shall be determined and paid by the respective governments appointing them.

2. The Secretary-General shall prepare and submit to the Commission an annual budget and such supplementary budgets as may be required covering all other expenditures of the Commission, including those of the Research Council, the Conference, the Central Secretariat, special research projects, conferences, surveys and other similar activities under Commission auspices. Upon approval of the budget by the Commission, the total amount thereof shall be allocated among the Member Governments in proportions to be determined by agreement. A joint fund shall be established by the Member Governments for the use of the Commission in meeting the expenditures estimated in the said annual or supplementary budgets. Each Member Government shall undertake, subject to the requirements of its constitutional procedure, to contribute promptly to this fund such annual and supplementary sums as may be charged to each as agreed.

3. The fiscal year of the Commission shall be the calendar year. The first budget of the Commission shall cover the period from the date of the entry into force of this Agreement to and including the 31st day of December, 1946.

4. The Secretary-General shall hold and administer the joint fund of the Commission and shall keep proper accounts thereof. The Commission shall make arrangements satisfactory to the Member Governments for the audit of its accounts. The audited statements shall be forwarded annually to each Member Government.

ARTICLE XVI
Authority to Appoint Committees and Make Regulations

The Commission is hereby empowered to appoint committees, and subject to the provisions of this Agreement, to promulgate rules of procedure and regulations governing the operations of the Commission, its auxiliary bodies, the Central Secretariat, and such committees as it shall establish, and generally for the purpose of carrying into effect the terms of this Agreement.

ARTICLE XVII
Relationship with Non-Member Governments in the Area

The Commission and Research Council in their research projects and in the formulation of recommendations shall bear in mind the desirability of cooperation in social and economic matters with other governments of the Caribbean area, not members of the Commission. The issuance of invitations to such governments to participate in conferences or other meetings sponsored by the Commission shall be subject to approval by the Member Governments.

ARTICLE XVIII
Relationship with United Nations and Specialized Agencies

1. The Commission and its auxiliary bodies, while having no present connection with the United Nations, shall cooperate as fully as possible with the United Nations and with appropriate specialized agencies on matters of mutual concern within the terms of reference of the Commission.

2. The Member Governments undertake to consult with the United Nations and the appropriate specialized agencies, at such times and in such manner as may be considered desirable, with a view to defining the relationship which shall exist and to ensuring effective cooperation between the Commission and its auxiliary bodies and the appropriate organs of the United Nations and specialized agencies, dealing with economic and social matters.

ARTICLE XIX
Saving Clause

Nothing in this Agreement shall be construed to conflict with the existing or future constitutional relations between any Member Government and its territories or in any way to affect the constitutional authority and responsibility of the territorial governments.

ARTICLE XX
Definitions

In this Agreement the expressions "territories" or "territorial governments" shall be deemed to relate to the territories, possessions, colonies, or groups of colonies of the Member Governments in the Caribbean area or to the administrations or governments thereof.

ARTICLE XXI
Entry into Force

1. This Agreement shall enter into force when notices of approval[1] thereof shall have been deposited by all four signatory governments with the Government of the United States of America which shall notify the other signatory governments of each such deposit and of the date of entry into force of the Agreement.

2. This Agreement shall have indefinite duration, provided that after an initial period of five years any Member Government may give notice at any time of withdrawal from the Commission. Such notice shall take effect one year after the date of its formal communication to the other Member Governments, but this Agreement shall continue in force with respect to other Member Governments.

In witness whereof the duly authorized representatives of the respective Member Governments have signed this Agreement on the dates appearing opposite their signatures.[2]

Opened for signature in Washington, on October 30, 1946, and done in quadruplicate, in the English, French, and Netherlands languages, each of which shall be equally authentic.

FORMAL MEETINGS OF THE CARIBBEAN COMMISSION

Meeting	Dates	Places
First	February 23–March 13, 1946	St. Thomas, Virgin Islands
Second	July 8–15, 1946	Washington
Third	December 10–14, 1946	Curacao
Fourth	June 23–27, 1947	Jamaica
Fifth	December 8–13, 1947	Trinidad
Sixth	May 24–29, 1948	Puerto Rico
Seventh	December 6–16, 1948	Guadeloupe
Eighth	June 13–18, 1949	Trinidad
Ninth	December 5–9, 1949	St. Thomas, Virgin Islands
Tenth	June 26–July 1, 1950	Martinique
Eleventh	November 24–December 14, 1950	Curacao
Twelfth	May 7–12, 1951	Barbados
Thirteenth	October 29–November 3, 1951	St. Croix, Virgin Islands
Fourteenth	May 6–10, 1952	Guadeloupe
Fifteenth	November 29–December 8, 1952	Jamaica
Sixteenth	May 11–16, 1953	Surinam
Seventeenth	November 30–December 4, 1953	Trinidad
Eighteenth	May 19–22, 1954	British Honduras
Nineteenth	November 29–December 3, 1954	Trinidad
Twentieth	May 14–23, 1955	Puerto Rico
Twenty-first	December 5–12, 1955	Aruba
Twenty-second	May 24–30, 1956	French Guiana
Twenty-third	December 10–15, 1956	Barbados
Twenty-fourth	May 22–27, 1957	St. Thomas, Virgin Islands
Twenty-fifth	November 22–29, 1957	Curacao

Twenty-sixth	May 28–June 2, 1958	Trinidad
Special[3]	October 8–9, 1958	Washington
Twenty-seventh	November 24–29, 1958	Trinidad
Twenty-eighth	August 10–15, 1959	St. Thomas, Virgin Islands
Twenty-ninth	December 9–15, 1959	French Guiana
Thirtieth	July 18–20, 1960	Puerto Rico
Thirty-first	September 5, 1961	Puerto Rico

WEST INDIAN CONFERENCE

Session	Dates	Places
Second	February 21–March 13, 1946	St. Thomas, Virgin Islands
Third	December 1–14, 1948	Guadeloupe
Fourth	November 27–December 10, 1950	Curacao
Fifth	November 24–December 3, 1952	Montego Bay, Jamaica
Sixth	May 10–19, 1955	Puerto Rico
Seventh	November 11–21, 1957	Curacao
Special	July 28–August 7, 1959	St. Thomas, Virgin Islands

CARIBBEAN RESEARCH COUNCIL

Meeting	Dates	Place
First	November 27–December 8, 1947	Trinidad
Second	May 27–30, 1949	Trinidad
Third	May 29–30, 1950	Trinidad
Fourth	July 16–19, 1951	Trinidad
Fifth	March 5–6, 1953	Trinidad
Sixth[4]	October 4–6, 1955	Trinidad

B. □ RULES OF PROCEDURE FOR THE CARIBBEAN COMMISSION

1. The meetings of the Commission shall normally be held in the Caribbean area and shall be attended by the Secretary-General. If the Secretary-General is unable to attend, he shall be represented by a deputy who shall be the Deputy Secretary-General whenever possible. The meetings shall be held in private unless the Commission decides otherwise. The minutes of the meetings shall be regarded as public documents but not as documents to be released for the purpose of publication unless so ordered by the Commission.

2. At each meeting of the Commission a tentative date and place shall be set for the next meeting. A definite date will be fixed by the Secretary-General in consultation with the Working Committee.

3. A provisional agenda for Commission meetings shall be prepared and circulated by the Secretary-General to all Commissioners sixty days before the date set for the meeting. Comments on the agenda by the National sections shall be forwarded by co-Chairmen to reach the Secretary-General not later than thirty days before the meeting. A revised agenda shall then be circulated to all Commissioners by the Secretary-General to reach them not later than fifteen days before the meeting. The revised agenda, which shall include all items requested individually or jointly by the co-Chairmen, shall be final, subject to amendment at the meeting.

4. In addition to meetings arranged in the normal course of the Commission's business, the Secretary-General shall call a meeting upon the request of any one or more National Sections provided that all the co-Chairmen agree. In the case of meetings convened under this paragraph the agenda shall accompany the Secretary-General's announcement of the meeting and the provisions of paragraph 3 shall not apply.

5. The Commission shall arrive at the decisions in accordance with the terms of Article VI of the Agreement provided that:—

(a) Any Commissioner who differs from his co-Chairman on any matter either of substance or procedure shall be entitled to have his views recorded in the minutes.

(b) Decisions on procedural matters shall be considered approved if agreed to by at least three of the four co-Chairmen.

(c) In the event of disagreement with regard to the classification of any question as substantive or procedural, the decision of at least three of the four co-Chairmen shall prevail.

(d) The Commission may set up such committees as it deems necessary and refer to them any questions for study and report. Such committees may be authorized to sit while the Commission is not in session.

British West Indian governments should be encouraged to use the secretariat of the Commission as a channel for inquiries which they may wish to have made in the United States on subjects within the Commission's terms of reference; the governments of American territories similarly to make use of the secretariat whenever convenient for inquiries of a similar character which they may desire to make of British official agencies.[26]

In the absence of a true joint secretariat these functions were carried on separately and not always uniformly by the respective national sections, with some of the burden carried by the jointly operated library. A great deal of the responsibility came to be assumed by the executive secretaries of the two sections in Washington.[27]

Native West Indians Added to Commission

There remains one final development for me to cover before I leave this discussion of the formal structure of the old A.A.C.C. On June 30, 1945, the two member governments issued the following joint communiqué.

For the purpose of associating the peoples of the Caribbean area more closely with the work of the Anglo-American Caribbean Commission and of including in its membership representatives of those peoples, it has been agreed by the Governments of the United States and the United Kingdom to increase the membership of the Commission from three to four members on each side.

This decision modifies the joint communiqué issued in Washington and London on March 9, 1942, when the Anglo-American Caribbean Commission was created.[28]

At the same time as this communiqué was issued the two governments made separate announcements with regard to their future plans for the Commission. The United States announcement said that the additional member of the American Section of the Commission would be nominated from Puerto Rico and appointed by the President. The British statement said that the British Government had full sympathy with the demand which had existed for some time for the appointment of a British West Indian unofficial member to the Commission.* The contemplated expansion of the Commission would permit the appointment of two such commissioners, as Sir Frank Stockdale had retired and one other British commissioner, Mr. A. J. Wakefield, had left his post in the West Indies.

---

*By the word "unofficial" with reference to Commission members or West Indian Conference delegates, the British meant simply individuals who were not themselves British government officials. There was no implication that such persons were in any sense less than full Commission members or delegates. In practice, however, "unofficial" was virtually equivalent to "native" or "Negro."

6. The Commission shall create a Working Committee which shall be composed of one Commissioner of each national section or his alternate appointed by the respective co-Chairmen. Minutes of Working Committee meetings shall be transmitted promptly to all Commissioners. All decisions recorded therein shall be accepted as interim decisions and shall be acted upon. If any Commissioner states in writing his disagreement with any decision of the Working Committee such decision shall be referred to the co-Chairmen, who will arrive at an interim decision in accordance with paragraph 5 of these rules. Such interim decision will prevail until the next meeting of the Commission. All decisions recorded in the minutes of the meetings of the Working Committee held between meetings of the Commission shall be submitted to the Commission for confirmation at its next meeting. The Working Committee shall appoint its own officers and, subject to such instructions as it may receive from the Commission, regulate its own procedure.

7. When the Commission is not in session the Working Committee shall—

(a) advise the Secretary-General on matters of policy and administration relating to the work of the Central Secretariat.

(b) consider and approve personnel policies of the Central Secretariat proposed by the Secretary-General, particularly as regards salaries, recruitment, and conditions of service.

(c) approve interim appointments to the Research Council and Research Committees.

(d) generally perform such functions of the Commission as may be necessary on an interim basis in order to expedite and coordinate the work of the Central Secretariat and the auxiliary bodies of the Commission.

(e) survey in cooperation with the Secretary General the items on the agenda so as to allow the discussion of these items by the Commission to proceed expeditiously and, whenever appropriate, indicate the implications of the various courses that can be taken by the Commission on specific items of the agenda.

8. The Secretary-General shall—

(a) provide the staff required by the Commission and its Committees, and by the Research Council and its committees.

(b) be responsible for keeping the Commission informed of any questions which may be brought before it for consideration.

(c) at any time, upon the invitation of the presiding officer of the meeting, make either oral or written statements concerning any question under consideration.

(d) make all the necessary arrangements for meetings.

(e) keep summary records of such meetings. These records shall be sent as soon as possible to all members participating in the meeting who shall inform the Secretary-General without delay of any changes they wish to have made. In the absence of any comment within a reasonable period the Secretary-General shall issue final minutes.

9. Any of these rules may be amended or suspended by the Commission, provided that the proposed amendments or suspensions are consistent with the Agreement for the Establishment of the Caribbean Commission.

Approved by the Commission, Third Meeting, Fifth Session, held at Curacao, December 13, 1946.

C. ☐ AGREEMENT FOR THE ESTABLISHMENT OF THE CARIBBEAN ORGANIZATION, JUNE 21, 1960

The GOVERNMENTS of the REPUBLIC OF FRANCE, the KINGDOM OF THE NETHERLANDS, the UNITED KINGDOM OF GREAT BRITAIN AND NORTHERN IRELAND, and the UNITED STATES OF AMERICA,

Having reviewed the work of the Caribbean Commission since the entry into force of the Agreement for the establishment of the Caribbean Commission, signed at Washington on October 30, 1946;

Recognizing that the Commission has done much to further regional cooperation in many fields, and has rendered valuable services in the Caribbean area;

Having considered the statements by representatives from the area calling for a revision of the Agreement for the establishment of the Caribbean Commission in the light of the new constitutional relationships in the Caribbean area;

Having considered that the purposes and functions as set out in the Agreement for the establishment of the Caribbean Commission should be the basis of a new organization designed to replace it;

Having noted the views expressed at the West Indian Conference convoked in Special Session commencing on July 28, 1959;

Having considered the draft Statute prepared by this Conference and transmitted to them by the Caribbean Commission;

Noting that the purposes and functions as set out in this draft Statute accord with those which were the basis of the Agreement for the establishment of the Caribbean Commission; and

Noting that nothing in this draft Statute is intended to alter or conflict with the respective constitutional relations between the Governments hereinbefore named and the prospective Members of the Organization respectively;

Hereby agree as follows:

ARTICLE I

1. The Contracting Parties agree upon the establishment of the Caribbean Organization in accordance with the Statute annexed to this Agreement.

2. The Republic of France for the Departments of French Guiana, Guadeloupe, and Martinique, the Netherlands Antilles; Surinam; the Bahamas; British Guiana; British Honduras; the British Virgin Islands; The West Indies; the Commonwealth of Puerto Rico; and the Virgin Islands of the United States are eligible to become Members, and are referred to in this Agreement as "prospective Members."

ARTICLE II

No provision of this Agreement shall be interpreted as affecting the present or future constitutional status of the prospective Members of the Organization or, where applicable, the present or future constitutional relations of any of the aforesaid prospective Members with the Contracting Parties.

ARTICLE III

On the termination of the Agreement for the establishment of the Caribbean Commission, signed at Washington on October 30, 1946, the assets of the Caribbean Commission shall be and are by virtue of this Agreement transferred to and vested in the Caribbean Organization. The Caribbean Organization is hereby authorized to assume at the same time the liabilities of the Caribbean Commission and shall be regarded as the successor body to the Caribbean Commission.

ARTICLE IV

The Agreement for the establishment of the Caribbean Commission shall terminate at the end of the first meeting of the Caribbean Council provided for in the Statute annexed to this Agreement.

ARTICLE V

1. This Agreement shall be subject to approval or acceptance by the signatory Governments. Instruments of approval or acceptance shall be deposited with the Government of the United States of America, hereby designated as the depositary Government, which shall notify the other signatory Governments of each such deposit.

2. This Agreement shall enter into force on signature of a joint declaration to that effect by the signatory Governments, following deposit of instruments of approval or acceptance by the signatory Governments, and after the Secretary-General of the Caribbean Commission has received notification, in accordance with paragraph 1 of Article IV of the Statute annexed to this Agreement, from not less than six of the prospective Members of the Caribbean Organization.

3. This Agreement shall have indefinite duration. Any Contracting Party may at any time withdraw from the Agreement. Such withdrawal shall take effect one year after the date of the receipt by the depositary Government of the formal notification of withdrawal and shall be without prejudice to any liability already vested in the withdrawing Contracting Party by or under this Agreement in respect of the period before the withdrawal takes effect. This Agreement shall continue in force thereafter with respect to the other Contracting Parties.

ARTICLE VI

This Agreement, done in a single original in the English, French, Netherlands, and Spanish languages, each version being equally authentic, shall be deposited in the archives of the Government of the United States of America. Duly certified copies thereof will be transmitted by that Government to the other signatory Governments.

IN WITNESS WHEREOF the undersigned, duly authorized, have signed this Agreement.

DONE at Washington this twenty-first day of June, 1960.

FOR THE GOVERNMENT OF THE REPUBLIC OF FRANCE:

Hervé Alphand

FOR THE GOVERNMENT OF THE KINGDOM OF THE NETHERLANDS:

J. H. van Roijen

FOR THE GOVERNMENT OF THE UNITED KINGDOM OF GREAT BRITAIN AND NORTHERN IRELAND:

Harold Caccia

FOR THE GOVERNMENT OF THE UNITED STATES OF AMERICA:

Christian A. Herter
Roderic L. O'Connor

D. ☐ STATUTE OF THE CARIBBEAN ORGANIZATION

WHEREAS the Caribbean Commission since its establishment in 1946 has done much to further regional cooperation in many fields and has rendered valuable services in the Caribbean area; and

WHEREAS since the establishment of the Caribbean Commission significant constitutional and economic changes have taken place in the area, and the peoples concerned have expressed their desire to accept increased responsibility in solving the problems of the area; and

WHEREAS in order to facilitate the continuance of social, cultural and economic cooperation in the area, it is considered advisable to establish a successor body, the Statute of which reflects these changes and the new responsibilities which the prospective Members (as defined in Article III of this Statute) have undertaken since 1946; and

WHEREAS the objectives herein set forth are in accord with the Charter of the United Nations;

NOW THEREFORE there is established the Caribbean Organization which is governed by the following provisions:

ARTICLE I
Establishment and Powers of the Caribbean Organization

1. There is hereby established the Caribbean Organization (hereinafter referred to as the "Organization").

2. The Organization shall have consultative and advisory powers and such legal capacity as may be necessary for the exercise of its functions and the fulfillment of its purposes.

ARTICLE II
Functions and Purposes of the Organization

Within the scope of its powers, the functions and purposes of the Organization shall be to concern itself with social, cultural and economic matters of common interest to the Caribbean area, particularly agriculture, communications, education, fisheries, health, housing, industry, labor, music and the arts, social welfare and trade.

ARTICLE III
Eligibility for Membership of the Organization

1. The following are the prospective Members of the Organization, and are hereby declared eligible to become Members:

The Republic of France for the Departments of French Guiana, Guadeloupe
    and Martinique
The Netherlands Antilles
Surinam
The Bahamas
British Guiana
British Honduras
The British Virgin Islands
The West Indies
The Commonwealth of Puerto Rico
The Virgin Islands of the United States.

    2. The Republic of France, as referred to in paragraph 1 of this Article, shall
be represented in the Organization by one delegation having three votes.

ARTICLE IV
Notification of Membership and Withdrawal

    1. Any prospective Member of the Organization may at any time declare by
notification given to the Secretary-General of the Caribbean Commission, or the
Secretary-General of the Organization, that it accepts the obligations imposed by
this Statute and that it elects to become a Member.

    2. Any notification in accordance with the preceding paragraph of this Article
received by the Secretary-General on or before the date on which the Statute comes
into force shall take effect on that date. Any notification received after the date
on which this Statute comes into force shall take effect on the date of its receipt by
the Secretary-General.

    3. Any Member may at any time declare by notification given to the Secretary-
General of the Organization that it elects to cease to be a Member. This notification shall take effect one year after the date of its receipt by the Secretary-General
of the Organization. On the withdrawal from the Agreement to which this Statute
is annexed of any Party to that Agreement, the Members for whose international
relations that Party is responsible shall cease to be Members of the Organization.

    4. Where a Member ceases to be a Member in accordance with paragraph 3
of this Article, such cessation shall be without prejudice to any liability already
vested in that Member by or under this Statute in respect of the period before the
cessation takes effect.

    5. The Secretary-General shall notify all Governments signatory to the Agree-
ment to which this Statute is annexed and all Members and prospective Members
of the receipt of any notification referred to in paragraphs 1 and 3 of this Article.

ARTICLE V
The Caribbean Council

    The governing body of the Organization shall be the Caribbean Council
(hereinafter referred to as the "Council").

ARTICLE VI
Composition of the Council

1. Each Member shall be entitled to send to each session of the Council one delegate and such advisers as it may consider necessary, but the Republic of France shall be entitled to send one delegation and such advisers as it may consider necessary. Such delegates or delegation, as the case may be, shall be appointed in accordance with the constitutional procedures of each Member. The Secretary-General shall be notified by the Members of the appointment of each delegate or delegation, as the case may be.

2. Each Member may at any time, by notification given to the Secretary-General, appoint a person to act as alternate during the absence of its delegate from any meeting of the Council. The Republic of France shall have similar rights with respect to its delegation. The alternate, while so acting, shall stand in all respects in the place of the delegate.

ARTICLE VII
Functions and Powers of the Council

Within the scope of the powers of the Organization, the Council shall:

(a) study, formulate and recommend to Members measures, programs and courses of action in social, cultural and economic matters designed to contribute to the well-being of the Caribbean area;

(b) assist in the coordination of local projects which have regional significance and in the provision of technical guidance on a regional basis;

(c) arrange for or provide technical guidance not otherwise available;

(d) promote the coordination of research on a regional basis;

(e) make recommendations to the Members for carrying into effect action in regard to social, cultural and economic problems;

(f) further cooperation with other international and national organizations and with universities, foundations and similar institutions having common interests in the Caribbean area and, subject to the principle expressed in Article XVII, may

(i) on behalf of the Organization, conclude technical assistance agreements with other international or national organizations, being agreements which every Member is competent or authorized to conclude and the conclusion of such agreements being dependent on a unanimous vote;

(ii) on behalf of the Organization, or as may be appropriate, on behalf of such of the Members as may make the specific request, conclude arrangements or contracts in pursuance of the aforesaid agreements;

(iii) conclude appropriate cooperation agreements with universities, foundations and similar institutions, and arrangements or contracts in pursuance of these agreements;

(g) summon such conferences, appoint such committees, and establish such auxiliary bodies as it may find necessary and desirable;

(h) direct and review the activities of the Central Secretariat and the afore-mentioned conferences, committees and auxiliary bodies;

(i) issue the staff rules of the Central Secretariat;

(j) issue the financial regulations of the Organization;

(k) appoint a Secretary-General in accordance with paragraph 5 of Article IX and paragraph 4 of Article X.

ARTICLE VIII
Meetings and Procedures of the Council

1. The Council shall establish its own rules of procedure.

2. Meetings of the Council shall be presided over by a Chairman, chosen from among the delegates to the Council.

3. The Council shall hold at least one meeting each year at which the annual budget for the ensuing year shall be considered. It is empowered to convene and hold meetings at such times and at such places as it may decide. The Chairman shall cause a meeting to be convened if requested to do so by not less than one-half of the Members. The first meeting of the Council (which shall be a budget meeting) shall be held at such time after the coming into force of this Statute and at such place as may be designated by the Caribbean Commission.

4. Meetings of the Council shall preferably be held in the territory of each of the Members in turn, and a similar principle, where appropriate, shall be fol-lowed with regard to all other activities of the Organization.

5. The first Chairman shall be elected at the first meeting and shall hold office until the end of the ensuing year. Thereafter the Chairmanship shall rotate in accordance with such rules of procedure as the Council may adopt, provided always that a Chairman shall not be of the same nationality as the preceding Chairman.

ARTICLE IX
Voting in the Council

1. Subject to paragraph 2 of this Article, each delegate shall be entitled to cast one vote, but the delegation of the Republic of France shall be entitled to cast three votes.

2. Matters of procedure shall be decided by the Council by a simple majority of the votes cast. Except as provided for in paragraphs 3, 4 and 5 of this Article, subparagraphs (f) and (i) of Article VII, and paragraphs 3 and 4 of Article XII, all other matters, including disputes as to the classification of any matter as procedural or substantive, shall be decided by a two-thirds majority of the votes cast. However, when a decision or recommendation is adopted by a two-thirds majority of the votes cast, any Member may declare that the decision or recom-mendation will not be applicable as far as it is concerned. Where, in respect of a matter to be decided by a simple majority of the votes cast, the votes are equally divided, the Chairman shall have a casting vote. If the Chairman does not in such a case use his casting vote, the motion for decision shall be lost.

3. The Council shall examine drafts of the annual budget and any supple-mentary budgets submitted by the Secretary-General. Voting on the total figure

of a budget, annual or supplementary, shall be preceded by a vote on each budget head. Each budget head shall be approved by a two-thirds majority of the votes cast. The total of a budget, annual or supplementary, shall be approved by a unanimous vote. In the event that it is not possible to obtain a unanimous vote on the budget for any year, the budget voted for the previous year shall remain in force and the Members shall continue to make the same contribution as they made during the preceding year.

4. The adoption and amendment of the Rules of Procedure shall require unanimity of the votes cast.

5. The appointment of the Secretary-General shall require unanimity of the votes cast.

6. For the purpose of this Statute, "the votes cast" means votes cast affirmatively or negatively. Abstentions shall not be considered as votes cast.

ARTICLE X
The Central Secretariat

1. The Organization shall maintain in the Caribbean area a Central Secretariat to serve the Council and its conferences, committees and auxiliary bodies.

2. The Secretary-General shall be the chief administrative officer of the Organization. He shall be responsible for carrying out all directives of the Council.

3. Subject to the staff rules issued by the Council and any further directives he may receive from the Council, the Secretary-General shall appoint and dismiss the staff of the Organization.

4. In the appointment of the Secretary-General and other members of the staff of the Central Secretariat, primary consideration shall be given to the technical and personal qualifications of the candidates. To the extent possible consistent with this consideration, the staff shall be recruited within the Caribbean area and with a view to obtaining equitable national representation.

5. In the performance of their duties the Secretary-General and staff shall not seek, receive or observe instructions from any Government, from any Member, or from any authority external to the Organization. The Secretary-General and staff shall refrain from any action which might reflect on their position as international officials responsible only to the Organization.

6. Each Member undertakes to respect the exclusively international character of the functions of the Secretary-General and staff and not to seek to influence them in the discharge of their responsibilities.

ARTICLE XI
Finances

1. The expenses of the Organization shall be borne by the Members in proportions to be specified in an appropriate arrangement arrived at unanimously by the Members.

2. The fiscal year of the Organization shall be the calendar year.

3. The Secretary-General shall prepare and submit to the Council the draft of an annual budget and such supplementary budgets as may be required by the Organization and shall submit them to the Members at least one month prior to

their discussion by the Council. Upon approval of the budget, the total amount thereof shall be allocated among the Members in the proportions arrived at in accordance with paragraph 1 of this Article. Each Member shall undertake, subject to the requirements of its constitutional procedures, to contribute promptly to a Joint Fund to be established by the Members such annual and supplementary sums as may be charged to each in accordance with the arrangement referred to in paragraph 1.

4. The Secretary-General shall hold and administer the Joint Fund of the Organization and shall keep proper accounts thereof. The Council shall make arrangements satisfactory to the Members for the audit of the accounts of the Organization. The audited statements shall be forwarded annually to each Member.

5. The expenses of delegates or delegations attending meetings sponsored by the Organization shall be borne by the Members whom they respectively represent.

ARTICLE XII
Observers

1. The Parties to the Agreement to which this Statute is annexed shall be entitled to send to all meetings held under the auspices of the Organization observers who shall have the right to speak but not to vote.

2. Any prospective Member of the Organization shall be entitled to send to all meetings held under the auspices of the Organization observers who shall have the right to speak but not to vote.

3. The Council may, if it so decides by a unanimous vote, and subject to the approval of the Parties to the Agreement to which this Statute is annexed, authorize the Secretary-General to issue to any Government having interests in the Caribbean area not being a Party to the Agreement to which this Statute is annexed an invitation to send observers to any meeting held under the auspices of the Organization.

4. The Council may, if it so decides by a unanimous vote, authorize the Secretary-General to issue to the organizations, universities, foundations and similar institutions as referred to in subparagraph (f) of Article VII, an invitation to send observers to any meeting held under the auspices of the Organization.

ARTICLE XIII
Relationships with Governments not Parties to the Agreement

The Organization in all its activities shall bear in mind the desirability of strengthening international cooperation in social, cultural and economic matters with Governments having an interest in such matters in the Caribbean area but not being Parties to the Agreement to which this Statute is annexed.

ARTICLE XIV
Immunities

Each Member undertakes to accord, so far as possible under its constitutional procedures, to the Organization, the Secretary-General and appropriate personnel of the Central Secretariat such privileges and immunities as may be necessary for the independent exercise of their functions, and to the Central Secretariat inviolability of its buildings, premises, archives and assets.

ARTICLE XV
Languages

The English, French, Netherlands and Spanish languages shall be the official languages of the Organization. The working languages shall be English and French.

ARTICLE XVI
Transfer of Assets and Liabilities of the Caribbean Commission

With effect from the termination of the Agreement for the Establishment of the Caribbean Commission under Article IV of the Agreement to which this Statute is annexed, the Organization, as the successor body to the Caribbean Commission, is authorized to take over all the assets and shall assume all the liabilities of the Caribbean Commission.

ARTICLE XVII
Saving Clause

No provision of this Statute shall be interpreted as affecting the present or future constitutional status of the Members of the Organization, or, where applicable, the present or future constitutional relations of any of the aforesaid Members with the Parties to the Agreement to which this Statute is annexed.

ARTICLE XVIII
Amendment of Statute

Amendment to this Statute shall require the unanimous approval of the Members of the Organization and of the Parties to the Agreement to which this Statute is annexed.

ARTICLE XIX
Entry into Force

This Statute shall enter into force immediately after:

(a) there has been received by the Secretary-General of the Caribbean Commission notification pursuant to paragraph 1 of Article IV from at least six of the prospective Members of the Organization; and

(b) the Parties to the Agreement to which this Statute is annexed have signed a Joint Declaration under paragraph 2 of Article V of that Agreement.

ARTICLE XX
Transitional Provisions

Until such time as the Secretary-General of the Organization is appointed and is able to assume the duties of his Office, the Secretary-General of the Caribbean Commission shall be the Secretary-General of the Organization with power to appoint a staff on a temporary basis.

E. ☐ LAW OF PUERTO RICO CREATING CODECA

AN ACT (No. 37, approved June 15, 1965)

To create a public corporation as a government instrumentality of the Commonwealth of Puerto Rico, under the name of "Caribbean Economic Development Corporation"; to define its functions, powers and duties; and to appropriate funds to said corporation.

STATEMENT OF MOTIVES

The Legislative Assembly—aware of the reality that Puerto Rico has gradually risen out of its former economic, social and cultural stagnation—believes that the fruits of the people's efforts that have made that growth possible should not be exclusive to our country and that we should share our experience with other democratic peoples throughout the world, most specially the friendly neighbor communities with which we have geographic, economic, social and cultural ties.

As an expression of its interests in this collaboration, it is the intent of the Legislative Assembly to create, through this statute, a Caribbean Economic Development Corporation which will benefit the inhabitants of Puerto Rico as well as all the inhabitants of the democratic communities of the Caribbean region, through the maximum utilization and development of the economic and human resources of all those communities, in agreement with the purpose of their closest mutual cooperation, aimed at the promotion of commerce, culture and education, and of all the social aspects referred to in this act.

The production of export goods has continually risen in Puerto Rico and the Caribbean during the past years, thus increasingly making more imperative the development of new markets and sources of supply in order to strengthen our economies. A public corporation dedicated to the promotion of greater trade cooperation and greater coordinated development of the Caribbean economy will be of considerable support to the rapid increase in the economic capacity and potentials of all the communities—which will benefit the development of better markets throughout the area—thus promoting greater economic and social stability and prosperity of these peoples, including Puerto Rico.

A corporation of this nature supposes the derivation of benefits in all walks of Puerto Rico's economic life, as well as of the other neighboring Caribbean countries, intensifying and coordinating production and the industrial, commercial and agricultural activity, thus providing direct benefits to labor as well as to management.

The Legislative Assembly of Puerto Rico, aware of the convenience of the foregoing, finds that the creation of the Caribbean Economic Development Corporation is in the public interest and, therefore,

BE IT ENACTED BY THE LEGISLATURE OF PUERTO RICO:

Section 1.—This act may be cited as the "Act of the Caribbean Economic Development Corporation."

Section 2.—There is hereby created a body corporate and politic, as a public corporation and government instrumentality of the Commonwealth of Puerto Rico, with the name "Caribbean Economic Development Corporation."

The Corporation shall have juridic personality separate and apart from every officer thereof and of the government of the Commonwealth of Puerto Rico and its agencies, instrumentalities, public corporations and political subdivisions; shall have perpetual existence; may adopt and use a corporate seal which shall be judicially noticed; and may sue and be sued.

Section 3.—It is the intent of the Government of the Commonwealth of Puerto Rico that the activities of the Economic Development Corporation benefit the inhabitants of Puerto Rico as well as all the inhabitants of the democratic communities of the Caribbean region, through the wise utilization and development, to the fullest possible extent, of the economic and human resources of all our peoples, in accordance with the principles of the closest cooperation between such countries, aimed at the promotion of commerce, culture and education, and of all the social aspects referred to in this act.

Section 4.—The Powers of the Corporation shall be conferred to, and exercised by, a Board of Directors composed of the following officials of the Commonwealth of Puerto Rico: the Secretary of State, who shall be Chairman of the Board, the Secretary of Commerce, and the Economic Development Administrator, who shall, in that order, discharge the duties of the Chairman of the Board during the Secretary of State's absence, and of two members appointed by the Governor, at least one of whom shall be from the private sector. These members selected from the private sector shall hold office for a term of two (2) years and until their successors are appointed and qualify. Ex-officio members may designate alternates, who must be approved by the Board.

Not less than three members shall constitute a quorum at the Board meetings, including, at least, a regular ex-officio member, who will preside; provided, however, that all agreements shall be adopted by the affirmative vote of at least three (3) members of the Board.

Section 5.—The Corporation shall exercise all such powers and duties as are necessary or convenient to carry out the purposes of this act, including, but not limited to, the following:

1.—To promote exchange and cooperation between the countries of the Caribbean region.

2.—To carry out surveys and research in the field of economic, social, cultural, or any other kind of cooperation.

3.—To administer programs leading to a greater exchange of persons and ideas between the Caribbean countries, including, but not limited to, developing and administering local scholarship programs, and administering scholarship programs of the United States, its agencies, territories, possessions or political subdivisions, of the states of the Union or foreign countries, to propitiate the promotion of culture, education, trade, industrial and agricultural development and the attainment of the other purposes of this act.

4.—To develop programs and activities designed to increase the commercial, agricultural and industrial production in all the Caribbean region.

5.—To grant service or other contracts and whatever other instruments necessary or convenient to the exercise of its powers.

6.—To grant economic and other incentives, so as to promote the rendering of services or creation of enterprises necessary for the attainment of the purposes of this act.

7.—To grant loans to promote the development of the economy of the Caribbean region, under such borrowing norms as may be established by the Board of Directors, which shall conform, as much as possible, to such norms as prevail for transactions of similar institutions.

8.—To provide technical and specialized services to governments and persons or public or private entities, local or foreign, and to request such services from said governments or entities.

9.—To determine, fix, alter, levy and collect rents, tariffs, fees and other charges for the rendering of services, use of properties or facilities, or for goods sold, lent or supplied, and to exempt from the total or partial payment thereof.

10.—To accept funds or economic aid of any kind from any natural or artificial person, or political entity, private or governmental, operating or functioning locally, internationally or in the United States of America, and to agree with such persons or entities as to the use of said funds.

11.—To borrow money and incur debts for its corporate purposes, under such terms and conditions as the Corporation may determine, with or without surety, to dispose of its liabilities evidencing such loans; to make, grant and deliver trust instruments and others with regards to any of such loans, incurrences of debt, bond issues, notes, mortgage bonds or other liabilities and by authority of the Commonwealth of Puerto Rico granted hereby, to issue its own bonds, notes, mortgage bonds and other liabilities in such manner, with the guarantee and under such redemption terms, with or without premium, and to sell the same at public or private sale for such price or prices as the Board may determine therefor.

12.—To guarantee payment of its bonds or any other liabilities by pledges, mortgages or any other lien or combination thereof, on all or any of its contracts, incomes, revenues or properties.

13.—To invest its funds in projects directed to benefit the Caribbean area.

14.—To acquire any kind and quantity of shares or other securities or interests in companies, corporations, or public or private entities; to exercise the rights connected therewith; and to dispose of such shares, securities or interests.

15.—To acquire any kind of property, in any legal manner, whenever the purposes of the Corporation so indicate, and to own, administer, lease, mortgage, sell, or in any other way dispose of, any property or interest therein, whenever the Board deems it necessary to the attainment of its purposes and in the public interest. The Corporation, however, may not grant title on real assets located in Puerto Rico without the Board's express authorization.

16.—To organize, purchase or in any way acquire and exercise partial or total control over subsidiary profit or nonprofit companies, associations or corporations, affiliated or associated.

The Corporation may delegate to subsidiary enterprises wherever it controls and keeps controlling more than half of the shares, any of its rights, powers, functions or duties as are deemed convenient by the Board to the purposes of the Corporation.

17.—To participate in the management, administration or functioning of local or outside enterprises.

18.—To adopt, amend and repeal bylaws for its internal functioning, the conduct of its activities, and the exercise of the powers granted thereto and duties imposed thereupon by law.

19.—The disposition of non-committed balances or surplus funds shall be subject to such determination as the Board may decide for utilization thereof.

20.—To have complete control and superintendence of its properties and activities, including the power to determine the nature and need of all its expenses and the manner in which they are to be incurred, authorized and paid, regardless of any provision of law regulating the expenditure of public funds, and such determination shall be final and definitive for all officials of the Commonwealth of Puerto Rico.

21.—To do all acts or things incidental, necessary or desirable to the carrying out of the powers granted to it by this act or by any other act in force in Puerto Rico.

Section 6.—Whenever the Corporation deems it necessary to take immediate possession of property to be expropriated in Puerto Rico, it shall request the Governor of the Commonwealth of Puerto Rico to acquire it, in behalf and in representation of the Commonwealth of Puerto Rico. The Governor shall be empowered to acquire, through any means authorized by law, and for the use and benefit of the Corporation, such necessary and convenient property and real chattels for the implementation of its aims and purposes. The Corporation shall previously make available to the Commonwealth of Puerto Rico the necessary funds to cover the estimated value of the property or rights to be acquired. The difference in value as may be decreed by the Court may be paid from the Commonwealth Treasury, but the Corporation shall be obliged to reimburse that difference. Once the total has been reimbursed, the title deed shall be transferred to the Corporation, by order of the Court and through evidence to that effect. In such cases as the Governor deems it necessary and convenient for the title to property or rights thus acquired to be registered directly in favor of the Corporation, so as to accelerate compliance with the aims and purposes for which it was created, he may request this from the Court at any time during the condemnation proceedings and the Court shall so order. The power hereby conferred shall not limit or restrict in any way the Corporation's own power to acquire property.

All movable or real property, and any right over, or interest in, them which the Corporation might deem necessary to its corporate purposes, are hereby declared of public utility. They may be expropriated for the use of the Corporation without the previous declaration of public utility prescribed by the General Law of Eminent Domain.

Section 7.—The Corporation's Executive Director shall be appointed by the Board of Directors; he shall hold office at the will of the Board, and until his successor is appointed and qualifies; and he shall perform all such duties and responsibilities as may be assigned to him by the Board pursuant to the Corporation bylaws.

These bylaws may provide that such powers and duties as the Board may deem proper to delegate, be delegated to the Executive Director.

No person may hold office as Executive Director of the Corporation who has a direct or indirect financial interest in any privately-owned enterprise which is in any way related to the Corporation, or who is engaged in any of the businesses in which the Corporation is engaged, or to which it provides capital.

All other officials and employees of the Corporation shall be appointed by the Executive Director, and all their powers and duties shall be determined pursuant to the Corporation bylaws. These bylaws shall prescribe the norms to govern all personnel matters. Said norms, insofar as compatible with the efficient attainment of the Corporation purposes, shall be analogous to those governing the personnel of the Commonwealth government.

Section 8.—All the Corporation personnel shall be comprised within the exempt service, as provided by the act creating the Office of Personnel of the Commonwealth of Puerto Rico.

Any official or employee who is a beneficiary of any retirement or insurance system, or savings and loan fund, and who is appointed to hold an office in the Corporation without any interruption in the service, shall continue enjoying such rights, privileges and obligations with regard to said systems, unless, within the term of one month after his appointment in the Corporation, such official or employee communicates to the respective authority his written decision to withdraw from said systems, it being understood that, in this case, he shall enjoy all such rights corresponding to persons who leave such systems. In the case of membership in retirement systems, the pertinent employer's contribution shall be made by the Corporation, pursuant to the provisions of the organic statute of the corresponding system.

Section 9.—The Corporation shall establish such accounting system as may be required for the adequate control and statistical record of all income belonging to the Corporation, or administered thereby, as well as all its expenses. All accounts of the Corporation shall be kept in such a manner that they may be separated according to the various activities it may carry out.

The Comptroller of the Commonwealth of Puerto Rico, or his representative, shall periodically examine all the accounts and books of the Corporation and shall report on his examination to the Legislative Assembly, the Governor and the Secretary of State.

Section 10.—All bonds issued by the Corporation and the income deriving therefrom shall be exempted from the payment of taxes or duties of the government of the Commonwealth of Puerto Rico and any political subdivision thereof.

Section 11.—The debts and obligations of the Corporation shall not be debts or obligations of the Commonwealth of Puerto Rico or of any municipality or political subdivision thereof, nor shall the Commonwealth of Puerto Rico or any municipality or political subdivision thereof be liable therefor.

Section 12.—The Corporation, and its subsidiary companies, associations or corporations over which the Corporation has total control, shall be exempted from the payment of all Commonwealth or municipal fees, taxes, duties or tariffs now required, or as may be required in the future. Said exemption covers the payment of license, patent, permit and registry fees, as well as the payment of fees for the execution of all kinds of documents; the carrying through of procedures of any kind; any registration or operation in the Property Registry, or in any other Commonwealth office; and the issuance of certificates by the Property Registry or any other office.

Section 13.—No injunction whatsoever shall be issued to prevent the application of this act, or any part hereof.

Section 14.—The Corporation shall, at the close of each fiscal year, submit to the Legislative Assembly and to the Governor of the Commonwealth of Puerto Rico a report on all its activities.

Section 15.—The sum of two hundred thousand (200,000) dollars is hereby appropriated to the Corporation, from unencumbered funds in the Commonwealth Treasury, for carrying out the purposes of this act.

Section 16.—Any agency or instrumentality of the Commonwealth government is hereby authorized to make available to the Corporation, either permanently or temporarily, equipment, office space, technical and professional personnel, and any aid or service deemed necessary for the efficient operation of the Caribbean Economic Development Corporation.

Section 17.—The Government of the Commonwealth of Puerto Rico hereby pledges to, and agrees with, any person or agency, whether federal, Commonwealth or foreign, subscribing or acquiring bonds or other obligations of the Corporation, not to mortgage, limit, or restrict the property, revenue, incomes, rights or any of the corporate powers essential for the Corporation to discharge its duties, until such time as said bonds or other obligations, regardless of date, and inclusive of the interest accrued therefrom, are totally paid and withdrawn.

Section 18.—If any provision of this act or its application to any person or circumstance be declared null by any court, said judgment shall not affect the rest of the statute.

Section 19.—This act shall take effect immediately after its approval.

F. □ THE CARIBBEAN ORGANIZATION—
THE FIRST THREE YEARS
(RADIO SCRIPTS)

THE ROLE OF THE CARIBBEAN ORGANIZATION

All over the world today, the leaders of the people are acting in accordance with one of the fables of a Greek slave, Aesop, who lived two thousand years ago. You will remember that Aesop used to entertain the beautiful ladies and wise men of his time by telling them short stories with a moral, and one of the stories which have come down to us is about the bundle of sticks. A father, the story goes, at the point of death called his five quarrelsome grown-up sons together and gave them each a single stick to break. Wondering a little what their father was up to, each broke the little stick he had received. The father then bound a number of these little sticks together and asked each one in turn to try and break this bundle if he could. Each one failed to do so and, with one of his last gasps for breath before he died, the father warned them that in unity there is strength.

In this series of broadcasts on "The Caribbean Organization—the first three years," I think it important to strike at the very beginning this note of *unity of strength* because this is the main purpose of the Organization and the reason why this centre for regional and international cooperation was set up in this part of the world to make a better life for you and me. The history of regional cooperation in the Caribbean is probably well known to every one of my listeners, but let us quickly run over the story to refresh our memories and to make it clear that what we have had—starting in 1961, three years ago—was a brand new beginning even though it continued from something else. This story and this purpose are extremely important for everyone of us in the Caribbean whether you work in the oilfields in Trinidad or you are a small farmer in Grenada, a shop clerk in Kingston, a young businessman in Guadeloupe or Curacao, a factory worker in greater San Juan, a wharfinger in Barbados or working on a ranch in the Rupununi of the Guianas. You may be anyone in the bewildering variety of our beloved Caribbean peoples with our rich potentialities for the future but you have a stake in the future which this story is planning.

Statistics and history can be dull things but let us look at a few of them. In 1942, America and England in the dark days of the war made an act of faith and founded the Anglo-American Caribbean Commission as a war-time emergency to encourage and strengthen social and economic cooperation and to protect the way of life of the English-speaking peoples in the Caribbean for whose destiny they were responsible. France and Holland were later invited to join this approach to remove poverty and improve prosperity in Caribbean countries and, four years later, in 1946, the Caribbean Commission was set up by these four metropolitan powers, America, the United Kingdom, France and Holland, with the clearly de-

---

Pamphlet published by Caribbean Organization, 1964.

fined objective of improving the economic and social well-being of the Caribbean peoples.

To ensure full participation by representatives of the Caribbean peoples, a West Indian Conference was held regularly every two years, at which the desires and comments of the peoples were expressed. Studies of the various aspects of Caribbean life were pursued by experts, so that a finger could be put on weaknesses of organization and upon the remedies to be taken. As time passed, the winds of change which were blowing around the world began to blow through the Caribbean also. The Three Antillean Colonies—French Guiana, Guadeloupe and Martinique—became French Departments and so became portions of France overseas. Surinam and the Netherlands Antilles obtained internal self government and equality of status with Holland in the tripartite Kingdom of the Netherlands. America entered into a special relationship with Puerto Rico which became a Commonwealth enjoying full internal self government. England, in the 1950s, encouraged a movement together of the majority of her colonies in the Caribbean, and the Federation of the West Indies was set up, however with the results known to us all.

These changes, quite naturally, were accompanied by a call for changes in the structure of the body for regional cooperation which had been set up in 1964, in order to bring it more in to line with the new constitutional relationships in the area. I shall not go into all the details and intricacies of the process—they would take a series of talks by themselves. The fact remains that in 1960, the four governments which controlled the Caribbean Commission entered into a new agreement which put the management of the body for regional cooperation more in the hands of the governments of the Caribbean countries. This means that the Caribbean Organization is now a grouping of governments of the Caribbean countries themselves, financed by and under the control of a Caribbean Council of government representatives, and it is concerned with economic, social and cultural matters of common interest to the Caribbean area. This is not a rich area and the standards of living are not up to those of advanced countries. This Caribbean Council decided to put first things first, and to concentrate on economic development. If the new constitutional relationships are to be meaningful and significant, then they must mean a better life for all.

It was agreed that there should be a Caribbean Plan for development in the area in these three fields. This plan was carefully devised to meet the special needs of the Caribbean area, but it was agreed that it should not be a supra-national plan imposed from above, but that each country should be free to pursue its own development programme independently, and the Caribbean Organization—the centre for regional cooperation—was directed to identify projects which could be accelerated and harmonised on a regional basis, and to plan steps for regional cooperation. This means that the Organization can say "why not let us plan to bring all the various aspects of planning tourist development in the Caribbean together, so that we can all increase the benefits of the industry to ourselves by the integration and development of the tourist industry in the Caribbean."

We have other broadcasts to follow in this series of talks on the first three years of the Organization's work, so all we want to do in this first talk is to show how the Organization came into existence and the main purpose behind it. The Organization is intended to be a focus and centre for Caribbean cooperation. It is created to meet the desires of the Caribbean peoples and that they should control the development of their own regional cooperation. It is therefore a body to be moulded and forged to their specific needs; the way they want it to help them, it is their creature. The value of the Organization is limited only by the boldness of vision and the imaginative planning of the leaders of the Caribbean peoples themselves.

Now, having said this, I want to say that we must be realistic and that there are many problems and forces tending to prevent regional cooperation from becoming a reality. First of all, in the process of inducing and increasing Caribbean cooperation, we are attempting to reverse the tides of history. We all know that over the past four centuries, history has carved the Caribbean up into four slices— the Spanish, the French, the Dutch and the British. The sunlit islands in this region between two great continental land masses were the targets of rivalry in the sixteenth and seventeenth centuries among European nations, and the tides of history swirled increasingly around their shores. Each island became a prize that was encouraged to look only to the metropolitan partner and to suspect or ignore each neighbouring island. With the administration came the language and the culture so that the populations lost any sense of belonging to a region but looked only to Europe as part of the Spanish, French, Dutch and British realms of influence, and gulfs of differences appeared in their habits and customs.

But there was an underlying unity in this diversity. The populations of the islands were the same stocks—an Amerindian base of Carib and Arawak peoples upon which a European layer of people was poured. Then, as the economic destinies of the region coincided with the destiny of the sugar industry, it became necessary to import peoples from Africa and, later, from India, China and the Far East to supplement the labour force. So the peoples of the Caribbean belong to the same stocks, despite the language and cultural differences. Now, that in the course of events, a new structure of political organization has come to the Caribbean, the time has come for us to mould a Caribbean consciousness through which the peoples of the region will naturally seek the assistance and cooperation of other parts of the region.

To some people it seems that this is an impossible task, but all over the world the nations and peoples who live in particular regions are finding that it is in their interest and to their profit that they should band themselves together into a group despite all that the past says to the contrary. We have been talking about European influences in the Caribbean. Ten, twenty, thirty years ago, it would have seemed inconceivable that some of the many embittered and antagonistic parts of Europe could have found a basis for coming together to form a united European economic community. Now the miracle has happened. I ask the question, if the European countries with their long bloody history of internecine strife can now make a regional approach, surely the lesson of economic unity, notwithstanding political diversity, cannot be lost on the countries of the Caribbean area.

This is the role and vision of the Caribbean Organization which is specially created as an instrument by which the governments of the area can work out ways and means of cooperation among themselves, for the lasting benefit of all. The role of the Caribbean Organization is to promote and develop all practical forms of regional cooperation in the Caribbean, especially those which will directly lead to a better life for our peoples.

May I just state briefly some facts about the countries served by the Caribbean Organization because of the history of our association. They are the three French Departments of French Guiana, Guadeloupe and Martinique; Surinam and the Netherlands Antilles; the Commonwealth of Puerto Rico and the United States Virgin Islands; British Guiana and the British Virgin Islands and eight of the ten former members of the Federation of the West Indies—Antigua, Barbados, Dominica, Grenada, Montserrat, St. Kitts-Nevis-Anguilla, St. Lucia and St. Vincent. The other two former members of the West Indian Federation—Jamaica and Trinidad & Tobago, have not joined the Organization. In all, we compare and analyse facts and figures relating to some 7 1/2 million people in one of the largest bauxite producing areas in the world which also counts oil, sugar and bananas among its principal products.

Laying the Groundwork

At the beginning of one of his books, the English novelist E. M. Forster placed a motto—"Only Connect." We can perhaps take this motto, "only connect," as being a summary of the guiding philosophy of the Caribbean Organization over the past three years.

Let us look at four examples which will show us the problems of the Caribbean as they exist today. They are Trade, Tariffs, Telecommunications, Transportation, and we will see the positive role of the Caribbean Organization in studying these problems with a view towards their ultimate solutions.

Let us take our Caribbean Trade, look at the patterns of Trade in the countries served by the Caribbean Organization. It was discovered that over the years each country had cultivated a flow of raw materials to, and an importation of manufactured goods from the metropolitan country with which it was associated—Surinam to Holland, Barbados to Great Britain, Martinique to France and so on. In effect, so far as established patterns of Trade went, we were in the Caribbean, to put it playfully,—as a commentator once said—"tied to our Mama's apron strings." This is, of course, to be expected in the history of the past, but with the evolution of constitutional relationships in the area, there was immediately a movement towards a more diverse trade pattern, and countries began to seek goods and markets in other countries, West Germany and Japan, etc.

As the body charged with the responsibility for regional cooperation, the Caribbean Organization asked the question, how much trade was going on among the various countries of the Caribbean, and it was found that this was on the average not more than 3% of the total trade of the region. Of every dollar's worth of trade moving to and from a Caribbean Country, only 3 cents went as trade with another Caribbean country.

It was felt that every effort should be made to improve and develop this trade within the Caribbean area, as a sort of first basis of regional cooperation, and the Organization began to ask these questions: in what goods and commodities could we properly encourage a greater flow of intra-Caribbean Trade and what were the best ways to do this.

In our next broadcast we will tell you more about the machinery of the Clearing House on Trade and Tourism Information that was set up to promote and develop trade within the Caribbean area. All we want to do now is to state this fact of trade among the Caribbean countries—that it is small and that it should be encouraged.

The next item we should look at is Tariffs. A survey was made of the existing barriers which prevent the free flow of goods from one Caribbean country to another. This study, prepared by Professor Stipec, with the cooperation of the Commonwealth of Puerto Rico, on behalf of the Standing Advisory Committee of the Caribbean Plan showed that as a general rule, around each island or Caribbean territory there had been built a wall of customs duties which shut out very many goods and commodities. If we are to encourage the growth and expansion of trade among Caribbean countries, the governments will have to take positive steps to reduce these tariff walls. The representatives of the various governments who form the Caribbean Council took careful note of these tariff barriers and it was agreed that, where possible, steps should be taken to reduce them in order to encourage a greater flow of intra-Caribbean trade.

How far have we got? We are looking at the foundations of regional cooperation in the Caribbean area, and we have seen so far that, as a result of our history, the patterns of trade for the greater part of our territories move along established lines and that they tend to move towards the metropolitan country with which traditionally the territory has been associated. We have also seen that, as a result of our Caribbean history, each country has built up a wall of customs duties to keep out the goods which can come from neighboring countries.

Let us recall the motto of "only connect" which we mentioned at the beginning of this broadcast. In the fields of telecommunications which is the third of the basic problems we are considering, it was found that there was little connection of a regional nature by telegraph and by telephone. We found the same characteristic that we have seen before, that each national grouping of countries is linked together, one to the other, and with either England or France, or America or Holland. Puerto Rico and St. Thomas can call one another on the telephone, and so can Barbados and Trinidad. But as soon as a businessman in a French Department seeks to communicate by telephone with a businessman in, say, an American or British territory immediately difficulties of communication arise, and these are not only difficulties of language. The main difficulty is one of telecommunications service—that adequate circuits are not available to link countries of different national groupings and to bring French, Dutch, British and American businessmen together.

I think I can say without fear of contradiction that in this field of regional telecommunications, the Caribbean Organization has scored a distinct success in its first three years. Realising the great degree to which this lack of proper cable and telephone services can hinder trade, the Organization took the initiative and sponsored, with the assistance of the United States Agency for International Development, a survey of the telecommunications needs of the Eastern Caribbean. The report was published and studied by all concerned. Then a year later, for the first time in history, the representatives of the State telecommunications agencies and private telecommunications companies operating in the area, (such as American Telephone and Telegraph Company and Cable and Wireless) sat around a table together with the representatives of the governments they serve, and very frankly and cordially everyone put his cards on the table and pooled plans for the future and the result is that by the end of next year we can expect to have a backbone of first class cable service running right through the Caribbean area. We are certain that the result of this meeting is a remarkable step forward and lays one of the main foundations of dynamic Caribbean cooperation.

The fourth problem we will look at is that of transportation—transportation by sea and by air. If one businessman can cable another in a neighbouring territory, if customs duties permit of the ordinary business of supply and demand being transacted and each can satisfy the other's needs, there remains the problem of getting the commodity from one Caribbean country to another by sea or by air.

The Caribbean Organization has been making a preliminary study of the transportation problems of the Caribbean, and the same pattern emerges—we find that the American trade patterns are linked together, and so in varying degrees, are the British and the French, and the Dutch. But there is very little sea transportation of an organized nature which links the whole Caribbean and which calls at American, British, French and Dutch ports. Of course, there is widespread recognition of this lack of transportation and this has led to a number of attempts being made to remedy this. For example: it was felt that the two West Indian ships, the Federal Maple and the Federal Palm were running between St. Kitts and Jamaica without full loads while it might be possible to arrange for passengers and cargo to be picked up in Puerto Rico or the U.S. Virgin Islands. As a matter of fact, a special study of this problem of sea transportation has been made under the auspices of the University of the West Indies.

We can mention also that a meeting of representatives of the various airlines serving the Caribbean has been called by the Secretary General in order to begin discussions on the important matter of special fares for regional travel.

Finally, in this talk on the foundations of regional cooperation in the Caribbean we should look beyond the study of the main problems to a special meeting which was organized under the auspices of the Caribbean Organization at the beginning of 1963.

The Caribbean Council realized that quite apart from studying the four problems we have touched on, and other problems as well, a positive step should be taken with regard to economic planning—so with the financial assistance of the Ford Foundation, which is here gratefully acknowledged, a Seminar on Planning Techniques and Methods was organized for the benefit of ministers of governments, government planners, and others at which economists of world repute lectured on basic topics and then discussed with the leaders of Caribbean society their application to the specific needs of the region. Among these lecturers were Professor Jan Tinbergen of Holland, Professor Sir Arthur Lewis of the University of the West Indies, now at Princeton, Michel Cointat of Paris, Dr. Rafael Pico of Puerto Rico and Alvin Mayne of the United States of America.

What took place at the Seminar was a concentration of intellectual power upon Caribbean planning needs. Economists called attention to the fact that the Caribbean units, especially the smaller ones are not viable by themselves, and that the only hope for the future where they were concerned was some sort of grouping. Some experts advocated a free trade area starting with a limited number of countries and a limited number of commodities. Others called for a new alliance, a Caribbean Common Market, and there was a demand for a consortium of the great powers traditionally associated with the Caribbean areas to bring the necessary financial assistance to the region.

So in these first three years of its existence, the Caribbean Organization has been laying the groundwork for the future, and putting down the foundations of regional cooperation in major areas.

The Development of Trade in the Caribbean

In the last broadcast, we looked at the ways in which the Caribbean Organization has been studying problems of the area and laying the foundations of regional cooperation. We mentioned then the patterns of trade which emerged from the history of the region, and which link the various Caribbean territories so securely with their metropolitan partners of the past. Today we will discuss the development of trade within the Caribbean area and the steps being taken to encourage its expansion.

When the Caribbean Organization was being established in 1961, the special needs of the region with regard to economic development were carefully examined and the idea of the Caribbean Plan was readily accepted by all member governments. If we want to put the meaning of this Plan in a nutshell, we can say that the Caribbean Plan is the expression of the will of the Members of the Caribbean Organization to work harmoniously together for the benefit of all.

Under the Plan, it was necessary to do three main things: to find out the obstacles which prevented true and lasting development from taking place; to identify the problems which had to be solved if this development is to take place; and to emphasize the policies which would allow development to follow. In the policies which have been discussed, formulated and re-emphasized at meeting after meeting of the Caribbean Council and its Committees, priority has been given to two main targets, the expansion of intra-Caribbean trade and the development of tourism. We shall be discussing the very important matter of tourism later in this series, so let us concentrate now on the matter of the development of trade which, as you know, is the very life-blood of a community's prosperity.

To make it easier for trade to take place between Caribbean countries, it was decided that a Clearing House should be set up in the Central Secretariat of the Caribbean Organization and charged with the special task of receiving and disseminating information on trade and tourism to government agencies and to business interests within the Caribbean area and even outside of it. The information may be of a general nature on the area as a whole, but it is more often specific information on trade. This could be the customs duties levied by country X on goods coming in from country Y or about transportation facilities, tariffs, formalities, and a host of other factors involved in trading in the Caribbean. Or it may be information on the demand for goods which are needed by a businessman in a particular island or it may be information concerning goods in supply which another businessman would like to sell.

Of course, it may be rightly said that many Caribbean countries produce the same things, like sugar, but you know, there had long been a suspicion that one of the main reasons why intra-Caribbean trade was only 3 to 4 cents in every dollar was because Caribbean businessmen just did not know what bargains and business opportunities were possible in other parts of the region. They could open their trade journals and see that such and such a commodity could be obtained in Holland or West Germany, but there was previously no journal to inform them of goods in demand or in supply in the Caribbean; no journal, that is, until the Clearing House on Trade and Tourism Information of the Caribbean Organization began to publish the Monthly Journal with its basic information on customs duties, etc., and the Weekly with its classified advertisements of opportunities to be snapped up by keen businessmen.

The Clearing House which started in 1962 has just completed the first two years of operation, and a survey has been made of its value to businessmen and to Chambers of Commerce throughout the region which has been most gratifying. This is one of the many instances of the value of information, showing that knowledge is power, particularly in the matter of the flow of trade.

The Clearing House survey disclosed that all correspondents found the trade opportunities on commodities and services to be of great value to them. Many exporters were able to find new markets as a result of the information supplied by the Clearing House. This is the precise reason for which the Clearing House was set up. Of course, with any information medium it is never possible to estimate 100% the value of the service. What we can say is that the Clearing House has been creating a better Caribbean consciousness, and bringing an awareness of trading possibilities to the attention of the businessman. Trade promotional work cannot be measured in practical results, because the businessmen themselves must do the business, but there is no doubt about these results and that is the reason why in all developed countries, the governments have expanded their trade information services during the post-war years and spent a lot of money for this purpose.

This point—that we must let facts be known—has been reinforced by a market analyst from Holland on the possibilities of expanding trade in fruits, vegetables and other food crops. Drs. de Boer spent six months last year visiting Caribbean countries and investigating the possibilities of expanding trade in these fields. At that time he was on secondment to the Organization by the Netherlands Government, at the request of the Government of the Netherlands Antilles. In his report he stated that, if Caribbean trade is to increase, it is the businessman who has to bring his skills into play to bridge the gap between supply and demand. Many businessmen said they would trade more with Caribbean countries if they had more information on what new markets were available, or where goods were available in sufficient quantities and of standard quality. If intra-Caribbean trade is to be expanded, then the work of market analysis must be continued from this centre of regional cooperation, strengthened to meet the needs.

Drs. de Boer has made a start, a valuable start, but as he pointed out in his report, the very complex work of market analysis must go on as a day-to-day routine, gathering figures and forecasting trends in order to assist governments and businessmen and farmers to expand production and to meet a shortage in one country by a shift of surpluses in others.

In recent months, there have been two important developments which we should notice in our review of the first 3 years of the Organization's work. The Clearing House is advancing from correspondence and publications to the face-to-face visit and to display, from correspondence to its logical development of Trade Missions and to the establishment of a permanent Trade Exhibition at headquarters.

Parties consisting of government representatives and businessmen have been moving freely from one Caribbean country to another, looking for trade opportunities and for ideas they can adapt to the improvement of their own businesses. For example: a mission went from Puerto Rico to Curacao and to Barbados and Trinidad. A group of young businessmen came from Martinique to see food processing factories in Puerto Rico. The design of small cottage-type hotel on the southern coast of Puerto Rico made a great appeal to legislators from Martinique. Because Puerto Rico has made considerable advances in the field of industrial development, the Chief Minister of St. Kitts came to look at light industry development and seek potential investors. These missions we have mentioned have all been organized with the assistance of the Caribbean Organization, and it is true to say that in this way we have been deepening the lines of trade possibilities within the Caribbean area. The dynamic world of business in the Caribbean area is quick to seize upon and follow up any information which leads to better trade.

A word now about the Permanent Trade Exhibition. For years, the Secretary General has cherished the thought that there should be at headquarters a full display of the very wide range of Caribbean products which already exist. From discussions in committee last year, it seemed at one time that we might think of a floating trade mart—equip one of the ships which travel through the Caribbean area, with all the Caribbean products available, so that it could be a commercial missionary floating from one port to another like an Ark upon the waters, taking this suite of showrooms where the inhabitants of our Caribbean countries could really see what the region produces. This attractive idea may or may not be realized in the near future, but at present a start is being made to mount a permanent Trade Exhibition in the Headquarters in Hato Rey. With the display will be all the relative information on prices, quantities available, names and addresses of manufacturers and exporters. Charts, photographs and diagrams will provide basic economic data on the various exhibiting countries.

This exhibition, in essence, will be a practical step forward in bringing to the attention of investors not only what is produced in the area and the possibilities of increasing such production for larger markets, but also what economically feasible projects could be entered into for the improved development of a particular country, group of countries, or the area as a whole.

We have been concerned in this broadcast with the way the Caribbean Organization has been promoting the development of trade within the region. This has been the work of the Clearing House on Trade and Tourism Information, an agency within the Secretariat, specially set up for this purpose of assisting government agencies and businessmen. We have also seen the developments taking place to improve its work.

THE IMPROVEMENT OF AGRICULTURE IN THE CARIBBEAN

From time immemorial the basis of wealth has been the land. It is the land which yields her increase patiently year after year to feed young and old, to renew the strength of the worker, and to provide the surplus of production which always is the beginning of trade with other countries.

Over the centuries, the Caribbean has always been an agricultural region. One-time sugar bowl to the world, its importance in the world economy declined with the rise of beet and the growth of the sugar industry in other places. In recent years, the countries in the Caribbean area have been trying to develop the industrial sector and to develop the tourist industry, and in certain territories, notably Puerto Rico, Jamaica and Trinidad and Tobago, important strides have been made in manufacturing. Agriculture, however, still continues to maintain its basic position as the foundation of the regional economy. Sugar is still the largest single employer within the agricultural sector, if not within the area as a whole, and sugar production remains the chief agricultural pursuit. But bananas, cocoa, beans, coffee, pineapple, tobacco, rice and citrus fruit maintain positions of importance.

In the three years of its existence, the Caribbean Organization has been engaged in many activities contributing to the improvement of agriculture throughout the region and it is possible to point to the main achievements in the field of regional cooperation which have accelerated the progress of Caribbean agriculture.

The first is the technique of the Demonstration Tour. There have been two Demonstration Tours since 1961, one on Vegetables and Food Crops which was held in Puerto Rico in February 1962, the other on Bananas held in Guadeloupe in February 1964. These Tours, both of which were carefully planned, and held in joint sponsorship with the governments of the territories concerned, have given a tremendous impetus to the farming community. In the Puerto Rican Tour, 15 countries sent 50 participants to observe the production, processing and marketing of vegetables and food crops (including fruits), and to exchange information and comment with each other on problems. Two years later, the Guadeloupe tour concentrated on Bananas alone; there were just under 300 participants drawn from 25 countries and emphasis was laid upon practices in the cultivation and marketing of bananas and projects of basic and applied research. Both tours provided an opportunity for the pooling of national resources on an unprecedented scale, and particularly in the case of the Banana Demonstration Tour, this was an outstanding success from the agricultural, scientific and commercial points of view. The contribution of the French government was most important, since specialists were brought from widely scattered areas in the world to meet experts from practically all Caribbean countries. There was therefore information covering a very wide range of disciplines of scientific and technical research, production and marketing. As a matter of fact, so enthusiastic were the participants over the Banana Tour, that it was suggested the Caribbean Organization should consider the arrangement of such tours as one of its primary functions and should devote the same kind of attention to other traditional primary products in the Caribbean, such as pineapples and other tropical fruits.

It is worth while making one final comment on the banana industry at this point. The banana, as the Secretary-General pointed out in his speech at the opening of the Guadeloupe tour, is second only to sugar as an agricultural industry and plays a great role in the area, since it provides employment all around the year and brings cash income to a wide range of farming communities, especially the smaller farmers.

The second matter for review is the visit to South Africa by an expedition under the auspices of the United States Department of Agriculture to collect grass species likely to be of value in the Americas. The background to this is short and simple. In a discussion in Jamaica in 1961, on the improvement of grassland in the Caribbean area, a report was made of a disease which was affecting the Pangola grass in Surinam. The point was made that the greater part of Pangola grass cover of the Caribbean area went back to one or two plants of Pangola grass which had been originally introduced into the United States from South Africa. The conference then registered concern at the risk that attends such a widespread use of material from such a restricted genetic base, since the possibility of selecting or breeding resistant varieties would be greatly restricted and one instrument for preventing the rapid disastrous spread of disease throughout the area thus rendered useless. It was recommended that as soon as possible an expedition should be sent to South Africa to collect other types of Pangola grass, for use in the Caribbean. The importance of Pangola will be realised when it is considered that nearly 1/10 of the total grass cover of the Caribbean is Pangola and that it is the main grass cover now used by progressive livestock farmers in the region.

The expedition to South Africa went early this year and as a result batches of grass species of the Pangola variety are now in quarantine in Puerto Rico and will be sent to Caribbean governments in the near future for observation and test. Some of these may well prove superior to the Pangola variety which is now so popular in the area and the selection and breeding of varieties for resistance to disease is now a practical possibility.

The third main development in regional agriculture which is of significance for the future is the trend towards establishing regional intra-Caribbean bodies, autonomous but cooperating with other regional bodies such as the Caribbean Organization.

It was in May 1963 that the Caribbean Food Crops Society was established. Its main objective was to stimulate the production and distribution of fruits, vegetables and other food crops, and so to improve Caribbean nutrition and living standards. It quickly attracted a membership coming up to 100 institutions and individuals drawn from all the Caribbean, Central America and the United States of America. It received strong support from the Caribbean Organization throughout the initial stages of its development, since its objectives marched along with those of the Organization as a centre of regional cooperation.

In its short existence so far, the Caribbean Food Crops Society has become a forum for the discussion and planning of research projects in many parts of the Caribbean. It has financed the tour of a specialist throughout the region collecting samples of food crops. It has initiated schemes of technical assistance, such as a survey of plant pests in the Caribbean area and a survey of papaya disease in St. Croix of the United States Virgin Islands.

This is only part of the record of this progressive body, the Caribbean Food Crops Society. Because science and research acknowledge no frontier, there is a movement to form a Caribbean Banana Growers Association arising out of the recent Banana Demonstration Tour. The British Caribbean Cane Farmers Association is attempting to enlarge its articles of association to bring into membership similar bodies and individuals in other national groupings. At a recent meeting, the British West Indies Veterinary Officers Association adopted a resolution favouring the establishment of a Caribbean-wide Association. One can, therefore, foresee a trend in all professional associations which will certainly enlarge the scope of regional cooperation.

We have selected these main points for discussion in this broadcast on "the Caribbean Organization—the First Three Years." Necessarily we have not stressed the routine work of arranging tours, providing information on problems of member governments in the field of natural resources, the very valuable assistance given by the Standing Advisory Committee on Animal Health and Production, etc.

But before we conclude, let us take note of one regional service which the Caribbean Organization provides in the field of agriculture. I refer to the annual document on the status of research into problems of animal health and production in countries served by the Caribbean Organization. The latest published document lists the studies dealing with grasses and legumes for fodder in the first section, and the second sets out the research on cattle and small stock.

THE CONTRIBUTION TO EDUCATION IN THE CARIBBEAN

In this 5th talk in the Series "The Caribbean Organization—the First Three Years," we are going to discuss the contribution being made by the Organization to the promotion of education and community welfare in the Caribbean area.

Last year the Secretary General of the Caribbean Organization, Mr. C. F. Beauregard, issued a message in support of the Freedom from Hunger Campaign. His opening sentences were (I quote) "The most important natural resource of the Caribbean area is its people. On them will depend to the greatest possible extent the success or failure of governments' plans for economic, social and cultural progress in these developing countries" (unquote).

Under the Caribbean Plan, it has been stated again and again that education is one of the most dynamic elements in the movement towards a better life for all. It transforms the individual, gives him better skills, and also it accelerates the rate of desirable social change. We have to build the services by which this better life in the Caribbean will flow and trained personnel at all levels are needed to maintain and direct these necessary services. Without trained personnel, little can be done with government funds and the capital of private enterprises in the promotion of economic development. Industrial development remains a vain hope unless trained personnel are available.

Last year, the Caribbean Organization arranged successfully a high level seminar on Planning Techniques & Methods—we have mentioned this before in this series of talks. But I want to go back to it to mention a lecture by Professor Arthur Lewis, then Vice-Chancellor of the University of West Indies. He gave a lecture at the seminar on the role of the Social Services in development planning. He made the point that education compared with the economic and productive sectors used to be like Cinderella in the fairy tale, but that in recent times Prince Charming has come to her rescue. A school of economists in Chicago have made calculations which set out to show that money invested in education is as productive as money invested in other natural resources of a physical nature. But it is a fact that it is difficult for many Caribbean governments to find the necessary capital to invest in education. This is why the Organization formulated a special programme of educational training to assist governments in implementing their development programmes.

Acting as donor country under the Caribbean Plan, the United States Government has made grants within the last 2 years to a total, so far, of nearly a third of a million dollars U.S. The money is spent to provide university training at graduate and post graduate levels for Caribbean personnel. This is the Caribbean Organization Fellowship Programme, and I'd like us to notice the major fields in which awards have been made. The purpose is to help bring the Caribbean rapidly from the 19th century and its complacencies into the modern world of electronics and economic equations.

Since agriculture is the basis of the economy in the region, scholarships have been offered in this field. We must help the Caribbean governments to grow two tons of cane or bananas, or what-have-you, where only one grew before.

Scholarships must also be offered in economics. This science of human behaviour going back to Adam Smith and his famous book "The Wealth of Nations," must be well known if governments and peoples are to improve their living standards and develop their gross national product.

Scholarships in engineering are also a priority. Caribbean nationals must be able to build airports, sea ports, modern roads, and bridges and to plan housing settlements.

A fourth priority is public administration. The 20th century has devised a variety of modern techniques to fit the making of decisions and their resulting public action into a democratic framework. The able young men and women of the Caribbean must be trained in these techniques of public administration.

Finally, there is teacher education. There is the saying,—if you educate an individual, you put him on the road to success. If you educate a teacher, you build a nation. The need to improve teaching skills was quickly recognized and it was decided that scholarships should be offered in this major field also.

I will give you some more information about this Programme since it is one of the most important single contributions to Caribbean regional development that the Organization has made in its first three years of existence. It was considered that the first choice of persons to be awarded these scholarships should belong to the governments themselves. So it was stipulated that governments should call for applications, make a short list of the persons applying in the fields they considered important for their country, and then send their candidates in to the Organization for final selection.

An independent Board of Selectors was then created. We got the four Universities in the region we serve to send representatives to make the final choice of applicants. They try to balance community needs against qualifications and to establish priorities. The awards are then made by the Secretary General on the advice of the Board of Selectors, after places have been obtained in Universities.

By October of this year, under the Caribbean Organization Fellowship Program, there will be some 80 students enrolled in universities in the Caribbean and in the United States of America, undergoing studies in order to go back to their countries and help bring their countries' development plans nearer their realization. At the end of 4 years, under this programme, there may be anything like 120 to 150 men and women who will have been trained in these basic development fields. This is nothing like the number of men and women in the area who would benefit from training, but at least they represent the beginning of a cooperative regional assault upon lack of direction and lack of training in the Caribbean. There is need, of course, for a further scheme in which technical and vocational training can be provided, since the value of this training scheme at university level will be enhanced when we have also trained a number of other persons at technical and vocational levels who will provide supporting services in the overall implementation of development schemes.

What we need to do at this present time is to determine all these education needs in relation to the needs of the region. This is why a survey of education and manpower needs throughout the Caribbean area is greatly needed and an approach has been made for collaboration and assistance by other international bodies in organizing such a survey.

In allied fields, training has been continuously going on under the auspices of the Caribbean Organization. Of special notice is a recent Regional Workshop on the Methods and Techniques of Cooperative Organization which was jointly sponsored by the International Labour Organization and the Caribbean Organization and which was attended by 23 participants from ten Caribbean countries. These participants were senior cooperative personnel, and they discussed practical problems affecting the development of the cooperative movement in their respective countries, and viewed at first hand the well-organized and successful cooperative institutions in Puerto Rico.

There is a great deal of other work going on to make the peoples of the Caribbean better fed, better housed, with better skills, more self reliant, and better equipped to face the future and to participate in their countries' drive for economic development. The major asset of the Caribbean is its peoples and they are being better prepared by the efforts of their own governments and also by the plans of the Caribbean Organization in regional cooperation, prepared for making a livelihood and for living gracious lives in the modern world.

THE CARIBBEAN ORGANIZATION AND TOURISM IN THE CARIBBEAN

Let me give you a vision of the future. The day that Emerson Jones and his wife, in Seattle, Washington, made the decision to holiday in the Caribbean they changed the pattern of their lives forever. Emerson Jones was a salesman in Seattle, on the Pacific seaboard. For years he and his wife had explored the Pacific in the summer months with a satisfaction and delight. Then one day he took home an illustrated brochure setting out the pleasure of holidaying in the Caribbean that he had picked up in a travel agency. That night he and his wife went through the brochure. They were keenly interested in history and they realized that the Caribbean was a rich and exciting treasure chest of history where they could move in the trail of Columbus from island to island and they could find traces of other great names such as Nelson and Alexander Hamilton and see the effects of historical developments under the impetus of French, Dutch, Spanish and British cultures. But they were interested also in blue seas and white sand glittering in the sunlight, and of these attractions there was an abundance in the Caribbean.

Of course, Emerson Jones and his wife were lucky. It was only the year before that the tourist industry in the Caribbean had been integrated, so they had a flat rate for travelling and staying anywhere in the region, enjoying the flavour of different cultures. The hotels were full but not overcrowded, the level of craftsmanship in the well-made souvenirs they found everywhere was excellent, so they could acquire easily little gifts for their friends at home. There was a fine level of courteous service in hotels, taxis and shops. They were glad to find that language was not a problem because the staff that served them was versed in all the languages of the region and best of all they found that their holiday brought them into contact with many tourists from Europe and many residents from other parts of the Caribbean who were holidaying in their own region.

Emerson Jones was interested in minerals in an amateur sort of way, so he found that the Caribbean was one of the richest bauxite regions in the world, Jamaica alone for example, having the largest known deposits in the world. Add to that, British Guiana, Surinam, and French Guiana. When he and his wife got home from the holiday, they talked about the trip with their neighbours and between themselves, and they aroused a great interest in the developing economy of the Caribbean and the rich variety of peoples they had found there. It was no wonder that Emerson Jones and his friends decided to start a company to invest in one of the many avenues for profitable employment in that area of the world, where they had spent such a stimulating holiday.

This is the sixth and last talk in the series "The Caribbean Organization—the First Three Years," in which we are telling the story of the difficulties and achievements of regional cooperation in this area. We have told the story of how the Organization came into existence by the will of the Caribbean peoples and their representatives and how it began to act as a focus of cooperation at government and popular levels. We have described the problems inherited from the operations of the past and the trends of history, such as the lack of communication and we have looked at the many ways in which a Caribbean consciousness is being forged by trade, training and technical cooperation on the international level.

In this last talk we are discussing the tourist industry and looking into the future at the benefits which will follow an integration of all tourist facilities in a well rounded and well planned Caribbean tourist development programme.

People sometimes look upon the tourist, clad in camera, sunglasses and Bermuda or Jamaica shorts, as an oddity to be endured, because he brings dollars into the economy, but there is so much more to it. A few years ago, the United States Secretary of Commerce described the tourist, camera and all, as a major factor in building international understanding and good will. Governments and Chambers of Commerce everywhere have learnt to recognize him as a person who may later return to make an investment in the economic development of the country, the beauties of which he has sampled.

The facts about the present Caribbean tourist industry are available. We know from studies that four countries in the Caribbean are able to attract more than 3/4 of the total tourist trade; in other words, Puerto Rico, Jamaica, the U.S. Virgin Islands and Trinidad & Tobago gained 83% of the tourist expenditure in 1961. We know that the remaining 17% of the tourist trade is shared among 15 other countries. So there is uneven development.

It is estimated that from America alone, there were 1 1/2 million visitors who came to the Caribbean in 1962 and that they spent $220 million U.S. Yet, this is less than 10% of the great flow of United States tourist expenditure in all parts of the world. When it is remembered that the Caribbean is a playground virtually on the American doorstep, one can see that with better organization of advertising and resources, it should be possible to attract a higher percentage of tourists. But this means that the image of the Caribbean areas as a prime playground of the Americas must be projected boldly.

Not only in the Americas can we expect to attract the attention of tourists. The rising prosperity of the European Common Market countries has encouraged a growing number of European tourists to go abroad on their holidays, and many of them travel to the United States of America. To many of these European tourists, it would be a great pleasure to take in the beauties of the Caribbean also, either on their way to, or from North America. This is a further market waiting to be tapped. Finally, there is the growing inclination on the part of the Caribbean peoples themselves to learn more of their region, to compare its beauty spots, to sample its history and to make the acquaintance of their hospitable neighbours. So we have the third possibility of expanding local tourism.

The Caribbean Organization has planned a project to integrate and develop the tourist industry in the Caribbean area. Under this scheme, a factual study of the present state of the industry would be made by a team of experts in order to analyse the market and assess the feasibility of harmonising and integrating all tourist development and including tourist promotion. The team would go from island to island studying the industry. After the results of the study have been made available, the proposal is to organize a seminar at which all the entities interested in tourism would meet to agree, if possible, upon the development of a common policy towards tourism at government and private levels. It would, of course, be necessary to retain and develop the individual characteristics of each island and territory, especially architecture, its carnival, menus and other aspects of cultural heritage, but the purpose of the project is to organize a more effective exploitation of the unique and varied physical and climatic attractions of the area, to expand the volume of traffic, to increase the expenditure in the less popular areas and to attract an increase in the volume of intra-Caribbean, North American, Latin American and European tourist traffic.

When the seminar is called, there should be present representatives of governments and government agencies, the financiers and builders of hotels, those associated with management in the hotel businesses, the airlines and the shipping companies which bring the visitors, the firms and organizations engaged on the publicity of the tourist trade of their region, the travel agents and tour operators who ensure that the visitors are satisfactorily taken to places of interest, the taxicab interests, the groups engaged on the manufacture of art and craft forms which become souvenirs for the tourists, the keepers of restaurants and cafeterias who feed the tourist. Last but by no means least, the vast organization of entertainment and sports which helps the tourists to relax and play. So you can see that there would be a massive confrontation of all interested in the expansion of tourism. And the purpose would be to discuss the problems and activities of tourism in order to develop a common policy of stimulation.

There is very much more that can be said about the Caribbean Organization and the first Three Years, but time and the exigencies of a radio series do not permit.

In these series, we have stressed the highlights of the problems and indicated the ground work which has been planned for the future—what we call the foundations of regional cooperation.

Anyone interested in learning more about any aspect of its varied operations can write the Secretary General at Box 1058, Hato Rey, Puerto Rico. We are always happy to answer enquiries.

All we need say here at the end of the series is that the Caribbean Organization is an instrument designed for regional cooperation brought into existence by the will of the Caribbean governments and peoples themselves, and waiting as an instrument to be moulded to their purposes, so that there will be a better life for us all.

G. ☐ EVALUATION OF CESCO PILOT PROJECT, 1966

By Norman G. Kerr, Superintendent of Education, British Virgin Islands

The great majority of the 2,400 children in these islands are taught in church or chapel buildings, used as schools. Of a total teaching force of roughly ninety, only twenty have been trained in colleges abroad. Most of the remainder are young women, a few are young men, who have passed straight from school into the teaching service, only very modestly equipped academically. Recruitment of teachers has been difficult for many years, scales of pay were not attractive and the problems of teaching in the conditions which prevail in the schools deters all but the most determined. "Wastage" from the service by promotion to administrative posts in the Civil Service, to commercial enterprises or by emigration from the territory has cancelled out the increase in numbers sent for training.

The shortage of trained teachers was aggravated, during 1966, by the efforts made to have local teachers trained for specialist work in the future. Three of the small group of trained teachers went to Britain for one-year specialist courses, two others left for University courses in Canada, a sixth for a University training in Puerto Rico. Three more young teachers were sent for training to the Leeward Islands Training College.

In these circumstances the offer of assistance from CESCO was warmly welcomed by Government and Education Department. The project co-ordinator visited the territory in February to gain first-hand knowledge of the needs of the schools and the problems to be met in satisfying them. It was decided that up to eight teachers could be absorbed in Tortola and that they should be competent teachers, adaptable to the difficult circumstances in which they would be required to work, with an interest not only in teaching but in teacher-training and able to fit into the restricted physical and social environment of a small, remote island.

As a shortage of trained and dedicated teachers is the common lot of Caribbean territories, it might have been expected that no response would be forthcoming from the member countries of CODECA to which the appeal was despatched. In the event the first volunteer from Puerto Rico, Miss Nerida Cruz, arrived in Tortola a few days before the Autumn Term opened, in time to join in an Island Teachers Conference, thereby meeting her new colleagues and finding out some of the problems of education in a small territory. Miss Dinah Evans from Guyana arrived three days later and began teaching on the following day. The happy coincidence of the arrival of two V.S.O. teachers from Britain enabled the Government to accommodate the four ladies in a furnished house in Road Town. Mr. Watson, an experienced teacher from Jamaica, arrived some weeks later and was placed in the large school at East End, some nine miles from town; a flat was rented for him within a half mile of the school.

At the end of the first term of work it is possible to make a preliminary assessment of the progress of this interesting experiment. Credit must be given to the three volunteers for their adaptability to the changed circumstances and environment in which they have found themselves. Coming as they all have, from large, progressive Caribbean territories with vigorous and expanding educational systems, the more primitive and restricted conditions in Tortola have tested their ability to fit into a new system. Faced with problems of crowded classrooms, poor furnishings, lack of materials and apparatus, they have adapted their teaching techniques, contrived and improvised their teaching materials and proved highly successful in their classroom work. Miss Cruz, as a Spanish-speaking teacher of English, readily transformed into an English-speaking teacher of Spanish and by her obvious enthusiasm stimulated a like enthusiasm among her classes at both Primary and Secondary level. Miss Evans, taking over a difficult, somewhat retarded group, in the large Road Town Primary School, has made a notable contribution by her persistent and conscientious effort in very difficult circumstances. Mr. Watson, accepting responsibility for the Post-Primary classes at East End filled an important vacant post in the school more than adequately and thereby relieved the Headmaster of a very difficult task.

It is difficult to estimate the beneficial effects on pupils in a small island community, of the close association for weeks on end, with a teacher from a different country. Curiosity and interest are aroused, questions are asked spontaneously, differences in speech, in manners and habits are noted and horizons are thereby imperceptibly broadened and insularity is eroded. In the long term these beneficial effects may prove greater than the immediate solution of a problem of teacher shortage.

But it is not only in their teaching that their contribution has lain. In circumstances where young inexperienced teachers have so little opportunity of seeing and hearing competent practitioners at work, their example in the schools has been of incalculable value. By taking an active part in the systematic "in-service" teacher-training programme, they have been able to disseminate, among groups of our young teachers, not only their own philosophies of education, but, perhaps more important, their methods of work in the context of the classroom conditions which prevail.

In the larger, social environment of the island community, our three CESCO teachers have made their impact. Where everyone knows everyone, it was inevitable that "foreign" teachers would incite considerable curiosity. The friendly relationship established with children in the classroom has spread to parents, relatives and friends outside the schools and by joining in community activities, attending church services, mixing in dances and swimming parties and setting excellent examples of "how teachers behave," our three young volunteers have established laudable relationships with our Virgin Islanders.

There have, inevitably, been problems. The most obvious arises from the discrepancies in financial rewards for what these teachers are doing. As each is paid his or her normal salary by the home Government and as salary scales vary widely over the Caribbean territories, it means that one may be receiving much more or less than another for doing the same job. As the British Virgin Islands are in the U.S. economic orbit, using exclusively U.S. currency, the cost of living is even higher than in U.S.A. and considerably higher than in most West Indian territories. Little is produced locally so the necessities of life are imported mainly from the U.S.A. and are consequently expensive. In these circumstances, it is possible that a volunteer may be called upon to make substantial financial sacrifices. It is true that the British V.S.O. teachers are, in a sense, less well treated as they are given only an allowance in lieu of salary, but they accepted these conditions as part of the V.S.O. project.

The question of transportation for the teachers has caused some slight difficulty. It was expected that teachers could be accommodated within easy walking distance of the school in which they taught and no allowance was made for daily transportation though it was understood that for journeys to other schools, to teacher-training classes or other extra-curricular activities, a vehicle would be made available. As the house occupied is a little over a mile from the school and as the only public transport available is by taxi at a cost of 50¢ per journey, the problem would have been acute but for the help of other teachers who own vehicles and have assisted with transport. This problem may recur early in 1967 as the teacher who has been most helpful is leaving the school. The V.S.O. teachers have bought a vehicle for their own use; since, however, they visit various schools, they will not be available to transport their CESCO colleagues to and from home at lunch time. A minor problem for Mr. Watson has been the irregularity of the postal service from Jamaica. More than three weeks passed before he received any communication from his own island; he is therefore not unnaturally worried as to how long his salary may take to reach him. Miss Evans too has found this a cause of some worry. Perhaps this matter could be dealt with through CESCO Headquarters.

From the foregoing it is, I hope, clear that, apart from the minor difficulties, inevitable in organizing any project, the pilot scheme on Tortola is a resounding success. The Government, the schools and the people are grateful to CODECA for the valuable assistance which has been rendered at a time of difficulty. As I shall very soon be leaving the Caribbean to return to Britain, I should like to add my personal expression of appreciation to CODECA and to the CESCO co-ordinator. I feel honoured that I have been able to assist in a small way in a project which may well set the pattern for future developments in Education in the Caribbean of enormous significance.

H. ☐ REPORT OF THE TRIPARTITE ECONOMIC SURVEY OF THE EASTERN CARIBBEAN (EXCERPTS)

CHAPTER II: A REGIONAL APPROACH TO DEVELOPMENT PROGRAMMING

IV.2.1. Part II of this report has set out a number of problems and restraints to growth that appear common to all of the islands of the Eastern Caribbean. In some cases the reduction of these restraints could come about through common policies and programmes voluntarily agreed to by the Governments themselves, e.g. removal of inter-island trade restraints, standardization and clarification of tax and incentive legislation, removal of restrictions on labour mobility. In other instances, positive measures to promote growth might also be undertaken through agreed common policies at a lower cost than would otherwise be possible if undertaken by each island separately, e.g. tourist promotion for the region, development bank for industry and housing, financing of production and market research for a wide variety of products common to the region, provision of certain marketing services. Finally, a number of specialized technical and commercial services could be provided or maintained at a higher standard of service if administered and financed through a common regional policy, e.g. inter-island shipping, income tax collection services, meteorological services, specialized educational services including the use of television, health and medical services, technical and consulting services relevant to water supplies, airport and harbour construction, road construction, cadastral surveys and land-use studies.

IV.2.2. If we now bring together the long list of common problems and growth restraints discussed in Part II and referred to above, several reasonably homogeneous groups emerge—

(a) the need for an active development organization capable of providing permanent services in market research and development and in industrial promotion including the service industry such as tourism;
(b) the need for long-term credit facilities for new industrial development, for housing, for agriculture and other primary industry development, and possibly for certain local government undertakings of a self-liquidating nature;
(c) the continuing need within the region as a whole for a variety of long-term and short-term technical and consulting services.

IV.2.3. In reviewing the kinds of development needs set out above, it is apparent that development assistance covering a wide variety of activities could be financed and administered for each territory separately. But having in mind the relatively small size of the individual territories and indeed the Eastern Caribbean region as a whole, and bearing in mind the enormous needs the world over for development skills and resources, it seems to us urgent that the planning and supervision of development activities common to all islands within the region be centrally programmed. The restraints to growth discussed earlier will not be overcome by sporadic efforts or projects which fail to achieve anything because of the lack of continuous supervision and technical services. What is needed is a consistent programme, no matter how modest, that will move forward gradually, and one that is close enough to local opportunities and requirements to be flexible. If development planning and activities were to be administered for the region as a whole by a single body it should then be possible to bring together various forms of external assistance offered by donor countries into an integrated and continuing action programme.

IV.2.4. Our recommendation therefore is that a single planning administrative organization be established under the joint sponsorship of the U.S.A., the U.K. and Canada, these being the countries which have demonstrated an interest in the economic development of the English speaking territories of the Caribbean in the past. This body, which we refer to below as a Regional Development Agency, would operate in separate divisions for various groups of functions. There would be one over-riding board of directors. The board would consist of representatives of the local island governments and of the participating overseas governments as well as the directors of the two divisions. The functions of the board would be to oversee and provide broad direction to the operating divisions. We think that two would be enough for the scale of development operations in the islands; a Technical and Commercial Services division and a Development Bank division. The budgetary process for each division should be separate so as to enable the Bank division to operate along commercial lines. In an operation of this size, it would seem to us that the functions of commercial development and the provision and development of the necessary technical and professional services could be combined in one division.

Financial Requirements

IV.2.5. It is anticipated that the bulk of financing for each division would have to be drawn from the overseas governments according to a formula agreed to in advance. Certainly this would be necessary in the case of the initial capital requirement for the development bank. In the case of the technical and commercial services division, it must be decided first of all whether the budget of the division is designed to absorb the total pooled commitments of the overseas governments for all current and capital projects for the region in a year. The latter approach may be unnecessarily rigid and demand too much prior agreement on cost sharing. This is a matter for the Governments involved to decide in the light of their own aid policies. But as a minimum the budget of the division must provide recurrent financing for its annual operational activities in the technical and commercial services field and for its responsibilities for forward planning. It would also act as the regional advisory body to overseas governments regarding priorities and the scheduling of major capital projects. We assign a very high priority to a body which is adequately financed to mobilize the practical and experienced skills necessary to build the tourist, industrial and market facilities required for a significant rate of growth in per capita incomes. For certain activities within the commercial development division, financial participation by local Governments on a shared basis would be provided for.

Functions of a Regional Development Agency

(1) Technical and Commercial Services Division

IV.2.6. An important part of the activities of this division will be tourist promotion and associated investment, the development of commercial market facilities for the primary products of the islands including the promotion of orderly trade within the region and between the region and elsewhere, and industrial promotion within the region including commercial enterprises in the primary industries.

IV.2.7. We have indicated in Part II the probable size of private capital required in new hotel and other construction if tourism is to grow at feasible rates. In order for investors to become interested on this scale, a great deal of active promotional work will be required. This will involve working towards a reduction of any obstacles or uncertainties at the local level such as land-use and zoning policies, site availability and land assembly, availability of public utility services, incentive and tax legislation, airport services and the like. The promotional programme will also involve direction of the advertising and publicity arrangements abroad, as well as the market studies and technical services necessary to seek out prospective hotel interests and to be able to present a factual prospectus.

IV.2.8. In Parts II and III of the present study, emphasis has been placed on the present slow growth of production and marketings of fish, livestock products and food crops for domestic consumption. Yet imports of such items are heavy for every territory. If these lines of activity are to make worth-while contributions to future growth and to viability then major efforts must be put forward to develop commercial marketing channels with an advanced system of communications connecting buyers and sellers. There is an urgent need as well for further development and co-ordination of the various receiving, storage, processing, shipping and delivery functions within each island as well as between islands. All of these matters will require the attention not of advisers alone but of operational people of energy and practical experience.

IV.2.9. Activities with regard to industrial promotion should be similar to those for tourism. It is again a matter of marshalling the relevant cost and market data for feasibility studies and of seeking out appropriate contacts locally or abroad in selected product lines. As a part of the groundwork for such activities, there is also the task of clarifying and expediting local planning and public services of interest to business in efforts to reduce unnecessary restraints to industrial growth.

IV.2.10. What has been referred to as a Commercial and Technical Services division would also be responsible for coordinating and providing the technical and professional services required in the various territories. This would apply to both long-term and short-term consultative needs and to public as well as the private sector. A regional agency of the type here envisaged should be close enough to local manpower resources to be able to identify specific shortages of technical staff, to stimulate action to meet them and to phase in local technical services wherever available. A regional agency, in planning and arranging for technical services, should also be able to minimize the unnecessary costs of duplication between territories and to make the most out of any specialized services made available.

IV.2.11. The commercial and technical services arm would also be responsible for the general supervision and conceivably part of the financing of any permanent commercial or social common services of the region which are not fully financed by voluntary agreements of the various territorial governments.

(2) Development Bank Division

IV.2.12. With respect to a development bank division of any over-riding regional planning and development body, the principal functions and modus operandi would be similar to many such larger organizations functioning elsewhere in the world. We think the operation should be conducted along strictly commercial lines once interest-free or low-cost capital has been subscribed to it. We see the requirements for zero or low interest-bearing initial subscribed capital as being an important one. If this is not achieved, then it will be virtually impossible for the bank to serve the projects of greatest need in development viz, new business ventures with little or no financial record, farmers or fishermen committed to undertaking production into commercial channels in new specialized enterprises or with the use of new specialized methods of equipment, medium and low income housing schemes, properly organized central water authorities and certain other self-liquidating public utility projects.

IV.2.13. We hope that by establishing a Development Bank within a Development Agency the islands would be enabled collectively to deal with certain international development agencies whose rules now exclude them on grounds of size. It may also be possible to interest private capital in any initial or subsequent capital subscription by offering a block of preferred shares of a type—possibly cumulative and participating—to private bank or other financial institutions. Such shares could carry a first preference as to earnings paid out as dividends up to a specified annual rate of return for each year, after which point all classes of shareholders would participate proportionately in any further distribution of earnings.

The General Case for a Regional Development Agency

IV.2.14. It is our conviction that the small islands of the Eastern Caribbean will have a very difficult time in development unless a more integrated approach is adopted to the mobilization and deployment of external assistance to development. Because of their small size, their degree of isolation and their continuous losses of trained manpower to higher income territories and countries, the islands will continue to be short of the intangible elements necessary to sustain rapid growth and change—elements such as the operating experience and skills needed in industrial marketing or service businesses; technical and professional skills generally; general administrative and organizational skills of the kind that benefit so much from frequent discussions with counterpart groups in such matters as health, education, marketing, civil aviation, public works, tax administration and a host of others. It is our belief that some kind of mechanism is needed within which overseas governments could lend the sustained initiative and organizational support as well as the tangible technical and capital requirements required for continued development. But to evoke this kind of sustained commitment on the part of overseas governments for each territory separately seems to us to be uneconomic and unrealistic. This is so because much of the prospects for development in any single territory will depend on an economy of effort in reaching decisions concerning a host of problems and needs common to all territories. Hence one of the important functions of a regional agency for development is that of providing a means for exchange of views and reaching a concensus regarding the general approach to be adopted for development in any particular sector of the economy. These are the decisions which can then be worked into the planning activities of the agency to be reflected later in activity programmes.

IV.2.15. We wish to stress one further point. Whilst we see many advantages to planning and administering a number of development activities on a regional basis, this does not imply in our minds that the particular private or public activities being assisted within each territory need necessarily be carried on in common with similar activities in other territories. This may be an advantage for some activities, but certainly not for many others. For example, there will be a continuing need for each of its territories to improve and extend their own school facilities. We think, however, that substantial economies in effort and time will be achieved by starting from the common educational requirements of all the islands and evolving a general plan or approach to meet these requirements. Having done this, the capital, technical and advisory services available for development can then be deployed throughout the various territories according to their distinctive needs. But the operation and direction of the various school systems will of course continue as always in local hands.

IV.2.16. The regional agency as we see it would act as the focal point for the development planning activities of the individual territories. Elements of the territorial plans would be incorporated into an overall strategy of development for the region by the agency. Budgeting for current activities in connection with development programmes would proceed accordingly, and approaches made to the sponsoring overseas governments for required capital assistance. The agency as a regional body would also be in a position to apply to or collaborate with other appropriate world or regional agencies or foundations interested in particular programmes. Nor is there any reason why an agency of the type envisaged here need be confined in all of its activities to the islands with which this report is concerned. But within the group, it would seem to us that each of the territories must be willing to commit themselves fully to the whole of the activities involved in any regional scheme, or to none at all.

IV.2.17. In arriving at our recommendation for a Regional Development Agency, we are fully conscious of the fact that setting up an organization solves no problems. The point is what the organization does. We have also borne in mind the danger that the Agency might have the effect of draining off into its service some of the scarce resources of trained manpower in the individual islands. We believe that this danger would be avoided to a considerable extent by the power that the Agency would develop to attract back highly trained West Indians now working overseas. But the danger exists, and the Governments of the U.K., Canada and the United States would have to accept the responsibility of meeting it by supplying in the early years a part of the staff that the Agency would need for its various activities.

IV.2.18. This leads us to a final point. We trust that we shall not be regarded in the islands as having been subtly influenced by our Governments into recommending some disguised form of federation, or as having invented a Regional Development form of federation, or as having invented a Regional Development Agency as a means of keeping them under outside tutelage. Anyone who believes this is deceiving himself. We recommend a Regional Development Agency because we believe that it is indispensable to the task of mobilizing the efforts of the islands in an effective drive for economic growth and viability. We recommend it for no other reason. We see the Agency as drawing initially on technical and other resources from outside and as involving the participation of our three countries. But we also envisage the gradual withdrawal of our three countries from the board and staff of the Agency as it proves and establishes itself. When this stage is reached and the Agency becomes an entirely locally-run operation, the islands may wish to dismantle it. But we do not think that they will.

☐ NOTES

INTRODUCTION

[1]Charles W. Taussig, "A Four-Power Program in the Caribbean," *Foreign Affairs* 24, no. 4 (July 1946): 699.
[2]Otto Pick, "The 'O' in NATO," *NATO Letter* 13 (December 1965): 14.
[3]Southeast Asia Treaty Organization, *Story of SEATO*, n.d., p. 30.
[4]Central Treaty Organization, Public Relations Division, *CENTO Makes Progress* (1961), p. 18.

CHAPTER 1

[1]Charles W. Taussig, "A Four-Power Program in the Caribbean," *Foreign Affairs* 24, no. 4 (July 1946): 701.
[2]Joseph M. Jones, "Caribbean Laboratory," *Fortune* 29 (February 1944): 256.
[3]*West India Royal Commission Report, Cmd. 6607* (London, 1945).
[4]Ibid., p. xiii.
[5]Ibid.
[6]Ibid., p. xvii.
[7]Ibid., p. 28.
[8]Ibid., p. 195.
[9]Ibid.
[10]Ibid., p. 220.
[11]Ibid., p. 174.
[12]Ibid., pp. 422, 423.
[13]Ibid., pp. xviii, xvi.
[14]Rexford G. Tugwell, "The Caribbean Commission: Notes on Its Beginnings," *The Caribbean: British, Dutch, French, United States*, ed. A Curtis Wilgus; Series One, vol. 8 (Gainesville: University of Florida Press, 1958), p. 266. Henceforth in notes this volume will be cited simply as *The Caribbean: British, Dutch, French, United States*.
[15]U.S., Congress, Senate, *Relieving Economic Distress in Puerto Rico and the Virgin Islands*, 78th Cong., 1st sess., Report 205, to accompany S. 981, pp. 1-4.
[16]Ibid., p. 1.
[17]Ibid., p. 3.
[18]Rexford G. Tugwell, *The Stricken Land: The Story of Puerto Rico* (Garden City, New York: Doubleday and Co., 1947).
[19]Ibid., p. 578.
[20]U.S., Department of State, *Second Meeting of the Ministers of Foreign Affairs of the American Republics, Habana, July 21-30, 1940*, Dept. of State Publication 1575, Conference Series 48 (Washington, D.C.: Government Printing Office, 1949), p. 3.
[21]Ibid., p. 75.
[22]U.S., Congress, House, *Acquiring Certain Naval and Air Bases in Exchange for Certain Over-Age Destroyers*, Message from the President of the United States to the Congress. 76th Cong., 3d sess., Document 943.
[23]Ibid., p. 2.
[24]U.S., Department of State, *The Caribbean Islands and the War*, Dept. of State Publication 2025 (Washington, D.C.: Government Printing Office, 1943), p. 14. Hereafter in notes this publication will be cited simply as: *Caribbean Islands and the War*.
[25]Quoted by Tugwell in *The Caribbean: British, Dutch, French, United States*, p. 268.

[26]Ibid., p. 269.
[27]*Caribbean Islands and the War*, p. 15.
[28]Ibid.
[29]*Report of the Anglo-American Caribbean Commission to the Government of the United States and Great Britain for the Years 1942-1943* (Washington, 1943), p. 3.

CHAPTER 2

[1]Bernard L. Poole, *The Caribbean Commission: Background of Cooperation in the West Indies* (Columbia, S.C.: University of South Carolina Press, 1951), p. 184.
[2]Ibid., p. 186.
[3]*Report of the Anglo-American Caribbean Commission to the Governments of the United States and Great Britain for the Years 1942-1943* (Washington, 1943), Appendix I.
[4]Ralph J. Bunche, *The Anglo-American Caribbean Commission: An Experiment in Regional Cooperation*, Mimeographed paper presented at the Ninth Conference of the Institute of Pacific Relations, Hot Springs, Virginia, January, 1945 (American Council Paper No. 7), p. 3.
[5]*Report of the Anglo-American Caribbean Commission to the Governments of the United States and Great Britain for the Year 1944* (Washington, 1944), 9. Hereafter in notes these annual official reports in this series will be designated simply *Report of A.A.C.C.*, with applicable year.
[6]First Meeting of the Commission, March 26-31, 1942, Trinidad.
Conference of Supply Officers, May 15-18, 1942, Jamaica.
Second Meeting of the Commission, May 26-June 6, 1942, Washington.
Third Meeting of the Commission, January 27, 1943, Washington.
Fourth Meeting of the Commission, August 17-23, 1943, St. Thomas, Virgin Islands.
Fifth Meeting of the Commission, March 20, 28, and 30, 1944, Barbados.
First Session, West Indian Conference, March 21-30, 1944, Barbados.
Sixth Meeting of the Commission, March 20-23, 1945, Washington.
Seventh Meeting of the Commission, July 25, 1945, Washington.
Poole, *Caribbean Commission*, p. 172.
[7]Ruth D. Masters, *Handbook of International Organization in the Americas* (Washington; Carnegie Endowment for International Peace, 1945), p. 16.
[8]*Report of A.A.C.C., 1942-1943*, p. 7.
[9]Ibid.
[10]Ibid., p. 8.
[11]Ibid.
[12]*Report of A.A.C.C., 1945*, pp. 18-19.
[13]Bunche, *Anglo-American Caribbean Commission*, p. 12.
[14]*Report of A.A.C.C., 1942-1943*, p. 10.
[15]U.S., Department of State, *Report of the West Indian Conference, Second Session*, Dept. of State Publication 2615 (Washington, D.C.: Government Printing Office, 1946), Appendix A, pp. 47-49.
[16]*Report of A.A.C.C., 1944*, p. 13.
[17]Ibid.
[18]Ibid., p. 14.
[19]Ibid., p. 16.
[20]Ibid., Appendix D.
[21]Tugwell, *The Stricken Land*, p. 638.
[22]Text of the Joint Statement, *Report of A.A.C.C., 1945*, Appendix C.
[23]Poole, *Caribbean Commission*, p. 196.
[24]*Report of A.A.C.C., 1944*, p. 10.
[25]*Report of A.A.C.C., 1942-1943*, p. 51.
[26]Ibid.
[27]Bunche, *Anglo-American Caribbean Commission*, p. 10.
[28]*Report of A.A.C.C., 1945*, p. 15.
[29]Ibid., p. 16.
[30]Ibid.

CHAPTER 3

[1] *Caribbean Islands and the War*, p. 5.

[2] Ibid., p. 18.

[3] Frances McReynolds Smith, "The Caribbean Commission: Prototype of Regional Cooperation," in *The Caribbean: British, Dutch, French, United States*, p. 279.

[4] Bernard L. Poole, *The Caribbean Commission: Background of Cooperation in the West Indies* (Columbia, S.C.: University of South Carolina Press, 1951), p. 200.

[5] Smith, *The Caribbean: British, Dutch, French, United States*, p. 279.

[6] *Report of A.A.C.C., 1942–1943*, pp. 17–18.

[7] Ibid., pp. 18–20.

[8] *Report of A.A.C.C., 1944*, pp. 30–31.

[9] Caribbean Commission, *Report of the Caribbean Commission to the Governments of the French Republic, the Kingdom of the Netherlands, the United Kingdom and the United States of America for the Year 1946*, p. 29. (Hereafter in notes these annual reports of the Caribbean Commission will be designated simply *Report of CC*, followed by the appropriate year.)

[10] Smith, *The Caribbean: British, Dutch, French, United States*, p. 281. Also, *Caribbean Islands and the War*, p. 45.

[11] Tugwell, *The Caribbean: British, Dutch, French, United States*, p. 265.

[12] Smith, *The Caribbean: British, Dutch, French, United States*, p. 280.

[13] *Report of A.A.C.C., 1942–1943*, p. 5.

[14] Ibid., pp. 12–13; *Caribbean Islands and the War*, pp. 28–31.

[15] *Caribbean Islands and the War*, pp. 32–34.

[16] *Report of A.A.C.C., 1942–1943*, pp. 13–14.

[17] Poole, *Caribbean Commission*, p. 206.

[18] Richard T. Whiteleather and Herbert H. Brown, *An Experimental Fishery Survey in Trinidad, Tobago, and British Guiana. With Recommended Improvements in Method and Gear* (Washington, D.C.: Government Printing Office, 1945).

[19] Anglo-American Caribbean Commission, *Guide to Commercial Shark Fishing in the Caribbean Area* (Washington: Kaufman Press, 1945).

[20] *Report of A.A.C.C., 1944*, p. 26.

[21] Werner J. Cahnman, "The Caribbean Commission," *Jewish Frontier* 14 (January 1947): 25.

[22] Carlton Skinner, "Self-Government in the South Pacific," *Foreign Affairs* 42 (October 1963): 137. Also: "South Pacific Commission," *International Organization* 18, no. 1 (Winter 1964): 213.

[23] Quoted in Anglo-American Caribbean Commission, *Caribbean Cooperation, A Series of Articles by A. D. Emmart, Associate Editor, Baltimore Evening Sun, Appearing in that Paper, May 4–11, 1943* (Reprint in pamphlet form by the Commission), p. 10.

[24] Joseph M. Jones, "Caribbean Laboratory," *Fortune* 29 (February 1944): 272.

[25] Quoted in Devere Allen, *The Caribbean: Laboratory of World Cooperation* (New York: League for Industrial Democracy, 1943), p. 37.

[26] A.A.C.C., *Caribbean Cooperation, A Series of Articles by A. D. Emmart*, p. 11.

[27] Ralph J. Bunche, *The Anglo-American Caribbean Commission: An Experiment in Regional Cooperation* (American Council Paper No. 7), pp. 18–19.

[28] Dexter Perkins, *The United States and the Caribbean* (Cambridge: Harvard University Press, 1947), p. 200.

CHAPTER 4

[1] *Report of CC, 1946*, pp. 11–12.

[2] Elizabeth H. Armstrong, "Report on the West Indian Conference," *Department of State Bulletin* 14, no. 359 (May 19, 1946): 843.

[3] Ibid., p. 844.

[4] Ibid.

[5] *Report of CC, 1946*, pp. 12–13.

[6]U.S. membership and participation in the Caribbean Commission was authorized by Public Law 431, 80th Congress.

[7]Bernard L. Poole, *The Caribbean Commission: Background of Cooperation in the West Indies* (Columbia, S.C.: University of South Carolina Press, 1951), p. 212.

[8]Caribbean Commission, *Serving the Caribbean*, an undated, pictorial pamphlet (Trinidad, Kent House), p. 2. This publication will henceforth be cited in footnotes simply as *Serving the Caribbean.*

[9]Preamble to Agreement. Article 52, Section I of the United Nations Charter states: "Nothing in the present Charter precludes the existence of regional arrangements or agencies for dealing with such matters relating to the maintenance of international peace and security as are appropriate for regional action, provided that such arrangements or agencies and their activities are consistent with the Purposes and Principles of the United Nations."

[10]Articles II, III, and IV.

[11]Article IX.

[12]Article XII.

[13]*Report of CC, 1946*, p. 18.

[14]Smith, *The Caribbean: British, Dutch, French, United States*, p. 287.

[15]Ibid., p. 295.

[16]*The Caribbean* 10, no. 5 (December 1956): 116.

[17]Caribbean Commission, *The West Indian Conference (Special Session)* (Trinidad: Kent House, 1959), pp. 3-4.

[18]*The Caribbean* 14, no. 4 (April 1960): 71.

[19]Caribbean Commission, *Report of the Secretary General on the Work of the Caribbean Commission, May, 1955 to August, 1957* (Trinidad: Kent House, 1957), pp. 10-11. Hereafter in footnotes the work will be cited simply as *Report of Secretary General, 1955 to 1957.*

[20]Ibid., p. 7.

[21]Articles 6 and 7, Rules of Procedure for the Caribbean Commission.

[22]*Report of Secretary General, 1955 to 1957*, Appendix II.

[23]Elizabeth H. Armstrong, "West Indian Conference: Fourth Session," *Department of State Bulletin* 24, no. 609 (March 5, 1951): 388.

[24]A. J. Poirier, "Conference Proves Stepping Stone to Improved Caribbean Economy," *Foreign Commerce Weekly* 34, no. 10 (March 7, 1949).

CHAPTER 5

[1]This presentation is based in part on the very excellent summary of Commission activities contained in the paper presented by Mrs. Frances McReynolds Smith at the Eighth Conference on the Caribbean, held at the University of Florida, December 5, 6, and 7, 1957. The paper is published under the title "The Caribbean Commission: Prototype of Regional Cooperation," in the volume *The Caribbean: British, Dutch, French, United States.* Much of the detailed data in this chapter is from her paper.

[2]*Serving the Caribbean*, p. 12.

[3]*Report of Secretary General, 1955 to 1957*, p. 28.

[4]*Serving the Caribbean*, pp. 14-16.

[5]*Report of Secretary General, 1955 to 1957*, pp. 48-49.

[6]*Serving the Caribbean*, p. 8.

[7]Annette Baker Fox, *Freedom and Welfare in the Caribbean: A Colonial Dilemma* (New York: Harcourt Brace and Co., 1949), p. 72.

[8]Elizabeth H. Armstrong, "West Indian Conference: Fourth Session," *Department of State Bulletin* 24, no. 609 (March 5, 1951): 389.

CHAPTER 6

[1]*The Caribbean* 10, no. 4 (November 1956): 78.

[2]Quoted in Smith, *The Caribbean: British, Dutch, French, United States*, p. 292.

[3]*Report of Secretary General, 1955 to 1957*, pp. v-vi.

[4]*Caribbean Commission Monthly Information Bulletin* 5, no. 9 (April 1952): 267. Arthur Chai Onn was the winner of a one-hundred-dollar prize for the best essay written about the work of the Caribbean Commission by a schoolchild of the area. The prize was offered by Mr. Jesus T. Pinero, former governor of Puerto Rico, and the contest was sponsored by the Commission.

[5]Annette Baker Fox, *Freedom and Welfare in the Caribbean: A Colonial Dilemma* (New York: Harcourt Brace and Co., 1949), pp. 231–32.

[6]*The Caribbean* 1, no. 1 (September–October 1961): 3.

CHAPTER 7

• [1]Smith, *The Caribbean: British, Dutch, French, United States*, pp. 296–97.

[2]At the fourth session of the West Indian Conference, which met in Curacao in November 1950, a resolution on this subject was submitted by Dr. C. B. Jagan, a delegate from British Guiana. The resolution was not adopted but the Conference agreed that it be included in the official report. It would have recommended that Article V be amended to provide that at least eight members of the Commission, including the four co-chairmen or their alternates, should constitute a quorum; and that Article VI be amended to provide that all decisions of the Commission should be taken by a majority vote of the members present. (Caribbean Commission, *West Indian Conference, Fourth Session*, Kent House, Port of Spain, Trinidad, 1951, pp. 83–84).

[3]Caribbean Commission, *West Indian Conference, Fifth Session*, 1952 (Trinidad: Kent House, 1953), p. 54.

[4]*West Indian Conference, Fifth Session*, 1952, pp. 88–89.

[5]Ibid., p. 90.

[6]Caribbean Commission, *West Indian Conference, Sixth Session*, 1955 (Trinidad: Kent House, 1955), pp. 77–78.

[7]Quoted in Smith, *The Caribbean: British, Dutch, French, United States*, p. 298.

[8]Ibid.

[9]Caribbean Commission, *The West Indian Conference (Special Session)* (Trinidad: Kent House, 1959), Introduction.

[10]Ibid.

[11]Ibid., p. 4.

[12]Ibid., pp. 4–10.

[13]Ibid., p. 26.

CHAPTER 8

[1]Henry Wells, "Constitutional Development in Puerto Rico," *Developments towards Self-Government in the Caribbean* (A Symposium Held under the Auspices of the Netherlands Universities Foundation for International Cooperation at the Hague, September 1954). (The Hague: W. Van Hoeve, Ltd., 1955), p. 76. Henceforth in notes this volume will be cited simply by its title: *Developments towards Self-Government in the Caribbean.*

[2]Ibid., p. 77.

[3]Ibid., p. 78.

[4]Arturo Morales Carrion, "The Historical Roots and Political Significance of Puerto Rico," in *The Caribbean: British, Dutch, French, United States*, p. 144.

[5]*Downes* v. *Bidwell*, 182 U.S. 244, 341.

[6]Wells, in *Developments towards Self-Government in the Caribbean*, p. 78.

[7]Morales Carrion, in *The Caribbean: British, Dutch, French, United States*, p. 163.

[8]Ibid.

[9]Wells, in *Developments towards Self-Government in the Caribbean*, p. 79.

[10]Morales Carrion, in *The Caribbean: British, Dutch, French, United States*, p. 164.

[11]Ibid.

[12]Ibid., p. 165.

[13]Wells, in *Developments towards Self-Government in the Caribbean*, p. 80.

[14] Ibid., pp. 81–82.

[15] Henry Wells, "The Nature of Puerto Rican Government and Politics," in *Developments towards Self-Government in the Caribbean*, pp. 134–36.

[16] *The World Today* 14, no. 5 (May 1958): 217–18.

[18] Luis Muñoz Marín, "Puerto Rico and the United States, Their Future Together," *Foreign Affairs* 34, no. 4 (July 1954), 546–47.

[18] United Nations Document A/C.4/L.300, quoted by Morales Carrion in *The Caribbean: British, Dutch, French, United States*, p. 166.

[19] Verbatim Record, Proceedings of the General Assembly, 459th Meeting.

[20] Alexander Brady, "The West Indies: A New Federation," *Behind the Headlines* (Canadian Institute of International Affairs) 17, no. 5 (January 1958): 102.

[21] Douglas Williams, "Constitutional Developments in the British West Indies," in *The Caribbean: British, Dutch, French, United States*, p. 7.

[22] Great Britain, Her Majesty's Stationery Office, *The West Indies: A Nation in the Making* (London, 1958), p. 8.

[23] Ibid.

[24] Ibid., p. 9.

[25] Ibid. The preamble to the Constitution simply affirmed the principle of "the greatest possible freedom of movement for persons and goods" within the Federation.

[26] The factual material in this chapter relating to the constitutional evolution of the West Indies Federation was gathered from such a wide variety of sources that individual footnote reference to each item would be virtually impossible.

[27] These provisions were modified somewhat in August 1960, by an Order-in-Council which conferred full self-rule on the West Indies Federation.

[28] Constitutional details for the most part from Great Britain, *The West Indies: A Nation in the Making*, pp. 11–15.

[29] Brady, "West Indies," p. 7.

[30] *Spotlight* (monthly news magazine from Jamaica) 21, no. 8 (August 1960): 9.

[31] *Newday* (Jamaica monthly news magazine) 4, no. 11 (November 1960): 15.

[32] Ibid.

[33] Kingdom of the Netherlands, *Surinam and the Netherlands Antilles: From Dependency to Partnership* (The Hague, 1955), p. 17.

[34] Ibid., p. 18.

[35] J. H. A. Logeman, "The Constitutional Status of the Netherlands Caribbean Territories," in *Developments towards Self-Government in the Caribbean*, p. 49.

[36] Kingdom of the Netherlands, *Surinam and the Netherlands Antilles*, p. 20.

[37] Ibid., p. 21.

[38] Ibid., p. 22.

[39] Ibid.

[40] Hans G. Hermans, "Constitutional Developments of the Netherlands Antilles and Surinam," in *The Caribbean: British, Dutch, French, United States*, p. 63.

[41] Kingdom of the Netherlands, *Surinam and the Netherlands Antilles*, p. 25.

[42] Ibid., p. 26.

[43] Hermans, in *The Caribbean: British, Dutch, French, United States*, p. 64.

[44] Ibid., p. 66.

[45] André L. van Assenderp, "The Netherlands Caribbean: A Study in Regional Autonomy," *The Caribbean: Contemporary International Relations*, ed. A. Curtis Wilgus; Series One, vol. 7 (Gainesville: University of Florida Press, 1957), p. 88.

[46] Franklin D. Parker, "Political Developments in the French Caribbean," in *The Caribbean: British, Dutch, French, United States*, p. 103.

[47] Eugene Revert, "Les institutions de la Martinique jusqu'a l'assimilation," in *Developments towards Self-Government in the Caribbean*, p. 43.

[48] Claudius C. Thomas, "Les Antilles Britanniques et Françaises: Structure et avenir politique et economique" (Unpub. Ph.D. diss., University of Strasbourg, 1960), p. 106. Translation from French is my own.

[49] Ibid., p. 107.

[50] *The Caribbean* 12, no. 4 (November 1958): 83.

[51]Ibid.
[52]Thomas, "Les Antilles Britanniques et Françaises," p. 111.
[53]Ibid.; p. 108.

CHAPTER 9

[1]The *Jamaica Daily Gleaner* of April 12, 1959, in a dispatch from Port of Spain dated April 11, reported: "Chief Minister Dr. Eric Williams told his press conference this morning that the Government of Trinidad and Tobago refused a request to contribute to the Caribbean Organization, successor body to the Caribbean Commission . . . . Dr. Williams, who before entering politics was an officer of the Commission said that, while the Organization might be of some value to other territories, his Government did not see it was of any value to Trinidad."

[2]For example, the report of a three-man commission appointed by the colonial secretary to consider the most suitable site for the capital, issued January 2, 1957. Also the report of a joint commission under the chairmanship of Sir Charles Arden-Clarke, issued May 14, 1958.

[3]The narrative material in this section of the chapter was furnished orally to me by the administrative secretary of the Caribbean Commission, after consultation with the secretary general. The information was taken directly from the relevant documents, which cannot be cited however because they are considered to be for the official use of member governments only.

[4]Editorial: "The Work Goes on," *Trinidad Guardian*, April 15, 1959. The newspaper accounts quite understandably confused two issues which were really separate: (1) the question of how much the West Indies Federation government could afford to contribute to the budget of the Caribbean Organization as a member; and (2) the separate question whether the government of Trinidad would pay certain headquarters expenses.

[5]Editorial, "A Decision in July," *Trinidad Guardian*, April 22, 1959.

[6]Caribbean Commission, *The West Indian Conference (Special Session)* (Trinidad: Kent House, 1959), p. 9.

CHAPTER 10

[1]Translated from Spanish by me. The published account of the West Indian Conference, seventh session, contains no mention of this statement by Puerto Rico.

[2]Puerto Rico's "ultimatum" to the West Indian Conference was preceded by missionary work on the part of Dr. Morales Carrion and others, extending over several years, to gain support for Puerto Rico's insistence on the change in the structure of the Caribbean Commission. Dr. Morales Carrion is reported to have visited Secretary of State Dulles and others in the Department of State, including the newly appointed United States co-chairman, Mr. Roderic O'Connor, in 1955 in connection with the matter. From that time on it was widely believed in the West Indies that the United States government's announced support for the proposed change was a result of Puerto Rico's insistence. There was also the belief that details of the proposed change had been drafted in Puerto Rico and presented to the United States government. In August 1956 it was reported that Norman Manley, prime minister of Jamaica, stopped in Puerto Rico overnight on the way to a conference in St. Lucia and that among the topics which he and Governor Muñoz Marín discussed was Puerto Rico's plan for the reorganization of the Caribbean Commission. In the fall of 1957, just before the seventh session, Dr. Morales Carrion made a trip to Jamaica and Trinidad for the purpose of explaining to officials of those islands the position which Puerto Rico was planning to take at the session with regard to the Commission structure. According to press reports he would have continued his trip to other islands except that an airline strike paralyzed transportation in the area.

[3]From an editorial, "A Crucial Conference," in the *Trinidad Guardian* of July 24, 1959.

[4]Several long-time employees of the Secretariat told me that this report was indeed true.

[5]*Trinidad Guardian*, November 25, 1958. Again I had to be content with oral assurance from Commission officials that the verbatim records of the meeting substantiate the newspaper account.

[6]Ibid.

[7]*Trinidad Guardian*, December 13, 1958.

[8]From Gomes's regular column in the *Trinidad Guardian*, December 7, 1958.

[9]Except that Puerto Rico voluntarily paid the rent for the Secretariat offices and the secretary-general's residence, plus certain other items, to the total amount of about $35,000, a sum which was not calculated as a part of the Commission's current budget. In other words these items, for 1961 did not have to come out of the organization's working funds.

[10]Caribbean Commission, *The West Indian Conference (Special Session)* (Trinidad: Kent House, 1959), p. 5.

[11]Ibid., p. 6.

[12]Ibid., Appendix VIII.

[13]While it is true that Puerto Rico's very liberal annual contribution to the Caribbean Organization was meant partly to cover the headquarters expenses, the fact still remained that Puerto Rico would contribute $140,000 to the total budget, and out of that total budget had to be paid the rent for office and residence. Puerto Rico's generosity was thus more than offset by the poverty of the other members plus the additional expenses of the San Juan location.

Puerto Rico's offer of $140,000 was calculated roughly as follows:

(a)	Rent for headquarters and residence:	$ 34,000
(b)	Additional contribution as host government:	$ 56,000
(c)	Normal contribution as a member:	$ 50,000
		$140,000

[14]I found one editorial comment to the effect that this budgetary reduction might not be a bad thing. The *Trinidad Chronicle*, in an editorial on August 7, 1959, wrote:

The new bird will not be arrayed with such healthy plumage as the old, since financial support for its existence will be considerably less than in previous years.

It would not be unfair to suggest that American influence in Puerto Rico will inject some well-needed vitality into the new organization, or at least make it more obvious exactly what the Commission stands for and what exactly it achieves.

Since its inception in the early '40's the Commission has helped largely in the exchange of ideas and information between the American, British, French, and Dutch territories in the Caribbean, as well as in development programs. The only flaw in this picture is the suspicion that all this could have been achieved with an organization a quarter the size and not nearly as expensive.

The Commission has been a splendid example of one of Parkinson's basic laws that subordinates multiply regardless of the volume of work produced. This fact has been tacitly recognized by the willingness of the new organization to undertake the same tasks on a much reduced budget.

[15]This first list was made up of: administrative secretary, statistician, chief translator, three translators, accountant, administrative officer, three technical officers, secretary, chief clerk, office assistant, five stenographers, three bilingual typists, proofreader, and bookkeeper.

CHAPTER 11

[1]Caribbean Organization, *Report of the First Meeting of the Caribbean Council*, held in San Juan, Puerto Rico, September 6–15, 1961, p. 1.

[2]Ibid.

[3]Ibid.

[4]Ibid.

[5]Ibid.

[6]Ibid.

[7]Ibid.

[8]Ibid.

[9]Ibid., p. 2.

[10]Information in these sections is adapted from "General Review of the Activities of the Caribbean Organization," in *The Caribbean* 4, no. 5 (December 1964). Supplementary details have been gathered from other Caribbean Organization publications and documents.

CHAPTER 12

[1]T. G. Mathews et al., *Politics and Economics in the Caribbean* (Rio Piedras, Puerto Rico: Institute of Caribbean Studies, University of Puerto Rico, 1966), p. 22.

[2]Ibid., p. 23.

[3]Ibid.

[4]Ibid., p. 21.

[5]Compiled from press reports.

[6]Mathews et al., *Politics and Economics*, p. 7.

[7]Ibid., p. 161.

[8]Ibid., p. 163.

[9]*Le Monde* (Paris), April 29, 1969, p. 12.

[10]Factual details such as these, as well as quotations from documents, in this section on the British Caribbean, are derived from the appropriate entries in *Keesing's Contemporary Archives*, unless otherwise indicated.

[11]For an analysis of why the Federation failed, see Amitai Etzioni, *Political Unification: A Comparative Study of Leaders and Forces* (New York: Holt, Rinehart and Winston, 1965), chapter 5: "A Union That Failed: The Federation of the West Indies."

[12]*International Conciliation*, no. 554 (September 1965), p. 77.

[13]U.S., Congress, Senate, Status of Puerto Rico: Hearings before the United States–Puerto Rico Commission on the Status of Puerto Rico, 89th Cong., 2d sess., 1966, Document 108.

Volume 1: Legal-Constitutional Factors in Relation to the Status of Puerto Rico
Volume 2: Social-Cultural Factors in Relation to the Status of Puerto Rico
Volume 3: Economic Factors in Relation to the Status of Puerto Rico

[14]United States–Puerto Rico Commission on the Status of Puerto Rico, *Status of Puerto Rico*, August 1966.

[15]As compiled and summarized by the writer from material in the *San Juan Star*, July 19, 20, 21, 22, and 23, and from the *New York Times*, July 23, 1967.

CHAPTER 13

[1]Andrew Viglucci, "The Caribbean: Today . . . and Tomorrow," *Sunday San Juan Star Magazine*, July 4, 1965.

[2]Margot Preece, "CODECA Is Met with Enthusiasm," *San Juan Star*, July 27, 1965.

[3]Caribbean Organization, *Report of the Third Meeting of the Caribbean Council*, held in Paramaribo, Surinam, October 3–8, 1962, p. 3.

[4]Ibid., p. 4.

[5]See, for example, Caribbean Organization, *Report of the Fourth Meeting of the Caribbean Council*, Held in San Juan, Puerto Rico, September 23–27, 1963, statement of the chairman of the French delegation, M. Georges Marie-Anne, p. 2.

[6]*Report of the Fourth Meeting of the Caribbean Council*, p. 6.

[7]In a personal conversation with me in June of 1966.

[8]*Report of the Fifth and Last Meeting of the Caribbean Council*, p. 4.

[9]Ibid.

[10]Ibid., p. 7.

[11]Ibid., p. 33. Details of the final meeting contained in the section are of course drawn mostly from the official report of that meeting.

[12]Caribbean Organization, *Final Report by the Secretary General to Member Governments of the Caribbean Organization on the Dissolution of the Caribbean Organization and the Liquidation of the Central Secretariat*, 1965.

CHAPTER 14

[1]Caribbean Economic Development Corporation, Puerto Rico, *A Proposal for an Informal System of Economic Coordination in the Caribbean*, submitted by the government of Puerto Rico, July 1965.

[2]This observation, and much of the analysis which follows, derives from extensive interviews which I had with Dr. Passalacqua and other CODECA officials in the course of my personal visit to CODECA headquarters in July of 1967.

CHAPTER 15

[1]Caribbean Regional Library, *Conference for the Establishment of a Bibliographic Center for the Caribbean*, held at Hato Rey, Puerto Rico, March 28–29, 1967, Official Records, p. 3.

CHAPTER 16

[1]Aaron Segal, *The Politics of Caribbean Economic Integration* (Institute of Caribbean Studies, University of Puerto Rico: Special Study No. 6; Rio Piedras, Puerto Rico: University of Puerto Rico, 1968).

[2]Ibid., p. 11.

[3]Ernst B. Haas and Philippe C. Schmitter, "Economics and Differential Patterns of Political Integration: Projections about Unity in Latin America," *International Organization* 17, no. 4 (Autumn 1964): 705. See also: Roger D. Hansen, "Regional Integration: Reflections on a Decade of Theoretical Efforts," *World Politics* 21, no. 2 (January 1969): 242.

[4]Haas and Schmitter, "Economics and Political Integration," p. 707.

[5]Quoted by Roger D. Hansen, "Regional Integration," p. 243.

[6]Segal, *Politics of Economic Integration*, p. 12.

[7]Ibid., p. 13.

[8]Ibid.

[9]Ibid.

[10]*Keesing's Contemporary Archives*, p. 22884.

[11]Ibid.

[12]Ibid.

[13]"CARIFTA: A Very Uncertain Picture," *E.I.U. Quarterly Economic Review*, no. 2, 1968, for the West Indies (May 23, 1968), p. 2.

[14]"CARIFTA: Birth by Stages," ibid., no. 4, 1968 (August 5, 1968), p. 2.

[15]Text of the CARIFTA agreement may be found in *International Legal Materials*, vol. 7 (1968). See also "CARIFTA Broadens Membership, Defines Product Rules," *Business Latin America*, July 4, 1968, p. 214.

[16]*E.I.U. Quarterly Economic Review*, no. 4, 1968, p. 3.

[17]"The First Months of CARIFTA," ibid., p. 1.

[18]U.N. document SF/310/REG.111.

[19]"The Regional Development Bank: The First Withdrawal," *E.I.U. Quarterly Economic Review*, no. 2, 1968, for the West Indies (May 23, 1968), p. 2.

[20]Letter dated July 15, 1969, to me from Mr. Paul Baxter Lanius, first secretary, United States Embassy, Bridgetown, Barbados. Also, briefing paper from the U.S. Agency for International Development, n.d.

[21]Briefing paper, U.S. Agency for International Development.

[22]"Barbados Joins the OAS," *E.I.U. Quarterly Economic Review*, no. 4, 1967, for the West Indies (November 14, 1967), p. 3.

Appendix A

[1]Entered into force Aug. 6, 1948, notice of approval having been deposited in behalf of: the United States, Mar. 8, 1948; France, Dec. 11, 1946; Netherlands, Aug. 6, 1948; and the United Kingdom, Mar. 4, 1947.

[2]The agreement was signed on behalf of the member governments on Oct. 30, 1946.

[3]Held in anticipation of the special session of the West Indian Conference which was to deal with the revision of the agreement for the establishment of the Caribbean Commission.

[4]The departure from the Commission staff of Dr. Eric Williams, now prime minister of the government of Trinidad and Tobago (see chapter 9), precipitated a reorganization of the research work of the Secretariat. Dr. Williams was deputy chairman of the Research Council and as such was head of the Secretariat's research branch. Upon his separation from the Commission the research work came to be decentralized among the other branches of the Secretariat. In time it came to be felt that no useful purpose would be served by further formal meetings of the Research Council. The Council remained officially an auxiliary body of the Commission, however.

□ INDEX